The Town of South Den.

The Town of South Denver

Millie Van Wyke

Its People, Neighborhoods and Events Since 1858

PRUETT

PRUETT PUBLISHING COMPANY
BOULDER, COLORADO

For information about permission to reproduce selections from this book write to
Permissions, Pruett Publishing Company, 2928 Pearl Street, Boulder, CO 80301.

Library of Congress Cataloging-in-Publication Data

Van Wyke, Millie.
    The town of South Denver : its people, neighborhoods, and events since 1858 / Millie Van Wyke.
       p.   cm.
    Includes bibliographical references and index.
     ISBN 0-87108-820-7 : $27.95. —ISBN 0-87108-813-4 (pbk.) : $19.95
1. South Denver (Denver, Colo.)—History. 2. Denver (Colo.)—History. I. Title.
F784.D84S688 1991

                                      978.8'83—dc2091-29372
                                            CIP

Printed in the United States of America

10 9 8 7 6 5 4 3 2 1

Book and book cover design by Jody Chapel, Cover to Cover Design, Denver, Colorado.
Cover Illustration: South Broadway in the early 1890s. From the *Denver Times*, August 16, 1895.

For

Don, forty-seven years in South Denver

for

Craig, Joan, and Jill, born there

for

Sue, Jamie, and Sarah, adopted into it

and for

The South Denver Dutch

Contents

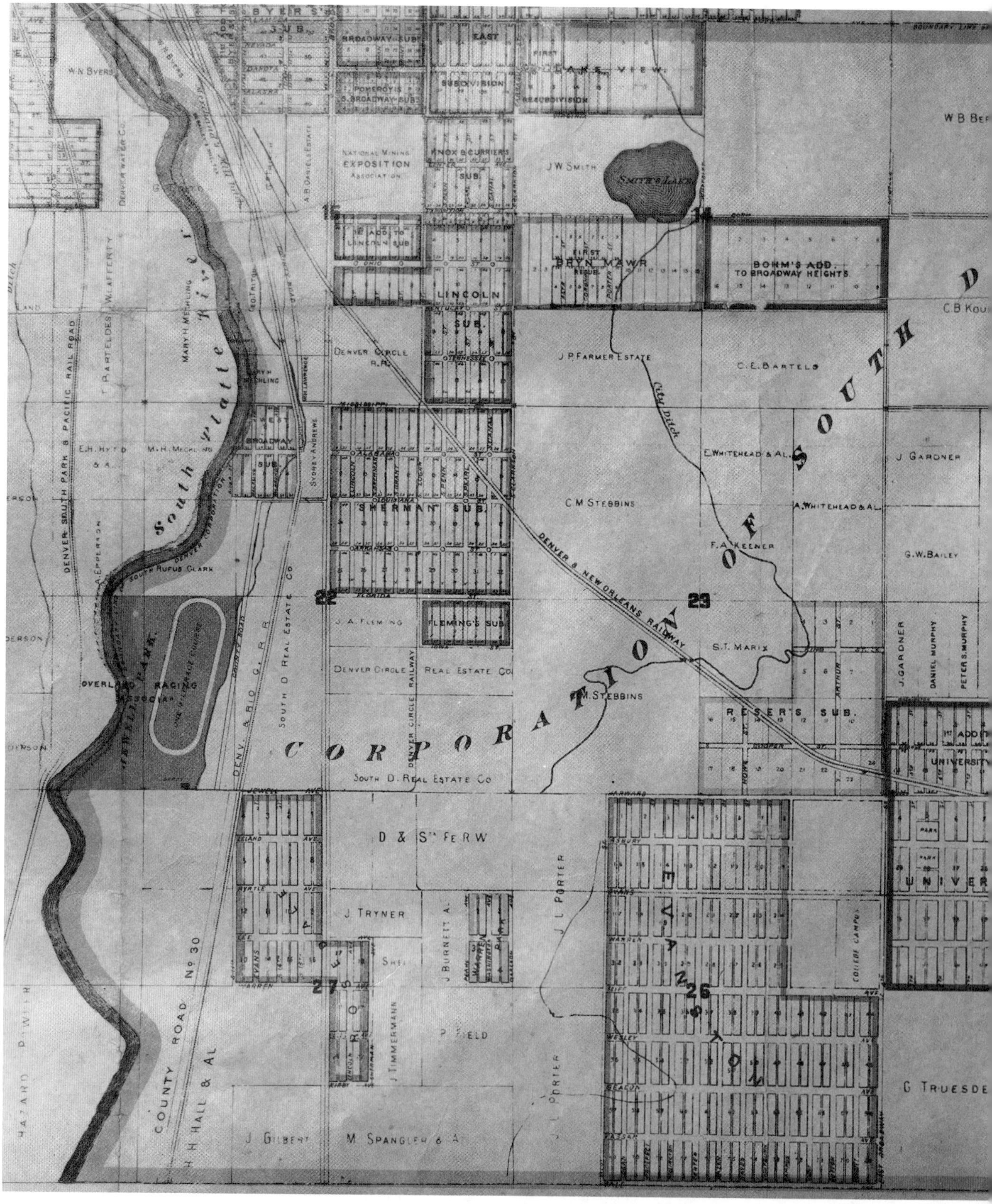
BYERS' SUB.
W. N. BYERS
BROADWAY SUB.
POMEROY'S S. BROADWAY SUB.
EAST SUBDIVISION
FIRST LAKE VIEW RESUBDIVISION
W B BE
DENVER WATER CO.
NATIONAL MINING EXPOSITION ASSOCIATION
A.B. DANIELS ESTATE
KNOX & CURRIER'S SUB.
J W SMITH
SMITH'S LAKE
RE ADD TO LINCOLN SUB.
FIRST BRYN MAWR
BOHM'S ADD. TO BROADWAY HEIGHTS
LINCOLN SUB.
C.B. KOU
DENVER SOUTH PARK & PACIFIC RAIL ROAD
T. BARTELDES
W. AFFERTY
MARY H. MECHLING
South Platte River
DENVER CIRCLE R.R.
J P FARMER ESTATE
C.E. BARTELS
City Ditch
WEST BROADWAY SUB.
SYDNEY ANDREWS
E.H. HYDE & A.
M.H. MECHLING
E. WHITEHEAD & AL.
J. GARDNER
C.M. STEBBINS
A. WHITEHEAD & AL.
SHERMAN SUB.
A. EPPERSON
RUFUS CLARK
F.A. KEENER
G.W. BAILEY
DENVER & NEW ORLEANS RAILWAY
SOUTH D REAL ESTATE CO
22
23
J.A. FLEMING
FLEMING'S SUB.
S.T. MARIX
OVERLAND RACING ASSOCIATION
OVERLAND PARK
DENV. & RIO G. R R.
DENVER CIRCLE RAILWAY
DENVER CIRCLE REAL ESTATE CO.
M. STEBBINS
J. GARDNER
DANIEL MURPHY
PETER S. MURPHY
RESER'S SUB.
CORPORATION OF SOUTH D
SOUTH D. REAL ESTATE CO
UNIVERSITY
D & S FE R W
J. L. PORTER
EVANSTON
J. TRYNER
J. BURNETT AL.
COLLEGE CAMPUS
27
26
COUNTY ROAD No 30
HAZARD P. WEIR
J. TIMMERMANN
P. FIELD
J. L. PORTER
H H HALL & AL
J. GILBERT
M. SPANGLER & AL
G. TRUESDE

Preface

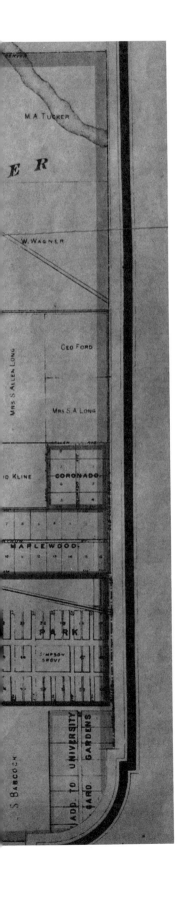

South Denver's history begins in 1858 when the Lawrence Party founded Montana City on the east bank of the South Platte River at what is now Evans Avenue. At that time all land south and west of Cherry Creek was considered "West Denver," Kansas Territory. Although by the early 1880s a more specific "South Denver" included all land south of Cherry Creek, my story is confined to the geographic area that constituted the original *Town of South Denver,* incorporated in 1886. Its borders were the South Platte River, Alameda Avenue, Colorado Boulevard, and Yale Avenue, the boundaries adhered to in this book.

Denver World's Map, April 1888

Montana City: First Town of the Pike's Peak Region

In the summer of 1858, several young gold prospectors, who would shortly become South Denver's first real estate developers, found themselves temporarily stalled in the San Luis Valley. Here, while waiting for news of more promising goldfields, they killed long hours by playing cards and telling stories around the tables at Fort Garland. These men did not much fit the stereotype of the rough, hard-drinking gamblers of the gold-rush era. True, they had succumbed to the gold-fever madness sweeping the country, and gold was what had brought them more than 700 miles on the Santa Fe Trail from Lawrence (in what is now Kansas) to this mountain valley. Although they had every intention of picking up their share of gold nuggets in the Pike's Peak country of Kansas Territory, their education and backgrounds had not prepared them for the hard digging that was producing so little. The gold they found around their camp twelve miles from Fort Garland amounted to only ten cents to every wagonload of dirt, and no amount of effort could make it pan out better. The men, though still hopeful for the big strike that would make them rich, gave it up for the time being and hung about the sutler's store at the Fort. Although Fort Garland, then in the Territory of New Mexico, was still uncompleted, it housed 154 men, including 78 mounted riflemen, and all the trappings necessary for a garrison erected to protect settlers. The post's trading store, erected outside the military post, was a square, red adobe building with a sod roof, white-washed mud interior walls, and board floors. It contained three living rooms, some storage rooms, and a barn. The store manager, or sutler, appointed by the U.S. secretary of war, stocked everything from Wiltshire hams to Mexican spurs, patent medicines to buffalo robes, stationery to saddles, and ammunition to cosmetics.[1] The sutler had furnished the parlors with tables and chairs, and glass tumblers were used in place of tin cups; the Lawrence men found it ever so much more pleasant than their mean mining camp in the brush.

Attorney William Parsons, survey engineer William Hartley, merchants John D. Miller and John Easter (who had organized and led the party), and newspaper typesetter William Boyer had swung picks and shovels alongside the others in the Lawrence party, but they had only partly invested their futures in the discovery of gold. They were more interested in developing towns. Within weeks, in fact, several of them would be involved in the platting and founding of the very first Anglo town in the region--Montana City, at the present Evans Avenue and the South Platte River. Others helped found St. Charles (later Denver) and Auraria, where Cherry Creek and the Platte River converge. A few invested in all of the towns.

Some would stay long after the gold rush waned, to help build a new state. Schoolteacher Jason Younker would become an alderman; Josiah

Hinman (an "accomplished gentleman"), a representative to Colorado's first constitutional convention; T. C. Dickson, a county commissioner; and wagon train captain John Tierney, a county assessor. As historian Jerome Smiley noted in 1901, "The Lawrence party did not develop any conspicuously successful miners in the year of 1858. As an aggregation the company seems to have taken more readily to the business of locating towns than to the heavy drudgery of prospecting."[2]

The Lawrence party of more than forty men and twelve wagons had left Lawrence the end of May 1858 to search for gold, with no more than rumor as their guide. They camped at the base of Pike's Peak in early July but found no gold there. Some passing mountain men told them of gold discoveries in the San Luis Valley, and off they went to try their luck. So far, their months-long adventure had led them to beautiful country and good times but little gold. And so they passed the time with U.S. Army soldiers who had just arrived at Fort Garland, spinning tales of fabulous brook trout caught in the clear valley streams and of their past experiences as soldiers themselves.

"We should probably have been there yet," Parsons wrote in 1872, "if another gold excitement had not arisen, for nothing else could start us. This time it was at Cherry Creek and we geared up and hurried off."[3] The Lawrence party retraced their steps, traveling fast now, "fearful, by reason of the rumors which we heard, that the gold would all be gathered before we could reach it. We passed Pike's Peak, through the pinery, down Cherry Creek and encamped in the angle formed by Cherry Creek and the South Platte." The next morning, after "seeing, handling and tasting" the gold there, they began to dig for their fortunes. For the third time since leaving Lawrence, they found little gold for their efforts. By noon, after half a day of sweaty, hard labor, they gave it up once and for all. Most of them "solemnly pledged each other never to do the like again."

While weighing the possibilities for new endeavors, attorney Parsons presided at the first trial ever held in the area. A gambler by the name of Vincent shot John Atwell during a game of monte, "the ball plowing along the left side of his head, but not breaking the skull," Parsons said. The victim had a Cheyenne wife. Vincent ran off but was caught in the brush by the Cheyennes, who turned him over to the Lawrence men. Parsons was selected judge, a jury was impaneled, and Parsons sentenced Vincent "to give Atwell his horse and Vincent to receive six days' rations and quit the country, on pain of being shot on sight." "There have been many able judges in Denver since my day," Parsons said in 1884, "but I venture to boast that justice has never been administered more speedily or satisfactorily than in Vincent's case."[4]

The Lawrence men wanted to build towns. "Being Kansas men, we commenced laying out town sites wherever there was room," Parsons said. They left Cherry Creek and went to Placer Camp on Dry Creek at the South Platte River near what is now Dartmouth Avenue in Englewood. Arriving September 4, about two weeks after William Green Russell and his party from Georgia had established the camp, the Lawrence party found it deserted; the Russell party had left it for more favorable prospects elsewhere. Some of the Lawrence party went back to the Cherry Creek–Platte River site, which had already become a rendezvous point for prospectors and miners.

Many members of the party decided to stay south, however, speculating that gold seekers who were sure to come in vast numbers could be induced to live in the town they would build and govern. They had only to find the perfect site for it. Heading north again along the east bank of the river, they examined and rejected several possible locations for their new home. When about a mile farther (near the present Iliff Avenue) they came to a lovely spot just south of where the river swept around a fabulous tip of grassy land (the present Overland Park), they knew they had found it. Here was "a beautiful point of land surrounded on three sides by the Platte River and heavy cottonwood timber, opening out on the southeast to the boundless plain."[5] The Lawrence men were enthralled with it. They went no farther.

It was here on the river's east bank that this group of gold seekers and businessmen believed lay the future of the Rocky Mountain West. After tying their horses to the cottonwood trees, they pitched camp and began to plan. Before the town could be laid out or construction on log cabins could begin, they needed to file a proper claim. Meeting the next day under the shade of the towering cottonwoods, they chose a name appropriate for a town that lay at the foot of a mountain: Montana (Spanish for "mountain") City. They organized the Montana Town Company and elected Beloit College graduate Josiah Hinman president and William J. Boyer secretary and applied for town incorporation papers from the governor of Kansas Territory. The paperwork done, they commenced to lay out the first organized town in the Rocky Mountain region, on the western edge of Kansas Territory. It was bounded on the east by the old Santa Fe to Fort Laramie trail (the present South Santa Fe Drive), on the west by the South Platte River, on the north by what is now Evans Avenue, and on the south by the present Iliff Avenue.

They began to build Lawrence Row. On November 2, the Kansas Company, a consolidated group of goldseekers from Missouri, eastern Kansas, and southeastern Nebraska, joined them, and a portion of the Leavenworth (Kansas) Company arrived a few days later. These two companies built Leavenworth Row and Kansas Row. They now had a fine town with proper streets, alleys, and lots and twenty log cabins that were ten by twelve feet with dirt floors and roofs made of sod-covered poles. The cabins were built of unhewn cottonwood logs, wood that tends to twist into all sorts of shapes in seasoning. Nevertheless, cottonwoods grew in abundance along the river, and their lumber was the only building material readily available. The first sawmill would not be built for another two years, and what lumber that could be obtained cost $100 a thousand. Nails went for $1 per pound, so the builders constructed the cabins in what is called the Lincoln Log style, the simplest and fastest method of erecting a cabin, chinking the logs inside with clay mixed with straw. Leather hinges held the doors in place. Few cabins had windows; those that did were covered with animal skins. The interiors were crude and designed to provide only the barest essentials--protection from the weather. They were lit at night with homemade candles and a variety of lanterns. Utensils, weapons, and tools were hung on wall hooks or piled in a corner. Tables and chairs were made of split logs and the miner's bed was either a pallet on the dirt floor or a simple wood frame with interwoven ropes that supported a mattress stuffed with grass or straw. Cooking was done on open fires outside the cabin.[6]

The town organizers had plans to build a square in the center of town. They boasted a butcher, a barber, a survey engineer, and a watchmaker as residents.

In the fall and winter of 1858–1859, Montana City had three rows of homes and up to 250 gold miners, town developers, and mountain men living in log cabins, tents, and makeshift dwellings under the trees. In fact, Montana City began to show signs of becoming the principal town of the gold region, and "for some weeks it was looked upon as a formidable rival to the cities projected at the mouth of Cherry Creek [Auraria and Denver]. Diggings that pay from one to four cents to the pan surround the locality, and when water is brought in, corner lots, streets and commons will give way before the miner's pick and rich pay, in shining gold, will be his reward."[7] Indeed, Montana City was "the nucleus of the gold-prospecting communities springing up, the commercial centre and Rocky Mountain metropolis."[8]

The founding of Montana City started with a chance encounter in the winter of 1857–1858. While visiting the Delaware Indians near Lawrence to buy meat for his butcher shop, John Easter encountered Fall Leaf, a young Indian who had just returned from the eastern slopes of the Rocky Mountains. There he had served as a guide for Colonel E. V. Sumner of the regular army in putting down an Arapahoe rebellion, and he had found some gold in a little stream of water when he got off his horse to get a drink. Fall Leaf ignited tremendous excitement in Easter's heart when he showed the merchant "quite a bunch of gold nuggets tied up in a rag." Could Fall Leaf find the place again? He said he could. Easter offered him $5 per day to direct a party to the spot. Fall Leaf agreed. In the ensuing weeks, Fall Leaf, who "bore certificates of honesty," revealed that "not the sands only, but the rocks and earth for miles around were studded--nay, filled--with particles, nuggets, even boulders of the purest gold." Besides, Fall Leaf carried about with him a "full-moon-sized silver medallion likeness of Franklin Pierce." And so the adventurers, wanting to believe, accepted his every word as truth.[9]

John Easter had gone West once before. Years earlier, as a youth living in Iowa, Easter had joined a band of gold seekers bound for California, and they traveled through portions of what is now Colorado on the way. The party never reached its destination and

Easter returned home. He later moved to Lawrence and opened his meat market. But Easter remembered the excitement of his earlier venture and leapt at the chance to repeat it. He "belonged to the class of men called soldiers of fortune . . . yet he was never a desperate character like some of the men who drifted to the frontier in the mid-century and later. . . . He had an adventurous spirit and he gathered around him others to whom the lure of gold was a powerful magnet."[10]

This young man, in fever pitch at the prospect of picking up gold nuggets lying there in plain sight and building the towns that were sure to follow, organized a company of "moving spirits" that winter. By the end of May 1858, they were ready to go. Ten ox-drawn wagon teams assembled early one morning, intending to travel the Santa Fe Trail's southern route for the

710-mile trip to the "Pike's Peak Region." But when it came time to head out, Fall Leaf was nowhere to be found, "and so we went without him," Parsons said simply. But not everyone joined in that lovely spring morning, as the train edged its way onto the trail. Easter, reluctant to leave without the only person who knew where they were going and how to get there, decided to stay and search for Fall Leaf. He appointed John H. Tierney, one of the oldest men in the group and one who had crossed the plains to California ten years before, as captain and sent the wagon train on its way. Easter and Roswell Hutchins stayed behind to search for Fall Leaf.

They finally located the guide, but Fall Leaf either refused outright to accompany the party or was incapacitated, depending on which of the various accounts about the matter is true. One version is that

This log cabin was erected in 1959 on the Montana City site (now Frontier Park), using logs from one of the 1858 cabins. *Photo by Millie Van Wyke*

Fall Leaf feared that the Indians of the plains would kill and scalp him if he showed up there again, probably because of his association with the Sumner expedition the summer before. Another story is that "Fall Leaf . . . was hired to pilot the company, but before the time came he took sick from an overdose of touse [sic] lightning,

John Easter. *Colorado Historical Society*

fell from his horse, and was otherwise demoralized."[11] Parsons agreed that Taos lightning (or "Mexican whiskey," distilled from wheat) was responsible. He added,

> a few days before the time set for our departure, Fall Leaf was attending a dance given by the dusky maidens of his tribe, and too much fire-water increased his natural desire to fight somebody, without conferring the requisite ability, and, as a consequence, he went home with broken ribs and other damages, and was compelled to forego the pleasure of leading us to that beautiful grassy canon in the big hills, where we could load our wagons with the golden treasure.[12]

Easter offered Fall Leaf every inducement he could think of to get him to come, but "when it came to a showdown, Mr. Fall Leaf refused to accompany us," he said. Dejected, Easter and Hutchins finally hitched up their mule team and left without him, overtaking the Lawrence party at Council Grove. After talking over their predicament and realizing that they had no idea where Fall Leaf had intended to take them or where he had found the nuggets, Easter's party decided to strike out anyway. They had come this far, and the promise of a gold-studded future in the West was too seductive for them to stop.[13]

This group of young, inexperienced, and now leaderless "boys" from Lawrence, Parsons wrote later, had

> lived upon the excitement of camp and field during the Border-Ruffian war just ended, and found their chief delight in the half-military, semi-savage routine of the "quarters," and the bewitching daily uncertainty as to what tomorrow might bring forth. They could not and they would not endure the monotony of the piping time of peace which had evidently set in. . . . During the winter and spring of 1858, they set out to devise ways and means to satisfy their craving appetite for vagabondry and adventure. The irrepressible Indian tale of exhaustless quarries of solid gold was whispered around in the very nick of time, and disclosed the opportunity which they so much desired.[14]

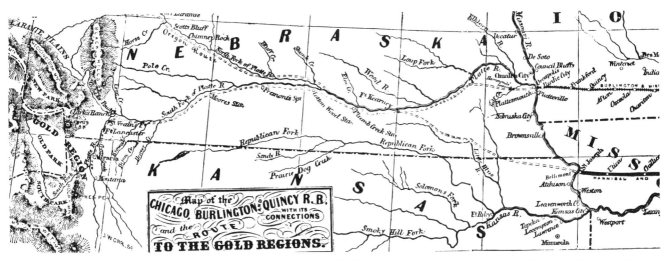

Chicago, Burlington & Quincy Railroad map showing 1858 "goldfields" of Montana [City] and Auraria. *Colorado Historical Society*

One of the men, Jason Younker, a schoolteacher, telegrapher, and carpenter, had been taken prisoner in that war but was released unharmed. For Younker and the others, a jaunt to the Rocky Mountains filled the bill. Once they had filed onto "the most wonderful highway of the world, the Santa Fe Road, more than two hundred feet wide and over eight hundred miles long and as smooth and well-beaten as a city street," the men became positively giddy with excitement, "profoundly commiserating the unhappy lot of those left behind, compelled, as they were, to endure the troubles and trials of civilization, wear clothes, eat cooked victuals with knives and forks, and submit to the galling restraints of law and order."[15] Although they were ignorant of the geography and topography of the plains, without a guide or guidebook, and not knowing where they were going or how to get there, "Still, we were happy. A rifle, revolver, one hundred pounds of flour, beans, dried apples, sugar, coffee and bacon, from a third to a half suit of clothes, ten pounds of tobacco, five gallons of whiskey, and about one-fourth of two yoke of oxen and a rickety wagon, was the interest of each man in the total outfit."[16]

At Council Grove, Captain James Holmes, his wife, Julia, and her brother, Albert Archibald, joined the group. Another family, Mr. and Mrs. Robert Middleton and their child, and two men (one named Cassidy, the other unknown) had been bound for Utah but were prevented from doing so by the prospect of a Mormon war; they had joined the group earlier at Dragoon Creek. Augustus Voorhees noted in a diary he kept throughout the trip that at this point the party had nine ox teams, two horse teams, one mule team, fifty head of cattle, forty-six men, two women, one child, and eight loose horses.

The Lawrence party "knocked around the country pretty much all summer," observing buffalo as far as the eye could see and bartering with Indians. For a cup of sugar and a little coffee, they could get a good buffalo robe. At Walnut Creek, Captain Tierney wisely advised Easter to pay the "toll" levied by the Indians on all people passing through their country, who they considered trespassers. Easter agreed, and "payment" of flour, sugar, coffee, and tobacco to the chiefs of four principal tribes representing 8,000 people and a ceremonial smoking of the peace pipe assured their safe passage into buffalo country.

"Let no man dare to charge us with lofty courage, enterprise or pluck, or commend our determination to hew our way to fortune," Parsons wrote. "We determined nothing of the sort. We simply intended to float around and let our fortunes find us." They first caught sight of Pike's Peak in late June. "It was to us everything. It stood for the whole country, from Mexico to our northern line. It represented gold, and plenty of it; it spoke of influence, power and position in our middle age, and ease and comfort in our decline. I think that with the first view of the celebrated mountain, we felt the first quickening of a definite purpose."[17]

On July 4, just shy of reaching the mountain, they celebrated the nation's birthday by firing a sunrise salute, reading the Declaration of Independence, making speeches, hoisting a flag, dancing, and setting off fireworks. Throughout the day they kept open wagons and open kegs. For a couple of weeks in early July, the party prospected at the base of Pike's Peak but did not find gold. Frank Cobb, John D. Miller, and Augustus Voorhees climbed to the top of Pike's Peak on July 8. Cobb wrote, "When we reached the summit we made a thorough search to ascertain whether anyone had ever done so before, but could find no indication that anyone had. We built a mound of stone and cut our names in wood, giving our names and date of ascent."[18]

Julia Holmes and her husband, James, also climbed to the top of Pike's Peak and remained there two days and nights. Julia, dressed in tight black pants, a hickory shirt, and a pair of moccasins, was the first woman ever to ascend the mountain. In a letter to her mother, written on the summit, she told how "nearly everyone tried to discourage me from attempting it, but I believed I should succeed and now, here I am. We brought a week's provisions, proposing to remain here and write some letters, etc."[19] Captain Holmes took a volume of Emerson's essays. Parsons wrote that Julia "slept upon the eternal snow, and wrote letters to the Eastern press dated at the summit. She did not claim to be a heroine, by any means; but if a record is to be made at all, it should be accurate, and I therefore register *our* woman's name. . . . She is probably the first woman who ever stood upon a point on the American continent anywhere near 14,000 feet above the level of the sea, and, for aught I know, the first who ever stood that high anywhere."[20]

Julia later served as secretary of the National Woman Suffrage Association in Washington, D.C.

The Lawrence party then headed south. The Middleton and Holmes families left the party along the way, and T. C. Dickson, who had been with the Russell party, joined it.

The San Luis Valley jaunt turned out to be another wild goose chase. Just when lounging about the Fort Garland store was getting tiresome, however, the welcome news came of gold at Cherry Creek and the Platte River.

With the Kansas Company in Montana City were Count Henri Murat and his wife, Katrina Wolf Murat, a colorful couple who had crossed the plains three times, riding over 10,000 miles since 1848, before settling there. The count claimed to be a nephew of Napoleon Bonaparte's king of Naples. The Murats loved Montana City. In a letter to a friend in Germany dated December 14, 1858, the count related that he and another young man

> felled the trees for our log cabin in six hours, and . . . tomorrow we shall have the cabin done ready for occupancy. We are not sorry for coming out here, for in the first place it is the most lovely country you ever saw. Gold is found everywhere you stick your shovel . . . and there is no doubt but the pay will be from ten to twenty dollars per day to the man. As I remarked above, gold is here plenty, and as soon as spring makes its appearance, the whole world will be in a blaze of astonishment at the riches that will be taken out of the earth. . . . We count now, all told, 250 men."[21]

At Montana City and later in Auraria, the count barbered and shaved the men's beards at a dollar a shave. Katrina ran a laundry business, charging an outrageous three dollars for half a dozen pieces of linen. The couple moved to Auraria in 1859, where the count built the El Dorado Hotel with David Smoke. The countess, "blue eyed, rosy cheeked, golden haired," was the cook and chambermaid. In May, when news came that an express line had been established between Leavenworth, Kansas, and Denver, she sewed the first flag to fly over the towns of Auraria and Denver City, from the roof of the El Dorado, the newcomers having forgotten to bring one. "From her trunk she took a red merino skirt purchased in Paris and other garments to make the stars and stripes. . . .

When the first stage coach arrived, this flag was the only one to celebrate the coming of rapid transportation."[22]

For the town developers, the summer and fall of 1858 had been fruitful. Parsons and five others, "having been elected to several offices each" in the many claims they had staked, set out to return to "the States" for the winter of 1858. They got lost and ran out of provisions. Along the way, they tried to convince the hordes of westbound wagons to go back home but suffered abuse and insults in return for their favor. It took five months and ten days to find their way home to Lawrence; only William Parsons ever returned, and then only for a brief visit in 1870. Parsons, a brilliant man who had learned Latin and Greek at age thirteen and graduated from Dartmouth two years before his trip West, made good use of his experiences. The same year that he returned to Kansas, he published a guidebook entitled *The Gold Mines of Western Kansas, Being a Complete Description of the Newly Discovered Gold Mines, Different Routes, Camping Places, Tools and Outfit and Containing Everything Important for the Immigrant and Miner to Know*. Although he advised travelers on everything from proper clothing to tools to trading with natives, he fully expected "to see thousands returning in a year or two discouraged and dissatisfied." He warned that

> sickness, misfortune and death will overtake and conquer many—crime, idleness and extravagance will involve in ruin hundreds besides their followers. . . . The exodus of honest, patriotic peace-loving citizens will be side by side with that of the gambler, horse-thief, and the more accomplished metropolitan desperado—and the shouts of honorable industry will be mingled with the curses and vile jests of the abandoned of every age and sex. But the good will surpass the evil.[23]

Few listened to his warnings; they then blamed him for their failure. "Thousands rushed to the mines in the wildest excitement, with every imaginable outfit, even to hand-carts and wheelbarrows and came crawling back poorer. . . . Forgetting that it was *their* excitement that exaggerated things beyond all reason, they everywhere denounced me as a liar and a cheat," he complained.[24]

From the day the Lawrence party established Montana City in September 1858, some of them had misgivings about the site, fearing that it was too far from major travel routes. These serious town builders decided, after scouting the surrounding country within a few days after arriving, that the area where Cherry Creek meets the Platte was the place of the future. They immediately had their surveyor, William Hartley, plat a one-mile square area on the east side of Cherry Creek. Frank Cobb drove the first stake and carried the chain to make the survey. The men joined up with two local men, John S. Smith and William McGaa, and went back to Montana City to draw up an article of agreement and constitution for St. Charles City on the "Upper Waters of the South Platte River at the Mouth of Cherry Creek, Arapaho County, Kansas Territory" among the nine parties. Four of the seven Lawrence men were elected officers: Adnah French was president; T. C. Dickson, secretary; Frank M. Cobb, recorder; and William (Nick) Smith, treasurer. William Hartley, Jr., Charles Nichols, and John A. Churchill served on the board of trustees.

But the Lawrence men were to lose their portion of the claim later. In October, "not expecting anyone from the States [to come West] so late in the season and being short of grub and money," Cobb said, all seven of them plus Dickson started back to the States, planning to return in the spring. They left McGaa and Smith to represent the St. Charles Company. At about 100 miles down the Platte, they met parties from the States en route to their claim site. Fearing their town might be confiscated by this group, "we sent Charles Nichols back to look after our interests and donate lots to induce these people to locate and build [under our charter]," Cobb said. The rest of them continued to Lawrence. But when Nichols arrived, he found that a party led by William Larimer had taken possession of their location and laid out a town called Denver City. To add insult, the claim-jumpers "threatened him with violence."

During their winter in Lawrence, the men succeeded in obtaining a charter for St. Charles from Governor S. Medary, dated February 11, 1859. But it was too late. When they returned to "St. Charles" in June, they found a bustling town being surveyed and platted as Denver City. French resigned as president of the St. Charles Town Company and John A. Churchill was elected to succeed him. They held a meeting in October 1859 to try to salvage their shares in the Denver Town Company, but they failed. St. Charles had disappeared into Denver City. McGaa claimed that the new Kansas territorial governor, James W. Denver, had sent a delegation to visit him and threatened to take St. Charles by force if McGaa did not hand it over willingly. The governor's representatives had also told McGaa that the Lawrence men (Cobb's party) "would be taken care of" and would not return. "Through threats and the influence of ardent spirits, I acquiesced," McGaa stated in 1866.[25]

The business of locating towns was moving forward. About the same time that Cobb's group set out for "home" for the winter, Lawrence men Giles Blood, Joseph Brown, John Easter, Roswell Hutchins, and William Regan also left Montana City in search of a more profitable location. They found it on the west bank of Cherry Creek, directly across the river from St. Charles. They immediately organized the Auraria Town Company and established Auraria, building their log cabins there or moving cabins to Cherry Creek from Montana City. Many Montana City residents joined one or the other of the new towns. William Chadsey, Howard Hunt, Peter Halsey, and possibly Joseph Brown of the Lawrence party were given a lot each, with the stipulation that they improve on it. Whether they built homes is not recorded.

The first attempt to establish a county in the area involved many Lawrence men. An act created February 7, 1859, established Montana County, which included Denver City in its boundaries. It appointed wagon train captain J. H. Tierney, William H. Prentiss, and A. D. Richardson commissioners to look after Montana County. Accounts of these elections and the process of dividing Kansas Territory into counties are sketchy and speculative, but it appears that Montana County was never officially recognized and was replaced by Arapahoe County. In March, an election of county officers included Roswell Hutchins as assessor. It is not clear whether the appointment was to Arapahoe County or Montana County.

At Montana City, those remaining passed the mild winter of 1858–1859 panning in the Platte River. On February 9, 1859, the Act to Incorporate the Montana Town Company in Arapahoe County, Kansas Territory, was granted by Governor Medary to Charles Nichols (who was also a founder of St. Charles City), Josiah Hinman, Jason Younker, Howard Hunt (who also had a lot in Auraria), William B. Parsons (who had long since fled), and J. H. Sweeney (who must have joined them later, as he was not a Lawrence man). The document is dated two days before the St. Charles incorporation was granted, thus making Montana City the first to be granted a charter.[26] The six men were empowered to make contracts, sue and be sued, and plead and be impleaded; they were authorized to have and use a common seal; they could acquire and hold any quantity of land not exceeding 640 acres; and they could plat the town into parcels, squares, and lots and sell, dispose of, and convey the same. Also granted to the town company was the power to construct courses, sluices, and ditches for conducting water from the South Platte River for mining purposes.

The Montana City incorporation "was the first political beginning in this region, for here was held the first election, which was the seed of future political movements that culminated in the present Centennial State."[27] Montana City and Auraria voters sent delegate H. J. Graham to Congress to obtain recognition for the new settlers as legal landholders. Although the various town companies simply moved onto Indian lands and acted as if the lands were in fact theirs, they had no legal right to it. Representing the Pike's Peak region, Graham "went on his mission to Uncle Sam as beggar for authority to act the role of squatter sovereign; to get rich by picking gold from the sand of the rivers; to plant civilization in the wilderness and found an empire."[28]

Count Henri Murat's prediction of spring riches never materialized. Even though Montana City was indeed the first town to exist, it became clear that its location was too far away from where the action was—the Cherry Creek–Platte River confluence. In the spring of 1859, residents of Montana City began tearing down their cabins and moving the logs by mule, horse, and oxen or simply floating them down the Platte and fishing them out at Auraria and Denver City, where they rebuilt their homes. By the summer of 1859, a few abandoned logs were all that remained of the town, the "string of shanties" having "been killed flatter than a wheat field—which it became in the ensuing spring," according to Owen Goldrick, Denver's first schoolteacher.[29]

Montana Town Company secretary William J. Boyer "took over" the town site and combined it with additional land for a ranch. In 1861 he sold the site for $750 and moved to Pony, Montana, a few years later.

The adventure over, the Lawrence men scattered. In 1859 John Easter and Roswell Hutchins built the second log cabin ever to be constructed in Denver City. It stood on what is now Eleventh Street between Wazee and Wynkoop. But Easter did not stay long. He went back to Leavenworth in 1861 and later traveled to Oregon and the Black Hills of South Dakota. He returned to Leadville in 1876 for eight years and then traveled to Wyoming and the Northwest again. He settled in the Cripple Creek District of Goldfield, Colorado, in 1894; he became its first mayor and later served as justice of the peace. Easter was respected and loved to such a degree that his birthdays were celebrated by the townspeople. He died in Goldfield on December 5, 1914, at the age of eighty-four. "Easter could not entirely get out of the habit of gold-seeking. In his closing years he made occasional prospecting tours into the hills, but he never succeeded in locating any valuable strikes around Goldfield. . . . Easter would have made a fortune if he had remained in Denver and held on to what real estate he possessed," wrote Eugene Parsons.[30]

Frank Cobb, who had returned in 1859 to try to salvage St. Charles, had taken what lots his claim-jumpers gave him "and made the best of it." At one time he owned 130 lots there but lost 92 when his bonds, kept in the city safe, were lost when the safe was swept away in the flood of 1864. Cobb left Denver at the outbreak of the Civil War and was with the Union army until its close. He returned to Colorado in his later years and engaged in mining.

Joseph Brown married William McGaa's widow and moved to the Pine Ridge Indian Agency in South Dakota. Adnah French, president of the St. Charles Town Company and originally from Brandon, Vermont, died poor in Santa Fe in 1872. John D. Miller settled in Pueblo, Albert W. Archibald in Trinidad, and Roswell Hutchins in Utah.

T. C. Dickson became a commissioner for Fremont County. Josiah Hinman committed himself to making Colorado a state; he traveled to settlements in El Paso and El Dorado counties to champion the cause. The few people who lived there were persuaded, and they elected Hinman to represent them to the first constitutional convention, held in November 1858. Hinman was elected a vice-president of the convention, and he may have helped draft its official documents. The *Denver Republican* noted that Hinman was a graceful writer, and his efforts in that direction were of great value to Colorado in its early days.[31] Hinman died in Vergens, Vermont, in July 1883.

Jason T. Younker spent a year "killing game and prospecting for gold" before deciding to farm along the Platte River near the Montana City site. He sold his farm in 1879 and moved to Denver. Younker served as an alderman for the Fifth Ward from 1881 to 1883 and was president of the Colorado Pioneer Association.

Today the Platte River, which has repeatedly flooded, recut, and rechanneled since 1859, flows quietly past Frontier Park, which now occupies part of the Montana City site. Only ancient cottonwoods and a replica of an 1858 cabin, built in 1959 with logs from one of the original log houses, exist where once a teeming, exciting cluster of dreamers worked, ate, slept, and panned for gold.

The Montana Town Company incorporators, believing they had made a mistake after all in choosing the site at what is now West Evans Avenue and the South Platte River, proved to be merely ahead of their time. The dream so dear to visionaries Boyer, Hinman, Nichols, Younker, Hunt, Sweeney, and Parsons—of a town that would someday develop into a valuable and desirable place to live—was sound, as it turned out. Twenty-seven years after the founding of Montana City, a new generation of "southsiders" mapped a three-mile-square city and incorporated it as the Town of South Denver. Like its predecessor, this town proved to be tumultuous and short-lived, but its people eventually knit themselves into a very special community, just as the Lawrence party had visualized.

The Southsiders

William Boyer's ranch on the former Montana City site was not completely isolated. Other settlers from the States also lived far south of Denver City as early as 1859. But gold was not what drew them to the area. These farsighted residents recognized early on that food, irrigation, newspapers, railroads, homes, schools, and churches would be needed long after the gold ran out.

Rufus Clark came to Colorado from Bedford, Iowa, with his wife, Lucinda, and their infant daughter, Mary, on July 11, 1859. Unimpressed with gold discoveries either in California or in the Pike's Peak region, Clark decided to seek his fortune in something less chancy and more down to earth: potatoes. He settled on a beautifully located and fertile 160-acre farm on the east bank of the South Platte River (now Overland Park) that ran from the river to what is now South Broadway and Florida to Jewell avenues and built a shack along the river for his family. Clark put most of the acreage into wheat, onions, potatoes, and other vegetables, and his first crop of potatoes was abundant enough to start him on his way to riches and earn him the nickname of "Potato Clark."

Clark had left his Connecticut farm family at age sixteen to sail on whaling ships in the South Atlantic and around the Horn into the Arctic, at one point becoming shipwrecked off the coast of Australia.

During his years as a sailor he became a "a confirmed drunkard, a slave to drink, so deep in the mire of sin and drink I never cherished a hope of getting out."[1] Nevertheless, his reputation as a trustworthy businessman and successful farmer got him elected to the territorial legislature in 1864, which met in Golden. It may have been during this brief stint in politics that Clark became acquainted with the governor at the time, John Evans, a man he would work closely with for many years afterward. Clark also served on the Arapahoe County School Board for one term.

Lucinda died in 1861, and in 1866, Clark married Mrs. Mary Gaff, who had a son of her own. Clark became wealthy from his potatoes and shared his good fortune with others. After the Chicago fire in 1871, he started for downtown Denver with a wagonload of potatoes to be donated to the stricken city. But the Salomon Brothers store provided eighty-pound sacks for Clark's potatoes and suggested that he auction his potatoes off and send the money instead. When word got out, other citizens contributed items—a silver pitcher, two boxes of cigars, five sacks of flour, a hat, boots, wine, a barrel of apples, a desk, and a box of oysters. The hat sold for $46. The first bag of potatoes brought $250, and the total raised from Clark's crop was $1,300. When everything was sold, Clark auctioned off the sale sign for $7. That night Denver's mayor sent a check for $7,220 to Chicago, an amount that included

Clark's auction money and other contributions from individuals.[2]

But alcohol continued to control his life until a dramatic religious conversion by the "gamblers' sermon" of Rev. E. P. Hammond in 1873 took away his desire for alcohol and turned him into a generous contributor to his church and the community. Clark became a staunch prohibitionist and a positive force in the affairs of South Denver.

Clark joined the United Brethren Church, and together with neighbors Emmet Nuckols and George H. Bryan formed the Nuckols Society of United Brethren to further the aims of the denomination. In 1874 they purchased a plot of land on the west side of South Broadway just north of the present Yale Avenue from Thomas M. Field for a token one dollar for church purposes. But the church failed to materialize and the society disbanded, so in 1886 the three men deeded the land back to Field. Rufus Clark also helped found the Salvation Army and, along with another man, donated a downtown building for it.

But Clark, "big and burly with an emphatic voice and bushy beard,"[3] retained all his old energies and mannerisms. Laborer C. A. Trease tended potatoes on the farm for only two months because he had "had enough" of one of the toughest fellows he had ever met. He insisted that Rufus Clark worked his horses and workers to death in spite of the fact that he had "got religion." In 1878 Mary drowned in a cloudburst that swelled the farm's irrigation ditches and flooded the fields. Trease said that "she was hurrying in from the field when the storm overtook her. When they found her she was dead, with her long hair all entangled in a barb-wire fence."[4] Four years later, Clark married Ella Perryman, who outlived him.

About the time that Rufus Clark was planting his first potato crop, William N. Byers arrived in Denver from Omaha with his wife, Elizabeth, their two children, and a printing press; he began publishing the *Rocky Mountain News* in 1860. Soon afterward, he bought land on the bank of the South Platte River between Alameda and Virginia avenues. The ranch was Byers's particular delight—"680 acres is low bottom that will produce well without irrigation—40 acres of that amount will be ready for cultivation this spring—10 remain in grass and 10 in timber. . . . Altogether it is one of the pleasantest and will be one

of the . . . best paying farms in this country."[5] In the fall of 1859 he built a temporary log house with a board roof. "The house had no floor and the grass roots were in evidence, the ground not even being smoothed off," Elizabeth wrote. "Most of the cabins at that time had mud roofs, but I didn't want my things ruined by water dripping from the mud roof for days after a rain. We had our belongings, including a cook stove . . . and with my nice silver, napery and our own things about us we felt quite at home and contented, crude as it was."[6]

After their move to downtown Denver in November, the family spent the summers of 1861, 1862, and 1863 at the ranch. Early one morning in June 1864, the river flooded, stranding them. As the waters rose, the family prepared to leave for higher ground. But while the gardener "went out on the plain to bring in the horses, the river suddenly cut through a low strip of land, leaving us marooned on an island," Elizabeth Byers wrote later. She continued,

> By this time our friends in town had become anxious about us, and reported our plight to Col. Chivington. The Colonel rode out and brought some soldiers from Camp, . . . returned to town and built a boat; probably a boat never was constructed in a shorter time than that one. It was put on one of Uncle Sam's military wagons and brought to our relief. . . . We were brought into town where Governor and Mrs. Evans kindly took us in and gave us a home for ten days.[7]

The Byers tried to return to the ranch, but the threat of another flood sent them back to Denver, where they took temporary rooms at the Colorado Seminary built by Governor Evans.

Elizabeth was appalled at the poverty-stricken stranded families, deserted wives, and homeless children she saw wandering the streets. She founded the Ladies Union Aid Society in January 1860 to help deserted children find homes and to provide other services.[8] In 1862 she knocked on the door of every downtown store and passed the hat at every saloon to collect money for the poor who had suffered terribly through a severe winter. "I stopped at the News office first. My husband laughed when I asked for a big, long pocketbook to bring home the contributions. I told him I was going to come back at four o'clock with $500."[9] William said she'd never do it. But at four o'clock she triumphantly returned to the *Rocky*

Elizabeth Byers at home, 151 South Washington Street. *Denver Public Library, Western History Department*

E. M. Byers Home for Boys, 64 West Alameda Avenue. *Denver Public Library, Western History Department*

Mountain News office with $519.

Thirty years later she was still at it. In 1893 she established the Working Boys Home and School at 1615 Lincoln, moving it to 1129 South Fifteenth (the present south Acoma Street) in 1898. By this time the Byers family had built a lovely red sandstone home at 151 South Washington Street, where William died on March 25, 1903.

William and Elizabeth had platted Byers Sub-division in 1874 (Alameda to Virginia avenues and Broadway to Bannock streets) and in 1905 Elizabeth moved her boys' home to a new building at 64 West Alameda Avenue near their home. Renamed the E. M. Byers Home for Boys, it was open to boys eight to twelve years of age whose parents were unable to provide for them. "No child is taken who has two parents living together, but only when the home has been broken up and they would be left uncared for to run wild most of the time at some lodging house or lonely farm or cabin."[10] The home kept an average of twenty-five homeless boys at any given time and on Sundays filled three pews at a nearby church, where they also presented an annual concert. Elizabeth Byers remained president of the E. M. Byers Home for Boys until her death on January 6, 1920. Her body lay in state at the Home for a day and the funeral was held in the main assembly room. The building was torn down in 1966.

Another investor in the new town, John W. Smith, came to Denver in June 1860 with a wagonload of construction machinery, looking for something to build. Like Rufus Clark, Smith knew that agriculture would be as important as mining in this new country; for that to succeed, water and irrigation ditches were essential. Smith watched with interest as the Capitol Hydraulic Company, which William Byers had helped to incorporate in 1859 with a capital stock of half a million dollars, began digging a ditch intended to transport water to the city from its headgate on Richard Little's land on the South Platte River near the present Bowles Avenue. Little was also the engineer for the ditch and founder of the town of Littleton. But Capitol Hydraulic encountered problems and completed only three miles of the ditch before abandoning the whole project a year later.

Smith knew that this ditch needed to be dug, and in 1864 he was awarded a contract for $10,000 and one-half of the capital stock of the Capitol Hydraulic Company to construct a new ditch wide enough and deep enough to admit the passage of small flatboats for the transportation of wood, coal, lumber, and other material into the city. In December Smith brought in a Rotary Canal Builder, a mammoth four-wheel outfit that looked like a combination fire engine, artillery wagon, mowing machine, and colossal steam plow, according to William Byers's *Rocky Mountain News*. This machine was manufactured in Illinois at a cost of $1,200, and Smith paid another $1,300 to ship it to Denver. In the spring of 1865 Smith harnessed eight or ten yoke of oxen to his canal excavator and began digging an open, unlined ditch three feet wide on the bottom and seven feet wide at the top, with steep sides. He began six and one-half miles above Littleton, with the ditch entering South Denver at the present Yale Avenue and Clarkson Street.[11] From there the ditch meandered to the north and east and then dipped into a natural depression (perhaps a former buffalo wallow) that Smith owned to create a lake (the present Washington Park's north lake). It exited South Denver at Alameda near Humboldt street.

The first water flowed through the 24-mile-long ditch in 1867, putting twenty or thirty thousand acres of good agricultural land under production through irrigation. The Capitol Hydraulic Company name had been changed to the Platte Water Company, with John W. Smith its agent, and the company, eager to show what irrigation could do for crop raising, convinced the already famous "Potato" Clark to help them out. Smith set aside 160 acres adjacent to Clark's farm as far east as Clarkson Street, gave him free access to the ditch water, and asked him to produce a fine crop of potatoes. Clark hired seventy-five men, ordered a batch of newfangled implements called potato forks, for which he had to pay freight of nearly two dollars each, and raised 16,000 bushels of potatoes. Word of his abundant fall harvest spread, and buyers came from as far as Cheyenne to pay two dollars a bushel for them.[12] The ditch company had proved the value of irrigation and in the years to come farmers and ranchers dug lateral ditches all along the banks of the ditch to water their crops, fields, lawns, and gardens. Trees and shrubs were also planted all along the watercourse.

Rufus "Potato" Clark. *Denver Public Library, Western History Department*

The city of Denver, however, was not happy with Smith's management of the ditch and complained constantly over the next years that the Platte Water Company did not maintain its ditch properly. Smith offered to sell the ditch to the city, which refused to purchase it for unknown reasons. Things came to a head in the summer of 1874, when Smith's ditch collapsed at its source in August, at the driest part of the season when water was most needed; had it not been for frequent showers, thousands of trees would have died.

This situation pointed up the danger of depending on a single ditch for the city's water supply, so six of Denver's aldermen began negotiations to construct a second major ditch out of the South Platte River, half of it to be owned by the city. This ditch would begin

above Brown's Bridge between Petersburg and Littleton and flow east of and approximately parallel to the river. The ditch would take the water after it had been used by Richard Little's Rough and Ready Mill for mill purposes and traverse twelve miles into downtown Denver, using about two miles of the unfinished Capitol Hydraulic Company's 1860 ditch for part of its course.

But John Smith's Platte Water Company and "its friends" Rufus Clark and Peter Magnes (founder of Petersburg, now part of Sheridan) successfully blocked the city's attempt by refusing to grant rights-of-way through their properties. Smith, of course, preferred to sell his own ditch to the city, and Clark and Magnes were not inclined to support municipally owned enterprises that could threaten their own private ditches and lands.

An exasperated William Byers, in his *Rocky Mountain News,* charged the company with forcing the sale on the city through negligence and could see no alternative to the city's buying the ditch: "It is a disagreeable truth, but one which might as well be openly confessed, that we are in the hands of this corporation and will be until this ditch is purchased. The sooner it now becomes the property of the city, the better."[13] The city purchased it in 1875, renamed it City Ditch, and eventually extended it to City Park for a total of twenty-seven miles. (Today the water is discharged from Chatfield Dam.) Smith leased his lake and property (now Washington Park's Smith Lake), twenty acres in all, to the city for ninety-nine years for $2,500. He was permitted to build an ice house and harvest the annual crop of ice and was required to keep the lake constantly filled and in order. The city also went ahead with its plans to construct a second ditch, which they called the Merchant's Mill Ditch. This ditch flowed from the South Platte River into Lake Archer, the city's reservoir, at about First Avenue, supplying Denver population with plentiful water until it was filled in about 1905.

During his twenty-three years in Denver, Smith, an Irish-Welsh man of varied interests, also built numerous planing, quartz, and flour mills across the state, the American House downtown, and Smith's Chapel at 900 Galapago Street. He was one of the directors of the Denver Woolen Mills and in 1880 organized the Denver City Steam Heat Company, forerunner of the

Public Service Company. He was also a promoter of the Denver Pacific Railroad and later president of the Denver, South Park, and Pacific Railroad. Pearl Street may have been named by Smith after Pearl Smith, daughter of his son Albert.[14] Smith left Denver in 1883 and died in 1895, leaving his Smith's Lake property to his daughter Laura, who had married Henry M. Porter, an entrepreneur and real estate investor like her father, in 1874.

After the brief gold rush of 1858 evaporated, Denver stagnated. In the 1860s, a fire, a major flood, and "Indian scares" contributed to its decline. But the arrival of the Kansas Pacific Railroad on August 18, 1870, linking Denver with the East Coast, brought prosperity to the town and to all of Arapahoe County.

General William J. Palmer's narrow-gauge Denver and Rio Grande Railroad came along a few months later and quickly became the most important railroad in assuring Denver's regional dominance. Palmer established the Denver and Rio Grande depot and shops at about Eleventh Avenue and chose three-foot-wide tracks over the standard gauge of four feet, eight-and-a-half inches, in order to run the railroad to mining camps and mountain districts. Palmer laid tracks south along the river, reaching Colorado Springs by October 1871, Cañon City by 1875, and Leadville in 1877, eventually linking Denver with Grand Junction. The D&RG, the first three-foot gauge track in Colorado, was instrumental in bringing manufacturers and businesses along its tracks and developing the western edge of South Denver as the industrial center it remains today.

Thomas Skerritt, who had arrived in Denver with his sixteen-year-old bride, Maria, in 1859 and grew massive apple orchards at his 600-acre Shadyside at Broadway and Sheridan Avenue (now Hampden), recognized the importance of a major railroad and of Smith's irrigation system and their impact on future growth. During the 1860s, farmers along the South Platte River as far south as Littleton struggled to survive the harsh economy, driving their teams and wagons either down County Road 30 (the present Santa Fe Drive) or over several miles of rough, undeveloped prairie to deliver produce to Denver markets. On April 25, 1871, Skerritt and twenty-two like-minded farmers, including Rufus Clark and Peter Magnes, petitioned the Arapahoe County commissioners to build a new

county road from Shadyside north to Jewell Avenue, where it would turn west and hook up with the county road.[15]

In May "road viewers" Richard L. Little, George Bryan, and county surveyor A. H. Deane examined the proposed road and recommended that the Jewell Avenue leg be eliminated in favor of continuing straight north to the very banks of Cherry Creek.[16]

The story of who actually constructed South Broadway (County Road 12) is unclear. Both the well-known and respected historian and author Alice Polk Hill, who moved to South Broadway the next year, and James O. Patterson, who also purchased property along the road five years later, stated that Thomas Skerritt, with the help of his four sons, Joseph, George, Harry, and Charles, "locked the hind wheels of his heavy farm wagon and, cutting into the sod, dragged a straight track, by the aid of section line stakes, from Shadyside to Cherry Creek. Dragging a heavy log behind the wagon for leveling, three times back and forth the entire route gave a plain road which became Broadway, called so from the first because of the width, 100 feet."[17]

The Skerritts were not to be stopped by a creek, either, even though the commissioners did not allocate funds to replace the bridge washed away in the 1864 flood. Indeed, Patterson said, "Cherry Creek in those days every now and then went on a rampage . . . so the Skerritts graded down their road and laid a heavy reinforced plank road on the creek bed so wagons could go across without sinking in the sand." This "surface" bridge, made of planks bound together on the edge, was about sixty or seventy feet long and

> had the advantage of the water running over it in flood time and not carrying it away. We had posts drove [sic] in the bed of the creek and a plank walk about ten inches or a foot wide, fastened to that. This walk was some two feet above the ground. It was allright to walk this narrow plank when the water was not running freely beneath you, but if it was you got dizzy. Mrs. John Dailey [wife of Byers's partner] tells me she tried to walk it one day when she found the swift running water was going to affect her, so she got down on her knees, and thus made her way over.

Even the horses fell victim to the hypnotizing swirl of the water beneath their feet. Patterson wrote,

I remember coming home one evening from town, I found the swift running water covered the whole creek bottom. It looked like the Missouri River, but I knew it was only about a foot deep, so I drove my horse in to it. When about a rod from shore, the horse stopped and fell flat over on his side, the running water had made him dizzy. I jumped out and got him loose from the wagon, led him out on the bank, and pulled the wagon out with much exertion.[18]

The new road and bridge finished, Rufus Clark, William Byers, and John Dailey planted shade trees along both sides of Broadway for nearly twenty-five blocks, from Cherry Creek at Fifth Avenue all the way south to Jewell Avenue. Thus the earliest "southsiders" had access to the city of Denver via this wonderful tree-lined boulevard and an adequate plank bridge. Patterson noted, however, that the main road leading south from the city was still the "old county road" (South Santa Fe Drive). "Broadway was not used much at first: In fact we all owned into the middle of Broadway, and only dedicated that portion of it when we platted our various additions." Shortly after completing the road, Thomas Skerritt went to work for the Arapahoe County commissioners as a road overseer, a position he held for many years.

In March 1873, the county commissioners awarded a contract to George W. Smith to build a proper bridge across Cherry Creek at Broadway. Smith's winning bid was $485, but the actual cost came to $728 by the time he finished it in July. In 1877 the commissioners decided to rebuild it, and on April 19, 1878, D. C. Crowell won the contract to build the bridge and stone abutment for $2,290. But in May 1878, before construction proceeded very far, Denver's second major flood (which some considered worse than the famous 1864 flood) took not only the bridge but also all the bank on the south side and the trees above Broadway, once again cutting off those hardy souls who lived far to the south of the city limits.[19] Defeated, Crowell sold all his materials back to the county, accepted $200 for labor expenses, and canceled the contract. By March 1879, the bridge still had not been replaced and fifteen petitioners demanded that it be done. The county agreed to fund half if the city of Denver paid for the other half. This was accepted and S. L. Robinson, low bidder at $3.90 per lineal foot, was ordered to complete it in sixty days. In 1882 private subscribers, among them Rufus Clark with his contri-

bution of $425, replaced this bridge.

Children in Arapahoe County schools' unincorporated "country districts" 2, 4, and 7 had access to public education as early as 1869. Early that year, Arapahoe County school superintendent Wilbur C. Lathrop had appointed Joseph Bennett acting treasurer of District 7, which ran from Alameda Avenue south to Littleton. East and west boundaries were not set at that time. On November 6 Lathrop granted W. H. Muir a teaching certificate, and Muir began teaching immediately, perhaps holding classes in a private home. Although thirty-five potential students ages five to twenty-one lived within District 7's geographic boundaries, not all of them attended school. School terms began in late fall and averaged four or five months, until boys and girls were needed to help on the farms and truck gardens.

The fledgling school district floundered financially, however, and a few months later, on February 16, 1870, its board of directors asked for an advance payment of $135 on future appropriations to pay Mr. Muir, as they had no funds in their treasury.

County schools (in what was then Arapahoe County) were formally established September 6, 1871, and the boundaries for District 7 were set, beginning at the South Platte River and Mississippi Avenue, east to Clarkson Street, south on Clarkson to Jewell, east to Colorado Boulevard, and south to Belleview Avenue, its southern border. Peter Magnes, who founded Petersburg and served as Arapahoe County commissioner in 1866, was elected president of the district. Thomas Skerritt was elected secretary, and George Bryan, treasurer. A frame schoolhouse had been erected on Louis Dugal's land at approximately Harvard Avenue and Santa Fe Drive in early 1871. By 1873, District 7 had sixty-three eligible pupils, so a second schoolhouse was erected at an unknown location. The two frame schoolhouses together cost $2,500.[20] A few years later a third school was added when Rufus Clark donated land south of Jewell Avenue and east of Santa Fe Drive in 1880, "to be used for a free public school." Presumably a third schoolhouse was erected on the site; perhaps, because the location was a short distance from the Harvard Avenue schoolhouse, this building replaced the old one.

The conduct of the schools was apparently satisfactory. Miss Corrine Cornell, teacher of the ungraded

Gallup country estate at Broadway and Alameda. *Littleton Historical Museum*

classroom at one of the schoolhouses, for example, was rated as an "excellent teacher, [who keeps] order and discipline. Instruction intuitive. Room and pupils clean and attentive" by the Arapahoe County school superintendent on one of his visits in 1880.[21]

Part of District 7, between Yale and Belleview, was incorporated into the newly created District 22 in August 1874, and the pupils were nearly evenly divided between the two districts. The census of District 7 was reduced in 1875–1876 to twenty-five pupils. (Land from Yale to Dartmouth was returned in 1884.)

District 4 lay north and east of District 7, from Clarkson to Quebec streets and Jewell to Sixth avenues. In the fall of 1869, eleven children attended school in a room of the L. Butterick house on the west side of Cherry Creek at about Kentucky Avenue. In late 1870, District 4 electors approved an assessment of five mills on the dollar to finance and erect a school on Levi and Millie Booth's farm on the other side of the creek, now known as historic Four-Mile House, 715 South Forest Street.[22] The Maple Grove schoolhouse was located southeast of the Booth residence near the apple orchard and a stand of maple trees, hence its name.[23] Treasurer H. Bohm reported

that construction of the frame building cost $491.46 and included five windows and two doors. School opened in November with three boys and three girls for pupils and Hezekiah Storms as teacher at a salary of $40 per month. Sarah E. Tibbals replaced Storms in 1873, Orrin Thompson taught in 1874, and Storms returned in 1876. That year the district repaired the building and moved it off the Booth ranch to the northeast corner of Holly Street and Colorado Avenue. When Lizzie McKenna taught in 1879, daily attendance averaged only 2.75 pupils.

Another grade school opened on Leetsdale Drive at South Holly Street in 1884. This school was also named Maple Grove and Hezekiah Storms taught there for the 1885–1886 school term. A District 4 school may have also existed in the Lakeview Subdivision on the present Steele Elementary School site. Its date of origin is unclear, but a community of seven houses existed there by 1886 and perhaps a school was erected to serve these families. Its name was changed from Lake View to Steele in 1912 and was probably torn down to erect Steele Elementary in 1913.[24]

Children in District 2, north of Mississippi and

west of Clarkson, went to the Eleventh Street School at Eleventh and Lawrence, built in 1861. They may also have attended Mrs. Nellie M. Dailey's school in her house in the vicinity of Third and Broadway, and later at Fourth and Bannock, but dates of these schools are unknown. As the Washington Park area became more settled, the children attended Lincoln School after 1891 or Myrtle Hill School (Washington Park), erected in 1893.

South Denver's Districts 2, 4, and 7 were absorbed into the Denver Public School system when the City and County of Denver was established in 1902.

Denver's early growth brought with it dirt and noise. Dust and grit filled the air, and soot from its northern smelters often blanketed the city. As late as 1880, no sewers existed, and the stench was unbearable. Dead animals lying in the streets were a constant annoyance, and runaway horses sent pedestrians scattering. Juveniles ran in packs, and adults committed burglaries daily. But most irritating of all of these unattractive blights was the existence of numerous saloons, which outnumbered churches by eight to one in 1870.[25] Families began to look elsewhere for relief. Suburbanization was already well under way in the Curtis Park neighborhood north of downtown Denver, as cheap, fast transportation in the form of horse-drawn streetcars became available there in the 1870s at ten cents per ride. As more streetcar lines were added, many prominent citizens moved north and hundreds of homes were built there. These "bob tail horse cars rocked up and down like a ship in the storm. When there was snow on the track they frequently left the rails, and then we got out and lifted them on," one rider said.[26]

By the early 1880s, however, developers began to steer growth elsewhere; when Patterson arrived in 1878, he noted that there were few houses between his house, near First Avenue and Broadway, and the Colfax Avenue jail. Patterson and others (including William Byers, who had sold the *Rocky Mountain News* two years earlier) who now owned considerable real estate around South Broadway and Alameda desired to see their community, which was then "bottom dog in the real estate fight," built up. An article in the *Rocky Mountain News* in 1880, written by Patterson, may have done much to persuade many to relocate across Cherry Creek to the south. A real estate

agent had told Patterson that "people were actually leaving the city [of Denver] because rents were so high and the price of property was so unreasonable," so he wrote the article to call attention to this "cheap, desirable, healthy and convenient locality" where residence lots went for $250 a pair. "The land is simply unobjectionable as regards the character of the soil, the water, the facility for irrigation, the

Avery Gallup. *Littleton Historical Museum*

freedom from malaria, the elevation, the magnificent mountain view. . . . No smelters or rolling mills drag their smoke over this region."[27]

Lovely residences and prosperous businesses crept south of Alameda Avenue along South Broadway in the early 1880s. Still in existence is a charming house at 1611 South Pearl, now owned by an investment company, and another at 1199 South Bannock, both built in 1880. Land not already owned by individuals was purchased from the Kansas Pacific Railroad, which had received a land grant of approximately 3 million acres for its 1870 Denver extension. The plots lay on alternate north and south sides of the track for twenty miles, including South Denver, making the Kansas Pacific one of the largest landowners in Arapahoe County. Horse-drawn streetcars never ran farther south than Alameda. Southsiders boarded the "little brown car" at Broadway and Alameda and made the trip to the Union Depot via Broadway and Sixteenth Street in thirty-five minutes.

For many years, George E. Kettle, whose Kettle Building survives in Larimer Square, and who settled near First Avenue and Broadway in the early 1870s, and John L. Dailey, William Byers's partner in the *Rocky Mountain News,* "fought the battles of this section alone and unaided," Patterson wrote. These battles centered on keeping saloons from crawling up South Broadway in the early 1880s along with homes and shops. Whenever residents heard of an attempt to get a liquor license, a delegation visited the county commissioners and the protest was sustained. So per-

William A. H. Loveland. *Colorado Historical Society*

Horace A. W. Tabor. *Denver Public Library, Western History Department*

sistent were they, backed by their money, Patterson wrote, that "the authorities generally thought the quickest way out of the thing was to grant us what we went for. There is no doubt but that this policy of ours has resulted in giving our community a better class of citizens than ordinary."[28]

In 1881 Avery Gallup, a businessman who erected the Gallup-Stanbury building, a Denver Landmark in Larimer Square, designed and built a large house on twenty acres on the southeast corner of Broadway and Alameda Avenue. He had built greenhouses on the Lincoln Street side the year before, and the Averys lived there in a rustic cottage covered with vines and exotic flowers while the larger house was being built. At their "country estate" on South Broadway, the Gallups planted rare trees, shrubs, and flowers around their new house and kept the lawn velvety, converting the grounds into a magnificent botanical garden modeled on gardens Avery had seen during his travels to Europe. The Gallups were famous for their lavish parties, and guests looked forward to each dazzling new floral arrangement that became the center of attention of each. The Gallups sold their Lincoln Street greenhouses to John L. Russell in the mid-1880s and built twelve more on fifteen acres on South Fillmore Street in University Park, near the railroad tracks, putting ten acres into nursery stock. Charlotte controlled the greenhouse business while Avery tended to their real estate interests throughout the state. Avery died in 1894 at the age of forty-seven; Charlotte moved to Littleton about 1900; and the house on South Broadway was torn down in 1909.

Growth south of Cherry Creek in the early 1880s also attracted the attention of investors hoping to capi-

Denver Circle Railroad engine. *Colorado Historical Society*

talize on it. One of them was William Austin Hamilton Loveland, who had promoted the town of Golden, helped organize the Colorado School of Mines, and built the territory's first railroad, the Colorado Central, in 1865. A politician who had chaired the 1861 and 1864 statehood conventions, he also served nine years in the territorial senate. In 1878 Loveland was the Democratic candidate for governor of Colorado but lost to Frederick W. Pitkin.

Turning to business, Loveland purchased the *Rocky Mountain News* a few months after William Byers sold it in 1878, and he began looking into an ambitious new railroad venture, this time a "rapid-transit" line right in the city. On November 16, 1880, Loveland, together with partners John W. Knox, George Tritch, and Henry D. Perky of Denver and Henry Hill of Iowa, incorporated the Denver Circle Railroad Company.

The object of this "Important Local Railroad Enterprise," Loveland wrote in his *Rocky Mountain News*, "is to build a narrow gauge railroad starting from a point in the center of the city of Denver and proceeding to a point not more than five miles in a given direction, and then making a circle around the city." He promised "elegant little passenger depots" at regular intervals, heated cars in winter, and cool open cars in summer. They would build the South Denver tracks first.

The primary purpose, of course, was to spur growth and enhance real estate values along the line, on land the Circle Railroad owners planned to buy. They dreamed of entire new suburbs—and great profits. For example, they envisioned that on the upper portion of West Denver (everything south and west of Cherry Creek) "a new city would spring up as if by magic if it had rapid communication." They would build up districts and populate people in healthy, comfortable homes, "many of whom would otherwise be huddled together in close quarters at a heavy rent in a central part of the city because the bread winner of the family had to be near his work." They proposed to lay out "gardens and parks and pleasant streets, where people can spend their evenings pleasantly in the summer months," their line bringing enjoyment within the reach of all. Future plans included building those very gardens and parks at strategic locations along the Circle Railroad.[29]

Millionaire Horace Tabor purchased 100 shares of stock in Loveland's Denver Circle Railroad Company and set the company up in his new Tabor Block downtown. Tabor had prospected for gold and operated grocery stores and post offices in Leadville and

Park County since 1858. In 1878 he was elected lieutenant-governor of Colorado, and then he was chosen to fill the last thirty days of Henry M. Teller's seat as U. S. senator. Tabor was defeated in the next senatorial election by one vote, and he went back to mining. In 1879 he and his partners struck gold in the Little Pittsburgh mine and it soon produced seventy-five to one hundred tons of ore daily. By 1880, the wealthy Tabor was interested in building up the state; the Circle Railroad venture with its possibilities for real estate development seemed an exciting investment, and he handed over the cash to Loveland's financial manager.

At the same time that Loveland's company began its railroad, it also began negotiations with the city to locate an Industrial and Mining Exposition along the tracks on South Logan street. Perky, a Nebraska lawyer who had recently moved to Denver, had suggested the idea of hosting a national mining exposition to the business leaders of Denver the year before and found them receptive. Now Perky and Loveland asked Horace Tabor to help them plan the construction of a hall for the exhibit along the railroad on their own land, which they would sell to the city. Tabor agreed and the three men began to plan a National Mining and Industrial Exposition.

The first organizational meeting, on May 14, 1881, was chaired by Wolfe Londoner, later Denver's mayor (1889–1891), and hailed as a "mass meeting of . . . a large number of the most notable residents here, as well as no inconsiderable a majority of those who represent the mining interests of the state."[30] They included Charles Kountze, Walter S. Cheesman, Horace Tabor, William Byers, J. S. Brown, John W. Smith, David H. Moffat, Jr., Governor William Gilpin, and Federal Judge Moses Hallett, all of whom hoped that the mining and industrial exposition would become an annual event in a permanent building.[31] All agreed that

> Denver today stands on a pinical [sic], the cynosure of the mining world. Her life, her development, as well as her phenomenal growth being due simply and alone to the growth and development of her mineral industries. . . . Denver may be said to live, move, and have her being through mines, for as their "output" is either rich or poor, so are the pockets of her inhabitants either filled to overflowing or empty. . . . For this reason, Denver is interested in the development of mining and the establishment of a home where the most beautiful products

of her soil may be lodged in safety, to be gazed at and admired.[32]

After many speeches and endorsements, an executive committee consisting of one representative each from mining, banking, railroads, the press, hotels, merchants, manufacturers, and state government interests was announced. Architect Willoughby J. Edbrooke, who had helped his brother Frank design the Tabor Block and the Tabor Opera House downtown, displayed a drawing of a building to house such an exposition, saying it could be done at a cost of $35,000 to $75,000.

An enthusiastic solicitation committee began immediately to raise funds. The Union Pacific Railroad contributed $10,000, and the Denver and Rio Grande $5,000. Tabor himself pledged $10,000 and invested over $30,000. Loveland was not far behind, although no dollar amount is known. Contributions poured in, so the city of Denver bought forty acres of land between Broadway and South Logan streets and Virginia and Exposition avenues from Loveland and Tabor's Denver Circle Railroad for $25,000 to build a magnificent exposition hall.

Meanwhile, the railroad plans went forward. In preparation for laying track down South Logan (then Kansas) Street, the Denver Circle Railroad Company purchased a large tract of land from Virginia to Mississippi avenues and Broadway to Clarkson streets (excepting a tract from Kentucky to Mississippi and Broadway to Logan). Most of the surrounding land was owned by Rufus Clark, who had purchased an additional 280 acres on November 3, 1881, to add to his 160-acre homestead. Clark's property now extended from Mississippi to Jewell avenues and the river to Clarkson Street (excepting a strip from Iowa and Florida, which later became Fleming's Grove Subdivision). Two weeks later Clark contracted with Circle Railroad owners Loveland, Knox, Perky, and Thomas Moulton to construct the tracks through a portion of this property. Instead of contributing cash, however, shrewd Rufus Clark offered Loveland and his partners 25 percent of all proceeds of the sales of all 280 acres. Once Clark had received "sums equal to the prices stated," the remainder of the land was to be equally divided between Clark and Loveland and the others. The Circle Railroad was to subdivide this into

National Mining and Industrial Exposition Building. *Colorado Historical Society*

blocks, lots, and tracts at their expense (for engineers and surveyors), and to sell the lots for not less than $100 per acre. (At this time Clark also purchased section 26, which was 640 acres, where the University of Denver now stands and which later would also need Circle Railroad services.)

With real estate titles and rights-of-way seemingly settled, construction of the Circle Railroad began in 1881. To handle its extensive real estate holdings, the Denver Circle Railroad owners incorporated the Denver Circle Real Estate Company in February 1882, and Loveland, Perky, Moulton, and Knox transferred their shares to the new company. At this point all the Denver stockholders except Loveland sold their interests to former governor Charles A. Jewell of Connecticut, Thomas M. Nichol of New York, and other eastern stockholders. Jewell died shortly afterward, leaving his real estate interests in the hands of Charles L. McIntosh, a director of the McIntosh and Mygatt Bank at Sixteenth and Curtis downtown. Nichol sold his interest to Theodore C. Henry, president of Colorado Loan and Trust, who was appointed president of the real estate company and general manager of the railroad company. In the process of all this transferring of stock and real estate, Horace Tabor's 100 shares of stock changed hands several times and disappeared into a tangle of legal difficulties that would cause grief for years to come.

The railroad opened for business on April 6, 1882. From the Circle's depot at Thirteenth and Larimer, the Circle Railroad tracks followed the west bank of Cherry Creek along Fourteenth Avenue, then turned south on what is now Inca to Third Avenue, east on Third, and south again on Cherokee Street to Bayaud, where it established its shops. Here the Circle divided, and one fork continued east on Bayaud and south on Kansas (Logan) Street, ending at Jewell Avenue. Two weeks after its maiden excursion, Loveland, Henry, and Clark platted their 160 jointly owned acres into Sherman Subdivision, the tracks running through the center of it directly alongside the exposition building site.

The cornerstone for the Willoughby Edbrooke-designed National Mining and Industrial Exposition Building, a stunning two-story hall of nearly 150,000 square feet, 500 feet long by 316 feet wide in the general form of a Maltese cross, was laid May 2, 1882. It contained a large exhibition hall supplied with an orchestra, a stage, private rooms, broad galleries, and a grand balcony. Plans called for a spur of the Circle Railroad to run right through the building for transporting exhibits. A tall stucco fountain featuring water cascading from the top stood in front of this magnificent building, which faced Logan Street, and a large number of ornamental houses of various sizes and styles, used for exhibits and other purposes, grouped around it.

A crowd estimated by the *Rocky Mountain News* at 15,000 to 18,000 showed up for the ceremonies, arriving by special Circle trains and by carriages, hacks, buses, and express wagons. The "march of dignitaries" began with a procession from the armory to the Circle Railway depot, where Denver's leaders boarded trains for the journey to the Exposition grounds. The parade included the chief of police and his aides, the governor's guard, the chief marshal, and the Loveland guard squadron, followed by ten carriages of state, county, and city officials and four fire department companies. They were joined at the Exposition Building by Board of Trade representatives. The new governor, Pitkin, along with former governors Gilpin, Evans, and Routt, shared the platform with exposition president H. A. W. Tabor, Denver mayor Robert Morris, and other prominent leaders. Governor Pitkin noted in his speech that the entire project was privately funded and did not receive aid from the state. It was a great moment for Horace Tabor. He had built the Tabor Block in 1880, the Opera House in 1881, and now he had made possible the beautiful Exposition Building. His name was now legendary.[33]

The mining exposition opened in August, again with a parade, inaugural ceremonies, music, and fireworks. Exhibitors from all over the United States showed their finest wares, and, according to Patterson, "the mineral exhibits far exceeded anything shown by Colorado at either the Chicago or St. Louis fairs."[34] The Argo Smelter north of Denver displayed thirty-seven silver bricks valued at $75,000 and one large brick at $55,000. On the grounds outside the hall, band concerts, bicycle races, and Ute Indian dances filled the afternoons. Japanese fireworks brightened the sky at night. The Denver Circle Railroad Company fenced in a tract of their land across from the hall at South Broadway and Center Avenue and built a baseball park on it. Here 350 fans watched the Denver Brown Stockings team, a team fielded by banker David Moffat's Denver Baseball Club that went by the name of the "Browns," lose to the Leadville Blues 30-5.[35] This site later became Union Park and in 1922 became Merchants Park, home of the Denver Bears.[36]

But the inevitable also happened. Almost as soon as word spread that the Exposition Hall would be built, saloon owners hastened to this new fertile ground, where competition was nonexistent and liquor licenses were manageable. The South Broadway merchants and home owners, successful in keeping saloons to a minimum so far, found themselves suddenly powerless to stop them. The commissioners were no longer listening. In the spring of 1882, Baron Walter von Richthofen, a Prussian who moved to Denver in the 1870s and helped develop and promote the Circle Railroad to advance his subdivision along its

route, incorporated the Sans Souci Park Company and constructed a lavish beer garden on the north side of Virginia Avenue between Broadway and Lincoln streets. The rustic building, surrounded by pavilions, gravel walks, flower beds, trees, a fountain, and rockery, contained a large concert hall where guests could listen to classical music while indulging in ice cream, strawberries, and imported wines. This was to be a resort for only the better class of citizens, and "an ample force of sheriffs and special officers were on hand at all times to preserve order and keep out dangerous, suspicious and disreputable characters." Public dancing, "thought to be a great source of immorality and a great inducement to the support of the disreputable," was prohibited in order to make the resort as pleasant as possible for the ladies and children.[37]

Other saloons, not by any means as genteel as Sans Souci, soon surrounded the Exposition grounds. Louis York moved his saloon from Seventh Avenue to the southwest corner of Broadway and Alaska Place and called it York Cottage. Horse dealer David Lauster and his wife, Mary, operated another saloon at Dakota and Broadway, and a man by the name of Parker owned another in the same general area. The Makin brothers opened their pub on the Logan Street side. Already long established was "Pap" Wyman's 1879 log roadhouse on South Santa Fe. Wyman was a tough, old-time marshal who had hunted for gold without success and turned to saloon keeping.

All this activity attracted the attention of Joe Lowe, gambler, drunkard, womanizer, and dance hall proprietor reputed to have had five wives, killed at least seven men, and already run out of two states. Joe began his business career as owner of the U.S. Saloon in Ellsworth, Kansas, in 1868 and quickly earned the nickname of "Rowdy Joe" for his tendency to act impulsively and get into barroom brawls. The town of Ellsworth then incorporated and passed liquor tax laws and ordinances that prohibited most of what Joe considered a normal life-style. He was soon arrested for mule stealing, robbery, running a house of ill repute, carrying guns, and drunkenness. Refusing to live in what had become a "too civilized" town, he and his common-law wife, Kate, moved on to Newton, Kansas, where much the same thing happened. From there the couple settled in Wichita, where they established a "dance house" outside the

Sans Souci Park. *Denver Public Library, Western History Department*

city limits at Delano. Here Joe ambushed and killed a dance-hall business rival by the name of Red Beard and went to jail. But one night he escaped, and Kate was arrested for aiding Joe's breakout. Joe took flight and Kate was released. The two met up in St. Louis, then departed for Denison and then on to Luling and later Fort Worth, Texas. Here, in 1876, Joe and Kate separated, Joe to marry Mollie Field. Joe and Kate each ran separate dance halls in Fort Worth, and it was Kate who now became known as Rowdy Kate, for her "disorderly houses" there.

In 1879 or 1880, Joe and Mollie landed in Leadville, Colorado, where Joe "shot John Timms and escaped punishment on account of the fact that Timms lived over a year and a day. Timms, however, eventually died from his injuries. Other men, it is said, were killed by Lowe, but their names and the details of the tragedies are unknown."[38]

In 1882, Joe and Mollie arrived in Denver and Joe picked the southeast corner of Jewell Avenue and South Broadway for his saloon/dance hall/roadhouse. Here on one of the main thoroughfares, he built Broadway Park and happily settled in as proprietor, bouncer, gun fighter, drinker, and brawler.[39] One account stated that Lowe had earned the money for this roadhouse by gambling in Leadville, but the *Daily News* claimed that Lowe had lost half the $40,000 he had with him when he moved to Leadville at roulette and the remainder in a mining venture, and that the penniless Lowe borrowed $1,000 from a Jim Bush to open Broadway Park.[40]

Loveland's Denver Circle Railroad Company, charging only five cents per ride, continued to struggle financially, even with the successful exposition. In the fall of 1882, Archie C. Fisk, a prominent realtor and president also of the Denver Land and Improvement Company, joined the Denver Circle Real Estate Company and replaced Henry as president. Fisk, Loveland, and Henry decided to build a huge amusement park and extend the railroad west on Jewell Avenue (named for Charles A. Jewell) to its gates. On October 22, Rufus Clark deeded seventy acres of his farm (Louisiana to Jewell avenues, South Platte River to the Merchant's Mill Ditch, next to the present South Santa Fe Drive) to the Circle Real Estate Company for $17,000, or nearly $250 per acre.

Fisk, Loveland, and Henry began to transform part of Clark's potato farm into "a beautiful and pleasant resort, with an abundance of native shade trees and an inexhaustible spring of pure living water. With walks and drives it can be made one of the most pleasant and attractive parks in the country." The main attraction of Jewell Park (now Overland Golf Course) was a one-mile horse-racing track and grandstand. By the end of May the track was being graded and finished under supervision of "gentlemen of the turf," and no expense was spared in making it one of the best in the world.

The promoters emphasized, however, that the racetrack was to be only a part of Jewell Park. A bandstand and a number of arbors were erected, a dancing pavilion was to follow, and plans called for a boating course, swimming pool, and open-air concerts. It was to be a family place with no saloons and no danger of "contacting dangerous or intoxicated persons." In June, Loveland, Henry, and the stockholders let a contract to Belmont and Company to operate the now finished park.

Getting to Jewell Park, which attracted pleasure seekers from miles around, was half the fun. The Circle Railroad ran special excursion trains from the downtown Larimer Street depot every half hour on Sundays and holidays. The little train was worked to capacity carrying merrymakers down Logan Street, turning west on the newly built section on Jewell and ending at a charming and ornamental depot in the park. In addition, tree-lined South Broadway was being upgraded by the county commissioners, and the "chief amusement" of the people of Denver was prancing up and down this wide boulevard, "the best drive in or out of the city and one of the best in the world, already the fashionable thoroughfare of Denver. Now that at the end of it there is a place to go to, it will be more popular than ever."[41] Horsemen and carriages could reach the grounds also by the old

Joe Lowe. From Rocky Mountain News, February 13, 1899. *Courtesy Colorado Historical Society*

county road (Santa Fe Drive) that ran along the Platte River. Whichever route they took, potential home buyers could not fail to notice the Circle Real Estate properties for sale along the way.

Once at the park, spectators were invited to visit Ed Chase's trackside betting and beer stand before settling down to watch harness races. "Big Ed" Chase had brought Denver's first billiard table to Denver in 1860 and operated saloons and the 750-seat Palace Theater downtown. He had been arrested numerous times on gambling charges but managed to escape conviction. Chase served on the city council in the late 1860s, and then he "specialized in organizing transients, prostitutes, street people derelicts, gamblers, winos of lower downtown to vote for his friends."[42] Such a man would not miss the opportunity to make a little money on horse betting.

Horses were driven, not ridden. A single horse was hitched to a high-wheeled sulky carrying the owner or driver. The horses were bred to be pacers or trotters, and their prosperous owners drove them around town in shiny buggies or, in pairs, carriages. Occasionally, professional jockeys raced the high-stepping pacers or trotters under saddle, but these races were not popular.

In November 1882, Rufus Clark decided to build a house on ten acres of his land north of the park. For

two years, Clark and Ella planned its architecture and finally decided to copy banker David C. Wyatt's house at Lincoln Street and Third Avenue, with a few minor changes. On January 15, 1884, Clark contracted with Henry H. Collins and carpenter James Cullin to build the nearly square brick house for $3,500. The house had a main hall that extended the length of the house, sliding doors that closed off the two parlors, an iron sink in an oak kitchen, a "good pantry with flour bins," and a clothes closet with shelf and hooks that was tucked under the stairs. The "good plank" window frames were fitted with bronze lifts, and doors and windows properly screened. All rooms except the kitchen were finished in grained walnut, and a blue tint was ordered for the walls. Last, a "neat brick privy built in the usual manner" stood at the end of the path in back.

For twenty-five years Clark had lived in a shack along the river with each of his three wives. Now, at age sixty, Clark finally had a proper home, at 1395 South Cherokee, later renumbered to 1398 South Santa Fe Drive. The house was torn down in 1957.

Rufus Clark Residence, 1398 South Santa Fe Drive. *Denver Public Library, Western History Department*

South Denver: Up for Grabs

Just east of Jewell Park, Pennsylvania oilman James Alexander Fleming, who was to build a stone mansion in what is now Platt Park and to play a major role in South Denver for the next decade, had also invested in real estate. Born on a farm near Crooked Creek (Creekside), Pennsylvania, on July 3, 1849, Fleming, while still in his teens, left the farm for northwest Pennsylvania's oil regions and began what was to become a rich career in oil, mining, real estate, and banking.[1] In the Oil City area, "he soon became known as 'Jimmy the Boy Operator' for his success in boring for oil and general knowledge of the oil belt. His counsel was sought in locating wells and when only nineteen years of age he supervised more than 150 engineers, drillers, gaugers and mechanics. By 1875, at the age of twenty-six, he was part owner of the Keystone Pipe Line Company."[2] Four years later, Fleming moved his wife and three sons to East Brady, Pennsylvania, not far from Creekside, but about this time he suffered the deaths of both his wife and his father, who died in May 1880. As the eldest son and already wealthy at twenty-nine, Fleming took responsibility for supporting his mother, two younger brothers, and four sisters in addition to his own boys.

Fleming decided that the family could prosper in the West, and with their future as well as his own in mind, he traveled to southwestern Colorado to look for silver or gold mines to buy, leaving his sons with his mother. His brother Thomas and uncle Robert

Morton may have accompanied him. On October 16 Fleming bought the Silver Point Lode on Engineer Mountain in the Uncompahgre Mining District of Ouray County for $10,000. The claim, originally staked in 1876, was a 300- by 1,500-foot piece of real estate on a cliff near the junction of Bear Creek and the Uncompahgre River southeast of Ouray. Two weeks later he applied for a silver patent, and in

James A. Fleming at an Elks convention in Ouray, Colorado, 1880. *Ouray County Museum*

Fleming mansion, South Grant Street and Florida Avenue. *Sketch from Denver Eye, January 1, 1890*

November he sold three-fifths interest in the mine to Pennsylvania investors, who incorporated the mine in December 1880 as the Buena Vista Mountain Mining Company with a capital stock of $80,000. Fleming held two-fifths' interest and agreed to manage the mine. But when the snows were too deep to begin mining operations, Fleming took the train to the thriving town of Denver to look for a residence site and explore the potentially profitable real estate market along Loveland's much talked-about Circle Railroad route, announced the month before. Fleming bought seventy acres of land between South Broadway and Clarkson streets and Florida to Mexico avenues for $4,000 in December 1880 and sold thirty acres of it, between Iowa and Mexico avenues, to the Denver Circle Real Estate Company less than a year later, in January 1882, for $6,000. He held the rest for later development of his

own Fleming's Grove Subdivision.

In the meantime Fleming mined the Silver Point Lode in Ouray. The lode's five-foot-wide vein was in quartzite formation, its pay streak from twelve to twenty-four inches and carrying galena with iron and copper pyrites in a quartz gangue. The mine, with a forty-eight-foot shaft, yielded eighty-five to ninety ounces of silver to the ton, and by August 1881 had produced 150 tons of ore. Fleming proudly displayed samples of his ore at the first National Mining and Industrial Exposition, although by then the mine was yielding only seventy-five ounces of silver per ton rather than the previous ninety.[3] As his mining and real estate achievements grew, James Fleming, traveling between his real estate business in Denver and his mining interests in Ouray, became a man of public note. The *Daily News* reported in May 1882 that he

The Town of South Denver

would "leave for Ouray today to look after his mining interests." More important, the article welcomed the news that "Mr. Fleming intends making Colorado his home."[4]

At last, Fleming was ready to bring his family from Pennsylvania, and for them, James built a lovely stone Queen Anne–style house on five acres of what is now Platt Park for $30,000 in 1882 or 1883. The architect of this spacious home, which is distinguished by its matching two-story towers, is unknown. When the mansion was finished, he brought to Denver his sons, William Porter, Charles, and Richard, ages nine to fifteen; his mother, Susanna; brothers Thomas H. and George R.; and sisters Sadie, Martha (Mattie), Elizabeth (Lizzie), and Nettie; the eleven of them settled in. The men put in a lawn and planted gardens and groves of fruit trees so skillfully that the park-like grounds soon became known as Fleming's Grove. The "Fleming's Grove, Circle Railroad, PO Box 2019" address appears in Denver's City Directory for the first time in 1884.

On March 31, 1883, Fleming platted Fleming's Grove Subdivision across the street from his home, bounded by Logan to Clarkson streets and Iowa to Florida avenues. With the help of his brother Thomas, a well-digger by trade, he drilled an artesian well on lots 38 and 39 of block 3 (about mid-block on the west side of South Washington Street) at a cost of $2,500, and he made the plentiful, pure water available free to buyers of his $80 lots.

The Circle Railroad ran conveniently down South Logan between Fleming's house and his subdivision, and James built a little train depot on the west side of the street. With water and public transportation now available, buyers soon took notice, and a little village, which also became known as Fleming's Grove, developed over the next two or three years.

Many of the houses in Fleming's Grove Subdivision were built by James's Pennsylvania cousins Jesse, Thomas Calvin, and Durbe Carson Fleming, who also followed James to Denver. The cousins, known as the Fleming Brothers, operated from their lumber yard on Ellsworth Avenue, built houses around the city and the Fleming Block at 68–74 Broadway, and opened the Fleming Brothers Bank at 103 Broadway in 1909. The Fleming Brothers were the first to sell houses on the installment plan, a method of financing that was popular immediately. They probably built their houses from pattern books, houses that were far more common than architect-designed dwellings.[5] In the boom times of the mid-1880s, they sometimes built whole blocks of houses at a time. "It seems to be no more trouble for them to build a house than it is for a cobbler to halfsole a pair of shoes," a neighbor remarked.[6] For the moment, James left the remaining acres west of South Grant Street undeveloped.

Early in 1884 James Fleming fell passionately and disastrously in love with a young woman sixteen years his junior by the name of Nellie J. Paddock. Nellie had moved to Denver after breaking her engagement to San Francisco musician Julius Heinrich. Here she met James Fleming and apparently an on-again, off-again love affair followed. At one point Nellie moved back to Rome, Illinois, and then spent some time in Chicago. James must have decided to give the nineteen-year-old gadfly up; he sent her a telegram to that effect in October 1884. Nellie wrote back that she needed her mother's consent to marry him but was "hurrying Ma up, for fear we may not get married at all." "Ma," however, favored the musician over Mr. Fleming and was balking. The exasperated Nellie, lamenting that "I don't believe any couple ever had such trials and tribulations as we do," was "coming to Denver if it kills me, whether it suits [you] or not, and I am determined to get married whether you are or not." She also made veiled, coy requests for money. She had pictures taken of herself, to send to James, and boasted that "the artist thought I was quite a good subject so took considerable pains . . . but they are too expensive, four dollars a piece."[7]

Two months later, on December 3, 1884, "Jim" and Nellie were married at the home of the First Congregational Church's pastor, J. Myron W. Reed, witnessed by a Mrs. E. Law and a friend of the Reeds, Miss Lizzie Dyo. Apparently none of James's family attended. James moved out of his mansion and into a boarding house at 338 Broadway, as Nellie, who was not ready to "go into housekeeping," wished. James enrolled Nellie in painting lessons and went about his mining and real estate business downtown and community affairs in South Denver while Nellie spent her days at the easel and "generally made her own bed and sometimes swept the room and sometimes not," according to the landlady. The couple took their meals with the owners and other boarders, mostly families, and often went out to places of amusement in the evenings, Nellie dressed in one of many lovely dresses Jim had a dressmaker fashion for her, and in jewelry and furs he bought her. When at home, the newlyweds were affectionate, even in the presence of the other boarders, and Nellie often sat on Jim's lap during after-dinner conversation. Only one thing disturbed Jim: Nellie insisted on wearing a bracelet she had received from her former fiancé and refused to take it off. Nellie also continued to correspond with several gentlemen friends in New York, Boston, and San Francisco, a practice unacceptable to her husband. Affectionate in public, their private arguments behind closed doors strained the marriage in its early weeks, and Nellie decided to move on.

On April 26, 1885, Nellie boarded a train for San Francisco, where her mother lived, telling "Jim," who bought her a new trunk and new clothes for the trip, she had to testify in a lawsuit there. Three weeks later she wrote Jim that she was not coming back. He went to San Francisco to persuade her to return, but when they met, her mother did all the talking, and he got nowhere. Nellie had moved back in with her musician, Julius. Shocked, Jim offered to move to San Francisco, but he learned that she "wouldn't recognize me even

on the streets" if he did. Nellie and Julius performed at the Mission Music Hall in San Francisco, she playing the piano and he the cello. Nellie was happy and was not coming back. Fleming continued to live at the boarding house, perhaps in hopes that Nellie would return.

By early 1884 the saloon situation in South Denver had worsened. Baron von Richthofen's hopes for Sans Souci as a respectable family resort had not been successful, and the baron, disgusted that his fine beer garden was not being patronized that first summer of 1882, instead threw a private party for gamblers, "fancy ladies," and sporting men of the town. "It was a crowded, lucrative, and long night, thoroughly enjoyed by a number of respectable men who would never after admit they had attended."[8] This incident altered the tone of Sans Souci and the baron sold it in October, only months after he had opened it with such high hopes. He never invested in South Denver again. The new owners, evidently more realistic about the public's tastes, vowed to "give more satisfaction" and lowered Sans Souci's standards to compete with its neighbors. A year later a Mrs. Jennings of New York paid $11,000 for Sans Souci and the *Rocky Mountain News* lamented that "the park will be run on the same principle as

This photograph was taken from the National Mining and Exposition building about 1883, looking north across Virginia Avenue (with fence) to Sans Souci Park, with the Gallup residence in the background (Alameda Avenue and South Broadway). The buildings along South Broadway on the left are taverns. *Denver Public Library, Western History Department*

heretofore—a resort for people of all descriptions."[9]

In March of 1884 South Denver residents, fed up with the disreputable York Cottage, the Lausters, and Joe Lowe's Broadway Park on South Broadway, Ed Chase's betting stand at Overland Park, and Pap Wyman's roadhouse on South Santa Fe Drive, formed the South Broadway Union Club "to take action looking toward the advancement of our public interests."[10] The club decided to fight liquor licenses as they came up for renewal, and Sans Souci became its first target. On June 5 they formally petitioned the Arapahoe County commissioners to deny Sans Souci a liquor license. They were unsuccessful, however, and the saloon flourished until the summer of 1887, when "instead of the usual seductive roadhouse signs and other outward embellishments calculated to deceive the public as to the true nature and intent of the place, there now appears on the main building in large and unmistakable letters the words 'Episcopal Mission.'" Sister Eliza, whose first mission had been at All Saints Episcopal Church in North Denver, conducted Sunday school, mothers' meetings, and a children's sewing and industrial school in the building for a few years while the rector of All Saints conducted Sunday services. The building burned down in 1893 and the grounds became known as Sans Souci Park; its still-lovely grounds were used for church picnics and outdoor parties for many years afterward.

Across the street from Sans Souci, the Exposition was also undergoing hard times. The 1883 Mining Exposition had not been as successful as the first one; it fell short of expectations in both exhibits and income. The corporation decided not to undertake a third one, but the Denver Chamber of Commerce was determined to keep it going and appointed from among its own members a board of exposition managers to undertake the 1884 exhibition. William A. H. Loveland was named president. Author Alice Polk Hill extolled the grand scheme and endorsed it with enthusiasm. Headed for the mountains on her way out of the city by train one morning in 1884, she wrote, "As we glided out of the city a splendid view of the Mining and Industrial Exposition was presented. This important enterprise . . . promises to grow in value with increasing years. It is said that the spirit of an age or country is written upon its industrial monuments, and this is Colorado's pride." She loved the narrow gauge

Circle Railroad as well: "We admired extravagantly the diminutive cars that swept along so gracefully and rapidly towards the Exposition building and to Jewell Park."[11] She was blissfully unaware that both enterprises were doomed.

The third Exposition opened September 1, 1884. Although it was better than the second, it was not equal to the first, and the hall closed permanently on October 4. So extraordinary and elaborate was the collection of minerals in the three exhibitions, Jerome Smiley noted in 1901, that it was hoped that somehow the bulk of it could be retained and eventually displayed in a museum of minerals in the city. Unfortunately, Smiley lamented, "there was no way opened to that most desirable end, and the great collection was scattered. Portions of it remained in Denver, other parts were bought to add to collections in the east, and the remainder taken away by exhibitors."[12]

Exposition bonds went up for sale and rumors flew that the building would be turned into railroad shops or a railroad depot, a slaughterhouse, or a smelter. One bond purchaser (who was perhaps a land developer with an eye to a new subdivision) wanted the building torn down and the property made into a residential area: he thought the building was "good for nothing except for the material in it." He estimated the property in 1887 to be worth $2,000 per acre and the whole thing, building and all, worth no more than $100,000.[13] A last-ditch effort to revive the building and bring back mining exhibitions seemed promising in the spring of 1888 when the *Denver Republican* announced that a potential buyer proposed to spend $2,000–$3,000 to restore the building to its original purpose. However, this person wanted to move the building to the heart of the city. That being unrealistic, "it would doubtless be better to utilize the South Broadway building than to have no permanent exposition at all."[14] Neither option materialized, though, and the grounds were sold to E. F. Hallack, John Knox, and John McDermott, who wasted no time platting the site into Exposition Addition on April 13, 1888. They tore down Willoughby Edbrook's splendid building and sold the outbuildings, which were moved off the property. But the land lay undeveloped, and by 1890 the area had become so neglected that sixteen neighbors petitioned the town to clean up "old tin cans and rags and old papers and other rubbish and a gang of dogs" surrounding a junk shop on the premises. The fountain remained a few more years, until the city destroyed it in 1902 when improving the streets. The Exposition Addition was later owned by Thomas S. McMurray, Denver's mayor from 1895 to 1899.

In March 1884, Loveland and Henry bought out the Denver Circle Railroad Company and the Denver Circle Real Estate Company's eastern stockholders' interests and became the sole owners. Jewell Park continued to be a success for Loveland and Henry.

The Denver Jockey Club, which controlled the racetrack, widened the track to sixty feet from the wire to the three-quarter pole, where it was widened to 100 feet, providing a magnificent homestretch. The track was regarded as one of the finest in the West. Nearly 100 horse stalls stood next to a splendid grandstand. The 1884 spring races, commencing on Saturday, May 10, offered a $10,000 purse and twenty-three races held over seven days. Trotting and pacing races, hurdles, and harness races were held under strict rules, and the entrance fee was 10 percent of the take. Jockeys, grooms, and stable boys were forbidden near the betting grounds, and craps and other gambling games were not allowed.

To the south of the track, an enclosed pavilion 135 feet by 95 feet with twenty-two stained glass windows was the scene of parties summer and winter. Benches and tables lined the walks and drives that meandered through thickets and groves along the riverbanks, and the mountain and country scenery was unforgettable.[15]

The Circle Railroad carried passengers to and from Jewell Park and was filled to overflowing on Sundays and holidays. In August 1886, 3,000 people came out to watch horse races and Professor van Tassel ascend in a gas balloon. He had filled the bag with gas at a gas main on Broadway and Eleventh Avenue, placed it into an express wagon, and weighted the basket down with rocks. As horses drew the wagon slowly along Broadway, it was completely surrounded by small boys all the way to Jewell Park. The professor had promised to take a local reporter up with him, but the pressure in the Denver main would not fill his balloon enough to support two people, so he left behind the reporter, who had "publicly made his last will and testament in anticipation of the ascent to heaven."[16]

The southern suburb attracted the attention of

Colorado Seminary trustees as well. John Evans, who had helped found the institution as the Methodist Episcopal Church's Colorado Seminary in downtown Denver in 1864 when he was Colorado's governor, had also founded Chicago's Northwestern University and its elite suburb of Evanston. He came to Denver in the spring of 1862 "as a man of great wealth and a figure of towering prestige and authority. For the rest of his life, he dominated Denver and Colorado affairs. . . . He was one of the founders of the University of Denver, and he built railroads, ran banks, joined the *News* editor [William Byers, also a university founder] in mining ventures, owned traction firms, real estate, and a wide variety of businesses. . . . Streets, chapels, and towns were named for him."[17] Evans was elected Colorado territorial governor in 1862 but resigned the

John Evans, territorial governor, railroad builder, and a founder of the University of Denver. *Denver Public Library, Western History Department*

governorship in 1865 to run for the Colorado senate on the chance that Colorado would be accepted as a state. President Johnson vetoed the act to form a new state, however, and Evans found himself holding no office at all.

Colorado Seminary failed to prosper; it closed in 1867 with a debt of $3,000. But its founders never lost hope that it would rise again, and for thirteen years they worked toward its revival as a fine university. Finally, in 1880, the seminary reopened in its downtown buildings as the University of Denver, which acted as the degree-granting body for Colorado Seminary. By now, however, Denver had become a crossroad of commerce and industry, and the university found itself in an environment not conducive to learning. The trustees hoped to find a new site away from the city.

An influential Denver couple, Bishop Henry White

Warren and his wife, Elizabeth Iliff Warren, were instrumental in the choice of University Park as the location for the university several years later. After their marriage in 1883, the couple became involved in the struggling Colorado Seminary, and in 1884 Elizabeth offered to donate $100,000 for the purpose of endowing a school of theology. She required, however, that the university seek a permanent location away from downtown Denver. Evans and the trustees instructed the university's financial agent, Rev. Franklin C. Millington, to begin the search for a suitable suburban location,[18] and in a very short time, he presented the board with three site offers—in Montclair, Barnum, and South Denver. Both the bishop and Elizabeth strongly supported the move south and showed their commitment by pledging to build their home near the campus, once the university made the move.

Elizabeth's first husband, cattleman John Wesley Iliff, had died young, leaving her with a vast fortune and a son, William Seward, by a previous marriage. John and Elizabeth had a daughter, Louise, and a son, John Wesley Iliff, Jr., who died at the age of sixteen months. Elizabeth had managed her husband's estate in superb fashion, and at the time of her marriage to Methodist Episcopal Church bishop Henry White Warren, she was supposedly the richest woman in Colorado. Elizabeth had arrived in Denver by stagecoach in 1868 to open a new store for the Singer Sewing Machine Company. Her inventory of seventy to a hundred sewing machines and some baby wagons sold respectably well, and she gained a reputation as a fine businesswoman by the time she was twenty-five. The bishop, a world traveler and mountain climber, was a widower with two daughters, Carrie and Ellen, and a son, Henry, Jr.

University president John Evans supported the Warrens' selection of University Park, for he realized that his Denver and New Orleans railroad, which sliced through the park along what is now Buchtel Boulevard, could be used to carry both students to the campus and home buyers to an elite academic community that he planned to have surround the university. Evans and his business associates had begun to lay the track in 1881; from the railyard and depot at Eleventh and Wewatta Street, they constructed the rails south along the river, then turned southeast, entering South Denver

at Alameda Avenue where it crossed Virginia Avenue, and swung diagonally to the southeast on its way to Galveston, Texas. Evans planned to eventually ship Texas cattle to stockyards he would build in South Denver.

Evans began negotiations with Rufus Clark for a parcel of Clark's land at what is now University Boulevard and Evans Avenue for a campus site. In November 1885 Rufus Clark offered to sell eighty acres with water rights between Jewell and Iliff avenues and Race (Campus) Street and University Boulevard to the trustees for $10,500 for use as a campus site. Further, ten additional property owners promised to deed other lands to the university, with the stipulation that:

> (1) within six months [by May 30, 1886] there shall be laid out and platted into lots or blocks, a Town site, to cover not less than two hundred acres of land, including the University site, of said Seminary; (2) that within one year there shall be planted and set out along the lines of streets and parks of such Town not less than one thousand forest trees; and (3) that at the earliest practicable time, in the judgment of the Board of Trustees of said Colorado Seminary, the main buildings of the Academic Department of said Seminary shall be erected on said University site, viz., on the east half of the northeast quarter of Section 26, Township 4 South Range 68 West, in Arapahoe County Colorado [on Clark's eighty acres].[19]

Although no mention was made in these bonds of prohibiting the manufacture or use of intoxicating liquors, the trustees had in mind a prohibition community of like-minded spirits. The idea of a group of people living in structured colonies was a popular notion on the East Coast at the time and the idea was moving west as land opened up. Based on the teachings of French socialist François Marie Charles Fourier, who died in 1837, the ideal community would consist of 400–1800 persons living in the center of a large and highly cultivated domain containing art, industry, and pleasure. Styles of living would vary in luxury and cost, but "the poorest person in the association is not only to be secure of comfort but his minimum of enjoyments greater than the present social arrangements can give princes and millionaires."[20] But by the 1870s it became evident that New England life-styles could not work in the West. Ethnic, southern, or religious settlements were also seen as failures. In the wild West, where alcohol threatened decent folk, a prohibition against liquor was more effective as an inducement to colonize than any other social force.

General Robert A. Cameron, Methodist, former physician, army officer, newspaper editor, warden of Colorado State Prison, and Colorado Seminary dean Joseph Shattuck, led the campaign for a similar colony in University Park. Both had been involved since 1869 in the founding of prohibitionist Union Colony (Greeley) with Nathan Meeker and Horace Greeley. Cameron, William Pabor, and Shattuck, with approval of the trustees and Rufus Clark, believed that a successful colony could be established in an urban setting as well. Residents of University Park would be "temperate with money to invest," as those in Greeley had been.

On November 30, 1885, the trustees began the process of setting up the "town" (colony) of University Park and complying with the requirements. They now had a $100,000 pledge from Elizabeth Iliff Warren (later withdrawn and reinstated), a campus site with room to establish a colony, and promised transportation. McIntosh's Circle Railroad Company, with Loveland as president, agreed "to build a [rail]road to the Park and run four trains daily directly to the campus if the trustees would locate where they wanted them to."[21] Clark also may have promised to hold the rest of his land between Jewell and Yale avenues and Downing to Race streets on the university's north, west, and south sides for future fund-raising possibilities and to develop another Evanston for him. With University Park on the east and Evanston on the west, the campus would be surrounded with the elite community that these men desired.

At the news that the university would in fact move south, some of Denver's most prominent citizens snatched up adjoining land on speculation. These investors, who purchased parcels of as much as 160 to 320 acres each on prairie land that ranged from Clarkson east to Colorado Boulevard and Alameda south to Jewell, included Charles and Luther Kountze (founders of the Colorado National Bank), their brothers Herman and Augustus Kountze, John Gonner, George Clayton, Charles Stebbins, Frederick Keener, David Kline, Margaretta Rice, and Alvin Daniels. Except for five houses and a school in Coronado (Florida Avenue and Colorado Boulevard), two houses

in Reser's 1883 subdivision (Florida Avenue and University Boulevard), and seven houses in the 1882 subdivision called Lake View (in the vicinity of Franklin Street and Alameda Avenue), this land was empty prairie and not improved upon or inhabited at that time.

In February 1886 the Colorado Seminary trustees began purchasing the first 150 acres for nearly $50,000, most with water rights; this purchase would not only establish the university but would also found University Park Colony through resale at higher prices. Already in hand were five lots outside the park, two of them donated by Robert Steele in January 1885 and four lots in East Denver purchased from Magdalena Arndt in July and John Farel in October, for a total of $13,550. In February 1886 Rufus Clark started the ball rolling anew by deeding his eighty acres to the Colorado Seminary on February 5 for $10,500 and donating $500 cash as well. An accompanying contract stated that if the Colorado Seminary carried out the November 1885 terms in good faith and sold lots at the rate of $125 per acre or reconveyed the unsold land to Clark within two years, the obligation was to be void. If these conditions were indeed fulfilled, the land on which the University of Denver buildings now stand could in fact have been "donated" by Rufus Clark, as is often claimed. Edwin G. Nettleton followed with a bond for deed in the amount of $1,500 for twenty acres outside the park near Hampden Avenue and Colorado Boulevard, and John Babcock, owner of 160 acres next to the park, deeded fifteen acres at about Harvard Avenue and Steele Street for $3,000 on February 10. William M. Dailey donated a small plot, William Cooke Faber donated six lots, and William Byers deeded four acres at $500 per acre in Byers Subdivision at Virginia Avenue.

The trustees now purchased land that would comprise University Park itself. Between February 9 and March 9, 1886, they purchased 320 acres of land adjoining the campus from Robert M. St. Clair and his sister, Mrs. C. F. (Esther) Truesdale, for $19,200 plus water, averaging $80 per acre for the land and water. Evans's Denver and New Orleans Railroad (renamed the Texas and Gulf Railroad), which entered the property at Jewell Avenue and Fillmore Street and sliced diagonally to the southeast and exited at Asbury Avenue and Colorado Boulevard, was already in place, and on March 3, 1886, Loveland's Circle Railroad

Company promised to extend the tracks east on Myrtle (Evans) Avenue as far as Milwaukee Street.[22] With double transportation to what was still a remote area, the trustees believed the buyers would come. John Evans dedicated University Park on Arbor Day in April 1886, giving the major address from the carriage of Walter P. Miller, who later played a critical role in bringing water to South Denver.

The university platted the 399 acres of land "under the name and style of University Park" on May 22, 1886, and Millington reported that this plot of empty prairie, from Campus (Race) Street to Colorado Boulevard and Jewell to Iliff avenues, had been laid out "with broad avenues and spacious parks . . . a town site with over 2,500 lots, including the campus site. One-fourth of each block in this town, which is known as 'University Park,' is to be retained in perpetuity for the endowment of the school, while the proceeds of the sales of the remainder will be devoted to other purposes at the discretion of the board of trustees."[23]

Three parks were included, and Colorado Seminary granted to the public the perpetual use of all of them. Observatory Park at this time took up only one block, from Evans to Warren avenues and Milwaukee to Fillmore streets. Asbury Park was laid out about half a block long on both sides of Asbury Avenue, from South Josephine to South Columbine streets. Another park, from Evans to Warren avenues and South Madison to South Jackson streets, was named Simpson Park after Methodist bishop Matthew Simpson. All three parks were planned with elaborate circular walkways, trees, and flowers.

The 100-foot-wide avenues were named for Bishop Francis Asbury (sent to the American colonies in the early 1800s by John Wesley and therefore the founder of American Methodism), former governor John Evans, Bishop Henry White Warren, and in memory of Elizabeth Iliff Warren's first husband, John Wesley Iliff, and of course for John Wesley himself. The last three avenues were named for institutions of higher learning: Yale, Vassar, and Harvard. The eighty-foot-wide streets were numbered from east to west, with Race (Campus) number one, University Boulevard number four, and Colorado Boulevard number seventeen. Corner lots were 30.75 feet by 150 feet, and others were 25 by 150 feet. The plat was filed the afternoon of May 22, 1886,

and signed by John W. Bailey, vice-president, and F. C. Millington, secretary, Colorado Seminary Board of Trustees.

Kittie C. Miller, wife of Walter P. Miller, signed the very first contract at $600 for four lots on May 28, 1886, but the deed was not recorded until January 1887, and the house they built on the property at 2160 South Columbine was not erected until 1889.

The first buyer in University Park, then, was John A. Clough, a University of Denver trustee and president of Colorado Savings Bank. Clough bought two lots on June 5, 1886, for $300. Because this was the first purchase in the park, the pleased Colorado Seminary trustees added two more lots, gratis, giving Clough the first four lots on the northeast corner of what is now East Evans Avenue and South Columbine Street. Here he built a house and supposedly installed a Mr. Bray to live in the house and "look after" the park while it was being developed. This much-remodeled and architecturally undistinguished house still stands at 2525 East Evans Avenue. Clough's deed stipulated, as did Miller's and all University Park deeds thereafter, that "intoxicating liquors shall never be manufactured, sold or otherwise disposed of as a beverage, in any place of public resort in or upon the premises," a clause lifted verbatim from 1871 Union Colony deeds. In case this agreement on intoxicating liquors were broken, the deed would become null and void and the premises would revert to the Colorado Seminary.

By August the trustees were selling inside lots at $300 a pair, or $150 each; agricultural lots went for $400 a pair, or $200 each. Finance administrator Millington acknowledged that this averaged a little over a thousand dollars per acre, but buyers were well aware that part of the asking price was in fact a donation to the university.[24]

Bishop Henry and Elizabeth Warren made good on their commitment to University Park by building the second house, Grey Gables, in 1887. This simple Queen Anne–style house at 2184 South Milwaukee, is still a gracious home today. The house next to it, number 2168, was built at the same time. University authorities sank a well across the street from the two houses that yielded about 1,000 gallons of water at 700 feet but then dried up. Without water, the houses were inhabitable, and they stood empty for two years. Apparently, no further attempts to search for water were made in University Park at this time.

While Evans's University Park was going forward, his Denver and New Orleans Railroad stalled financially. The tracks ran alongside a section of land known even then as the Mexican Diggings, on the east bank of the South Platte River just south of Virginia Avenue (the present Robinson Brick site). Here the famous John Simpson Smith, who had come west in 1826, married a Cheyenne woman and became a chief of that tribe before working as a trader, trapper, and guide. Supposedly he discovered a considerable amount of placer gold on a couple of acres here in company with a party of Mexicans. The spot became known as the Mexican Diggings or Spanish Diggings. A year later, William Green Russell's party from Georgia established a camp there and mined as much as ten dollars' worth of gold dust a day before exhausting the site and moving farther south.[25]

This now-historic site became part of the Denver and New Orleans Railroad's grant, but by April 1885, the railroad had not paid the 1884 taxes on the eight acres of land and the county sold it on March 13 to George Tritch, president of the German National Bank and member of the railroad board. In June Tritch sold it to University of Denver vice-president John W. Bailey, who had incorporated the John W. Bailey Milling, Amalgamating and Mining company in December 1884 with a capital stock of $2 million. Bailey incorporated the Bailey Reduction Company in April 1885 and erected a smelter on the property. Bailey, who had moved to Colorado from New York about 1871, was a principal owner of the Recine Boy mine in Silver Cliff and partner in several mines near Ouray. By 1879 he was wealthy enough that "making a living is no longer a problem with him," according to the *Rocky Mountain News*.[26] He had been looking for a stamp mill site for some time, having the machinery built back east. The mill consisted of forty stamps driven by a 200-horsepower engine; each stamp had a capacity of two tons of ore per day. However, the stamp mill failed, and Tritch's German National Bank repossessed the property.

Evans's railroad went through a number of reorganizations during its nearly seventy-five years of existence. In 1886 Evans consolidated it with the Fort Worth and Denver Railroad and, even though its legal name changed to the Texas and Gulf Railroad, for several decades it was known simply as the Fort Worth Railroad. The Union Pacific took it over in 1890; still later it became the Colorado and Southern Railroad and ceased operation altogether in the mid-1950s.

While University Park waited for settlers, Fleming's Grove and the subdivisions along South Broadway, blessed with plentiful water and public transportation, bustled with activity as solid communities of homes, schools, and churches were being established. James Fleming, elected president of School District 7 in early 1883, was likely responsible for its first school, Fleming's Grove Elementary. Fleming initiated school bonds of $4,800 redeemable after five years and payable over fifteen years at 7 percent interest. These bonds were used to build a brick schoolhouse on the corner of South Grant Street and Colorado Avenue in 1885 on land donated by William A. H. Loveland; Theodore C. Henry; Loveland's sons, Will L. and Frank W. Loveland; and J. R. and Hattie Mulvaney. The Fleming's Grove schoolhouse contained only first and second grades, about forty students. The first teachers were Mrs. Ida Johnson and Miss Kate D. Harris.[27] Whether the school was classified as graded or ungraded is unknown, but the monthly salary in a graded school in 1885 was $108.07 for a male teacher and $67.63 for a female teacher. In ungraded schools men earned $54.78 per month and women $49.37.[28]

By 1886, there were enough folks in Coronado, a forty-acre market gardening community east of University Park, to warrant a second school. This subdivision had been platted on October 26, 1883, by Henrietta C. Long, who named the streets after herself

John Babcock, town trustee, state legislator, and philanthropist. *Colorado Historical Society*

and her husband, S. Allen Long. Boundaries were Henrietta (Colorado Boulevard), Allen (Florida Avenue), Long (Monroe Street), and Mexico avenues. Colorado Avenue (Jackson Street) ran through the middle of it. The Longs also owned the forty acres immediately to the north and later platted it into Coronado Heights. In early 1886 John S. Babcock spearheaded the effort to get not only a school but also a school district of its own for Coronado.

Babcock had settled in Littleton in the early 1880s. In February 1885 he purchased 160 acres south of Coronado (Iliff to Yale avenues and Steele to Colorado Boulevard) for $20 an acre or a total of $3,200. Babcock and Franklin C. Millington, the University of Denver's financial officer, platted the east half (Colorado Boulevard to Monroe Street, Iliff to Yale avenues) into University Gardens on November 30, 1885, and divided it into large lots, 634 feet deep and 330 feet wide. The lots sold well to investors speculating on the University of Denver's move to University Park, but the first house was not erected until 1912, on the corner of Iliff and Monroe. This small house was replaced in 1929 by the present two-story, ten-room house, known to neighborhood children as "the castle" because of its Victorian tower and the high concrete wall on two sides.

Three years later, on April 24, 1888, Babcock, together with Andress M. Rader, George S. Welch, and Jacob M. Murphy, platted part of the west half into Asbury Park, from Beacon (Harvard) to Yale avenues, and Babcock (Monroe) to Coke (Steele). North-south streets were named Advocate (Adams), Tamzin (Cook), and Ellsworth (Madison) streets. For himself, Babcock reserved a large plot on the corner of Cook Street and Iliff Avenue. A lateral canal that had been cut from the High Line Canal in what is now Eisenhower Park flowed down the present Colorado Boulevard. From this canal Babcock cut another ditch that ran along the south side of Iliff Avenue, perhaps as far as University Boulevard, which became known as the Babcock Lateral.

Most people throughout the city called City Ditch "the big ditch" to distinguish it from these smaller streams (laterals), which brought trouble as well as water to families:

> Mothers scolded small boys who waded in them on hot summer days despite the broken glass. The boys loved to make water wheels and would sometimes divert the streams to private projects not appreciated by property owners farther down the street. Drinking water being scarce, some grown people drank ditch water and swelled the ranks of typhoid patients. This despite the fact that the streams were often choked with litter. The newspapers occasionally asked that fetid matter cleaned from the ditches should not be left in piles along the streets to contaminate the air.[29]

By 1882 these conditions forced the city to hire water police to control the use of the laterals and keep them clean, but their job was impossible; physicians persuaded the city to fill up some of the ditches. By 1898 most of the lateral ditches, including the Babcock Lateral, were filled in and had disappeared, and the city installed a water tank at Iliff Avenue and Colorado Boulevard to provide water to University Gardens and University Park residents.

A natural ditch that ran through the south portion of Babcock's property along Vassar and Harvard avenues was left untouched, however. Children sailed boats in "the slough," as it was known, during the summer and skated on dammed-up ponds in the winter. It is known today as Harvard Gulch for the street it parallels. For many years the ditch lay idle, the stretch of land considered "so undesirable as to be nearly worthless," said Denver parks planner Saco De Boer in 1923. De Boer saw possibilities, however, and recommended that park roads be built "north and south of the gulch and the low area between them treated as a series of lakes with the water running over cascades from one level to the other. One large lake [in what is now De Boer Park] can be set aside as a swimming pool." He proposed to continue this "Fen Parkway" all the way west to the Platte River, and east to the High Line Canal at Holly Street.[30] De Boer's plan never materialized, and as the area urbanized, the ditch overtaxed the drainage system and caused occasionally severe flooding. Four heavy downpours in 1956 inundated every north-south street along its banks, from South Broadway to South University. Prof. Robert H. McWilliams, head of the University of Denver's Department of Sociology for many years and a member of the Denver City Council for eight years, was instrumental in instituting plans for the Harvard Gulch project to contain the flooding. A special bond election in 1967 financed the construction of concrete lining along that section and the enclosure of the gulch in a

Coronado School, Jackson Street and Florida Avenue, erected in 1886. The Coronado Methodist Mission also met here on Sundays. Note the skinny whitewall tire in the tree of this 1931 photo. *Photo courtesy of Anna Varga*

ten-foot conduit from there to the river. The section between Colorado and University boulevards remains unlined and delightfully natural in its appearance. Bicycle paths follow Harvard Gulch through McWilliams and De Boer parks and children still sail sticks and boats in it and pick dandelions along its banks in the spring.

Perhaps it was Babcock's own limited, seventh-grade education that spurred his interest in education and led him to help establish two schools—Coronado and University Park. In 1886 he led the drive to carve District 35 from parts of Districts 4 and 7 with the help of Theodore Petzoldt and William E. Thompson, setting its boundaries at Mississippi and Dartmouth avenues and University Boulevard and Quebec Street.[31] The petition was approved by Superintendent John L. Fetzer

on March 22, 1886, and the new school board purchased lots on the southeast corner of Florida Avenue and Jackson Street from the Longs on September 27. Here they built a single-room, red brick schoolhouse at what was then 1495 South Jackson Street. William Thompson was its first and perhaps only teacher. By 1888 District 35 showed twenty-five males and eighteen females between the ages of five and twenty-one living in the district.

There is no record of the school board officers for 1886–1888, but John Babcock was president from 1888 to 1891 and very likely from 1886 as well; William B. Simms was treasurer from 1888 to 1891. Secretaries were attorney John Hipp (1888–1890) and Charles M. Taylor (1890–1891).

Theodore and Katherine Petzoldt, garden farmers

on South Dahlia Street near Louisiana Avenue, had two attractive daughters in the school that they had helped organize. Teacher Thompson married their sixteen-year-old, Minnie, and school founder Babcock married Maggie, who was fifteen years younger than he.

The schoolhouse was probably used at least until University Park Elementary was constructed in 1893 at Iliff Avenue and St. Paul Street in the same district, on land donated by Babcock. But the Methodists established the Coronado Mission in the schoolhouse and met there on Sundays until 1903. The building was then sold to a private party in 1904 or 1905, and it may have been vacant for several years, until George P. Varga, Sr., bought it. Varga and his wife, Anna, had emigrated to the United States from Czechoslovakia with their families and met in an English class at Emily Griffith Opportunity School. George worked for the Mountain States Telephone and Telegraph Company, and he noticed the property for sale one day while making his rounds. He and Anna purchased the six lots from Kate Smith just before the Crash of 1929. They later sold two of the lots, tore the schoolhouse down, and built a lovely brick house on the site, facing south (3737 East Florida Avenue), in 1935. In its construction the Vargas used some schoolhouse bricks to finish the interior, and they moved a five- by ten-foot, six-inch-thick flagstone slab from the front of the schoolhouse to their front door on the south. George died in 1970;

Anna lives in University Park.

Although neighborhoods were developing nicely by the mid-1880s, the saloons that had survived the closing of the Exposition Building flourished. James Fleming was particularly annoyed with Joe Lowe's thriving Broadway Park, situated on the Circle Railroad and close to Jewell Park, and so close to his own house he could probably hear the revelry at night. By the fall of 1885, these establishments became "notoriously annoying to the better class of citizens whose homes were near, and it was evident that all this beautiful section which by nature was destined to be filled with the homes of our best and most enterprising citizens was going to be rendered almost valueless on account of these nuisances," stated the *Denver Eye*.[32] As the problem became increasingly intolerable and help from authorities less reliable, one or two citizens even made arrests and prosecuted the parties at their own expense. "But it did no good, for the [county] commissioners would give no aid, so it became evident that a different course must be pursued to rid this region of these great blemishes on its fair face."[33]

James Fleming, Avery Gallup, and Rufus Clark, perhaps among those who pursued and harassed the "liquor element" on their own, were already working on that "different course." The three men got together and began to come up with a strategy for saving the community.

Picnics such as this one at Jewell Park in 1884 likely goaded temperate citizens into attempts to ban alcohol. *Denver Public Library, Western History Department*

The Corporation of South Denver

Fleming, Gallup, and Clark's "different course" developed with amazing speed into a concrete plan to "incorporate a town and pass ordinances such as would be equivalent to prohibition."[1] For their town, the three men decided on a three-mile square section of real estate that included their lands as well as hundreds of acres of empty prairie. Boundaries of the town would be Alameda Avenue, Colorado Boulevard, Yale Avenue, and the South Platte River, which would provide University Park with the legal entity it needed for its colony and an environment free from saloons.

In early 1886 the men enlisted the support of resident property owners John S. Babcock, gardener George E. Dunlap, builder and painter August H. Gamage, court stenographer Henry F. Jolly, florist John L. Russell, and attorney John Hipp. The group put together a proper petition in favor of incorporation and circulated it among the 150 inhabitants living within the boundaries of the proposed town to secure the necessary thirty votes.

Nonresident Denver Circle Real Estate Company owners William A. H. Loveland and Theodore C. Henry, as well as Charles L. McIntosh, who represented Governor Jewell's interests in the Denver Circle Railroad Company, supported the incorporation as a way to advance their real estate interests. But another group, the thirteen nonresident landowners who had invested so heavily in South Denver the year before, watched the proceedings with alarm. Ineligible to vote, and therefore momentarily powerless, this group of bankers, investors, and businessmen nevertheless vowed to defeat any such idea, one way or another.

Saloon owners, of course, were outraged. The "liquor element, strong and determined for a fight," and supposedly backed by the "brewing and wholesale liquor interests of the city of Denver" naturally railed against the planned prohibition suburb.[2] But forty men (women did not yet have the vote)—ten more than needed—signed the petition to incorporate the Town of South Denver and the jubilant organizers pressed on. They hired George W. Allen, a former Pennsylvania legislator who later became a District Court judge, to act as their attorney. Then they surveyed the land and drew up a map, all at their own expense.[3]

On June 16, 1886, James Fleming and the other thirty-nine signers filed the surveyed plat, incorporation map, and petition in Arapahoe County Court, asking that the territory and its 150 inhabitants be incorporated into a town under the name of *South Denver*. The court accepted the application and appointed Rufus Clark, Frederick W. Johns, John L. Russell, John S. Babcock, and Samuel H. Seccombe commissioners, to act as clerks in an incorporation election to be held six weeks later, in July.

The commissioners printed handbills notifying everyone of the coming election and posted them in

Map filed with Fleming's petition to incorporate the Town of South Denver, June 16, 1886. *Colorado State Archives*

stores and other public places. Now the serious campaign for votes began. Prohibitionists assured the people that incorporation was for their own protection against saloons and appealed to their sense of commitment to a legal community. The "liquor element" campaigned just as hard against incorporation, appealing to those who felt that all this goodness and uprightness was just a touch too confining. Joe Lowe had been forced out of two states already, not by gun-toting enemies but by ordinances and laws, and he was not about to let that happen again, at least not without a fight. Lowe, York, Lauster, and Wyman tramped up and down South Broadway trying to persuade their neighbors to vote no.

On July 31, 1886, supporters and saloon keepers alike showed up at the vacated exposition building to vote. Pap Wyman, Louis York, Joe Lowe, and David Lauster were not far behind their enemy, incorporation leader and prohibitionist James Fleming. But their votes failed to carry the day. Of the 104 electors who cast their ballots, sixty-five voted for incorporation and thirty-eight against. One vote was cast blank.[4] The "liquor establishment" lost this round but was far from ready to give up the fight.

On August 9, the court declared the Town of South Denver to be an incorporated town, and the secretary of state filed the incorporation papers on August 14, 1886. Almost immediately, the second set of opponents, nonresident landowners, made their move. All told, they owned 840 acres and their investment had been validated: with the university moving its campus south they stood to reap considerable real estate profits. As an unincorporated district, taxes were not an issue; if incorporated, however, they would be forced to pay taxes for a developing town but would receive nothing in return, because their own property was vacant and none of the owners lived within the boundaries. Led by city leader and former *Rocky Mountain News* owner William Byers, they hired the Bartels and Blood law firm and prepared to challenge the incorporation with all the power and influence their standing in the community could muster.

The residents of this brand new town knew nothing of this. On September 4, the voters went to the polls again, this time to choose their leaders. James A. Fleming was elected the first mayor, and John S. Babcock, Frederick W. Johns, Avery Gallup, George E.

Dunlap, and August Gamage were elected trustees. Fleming and the trustees were paid a token $1 per one-year term, as was Rufus Clark, the treasurer.

The town council held its first meeting September 18 in the cavernous exposition building and commenced to organize their town and appoint officers. Elias Broadwell became the first police magistrate, and Alex Miller, a rather volatile man who had problems staying out of trouble himself, became town marshal and dogcatcher. For these services, Miller earned $65 per year plus $2 for each arrest he made. Henry F. Jolly was elected clerk and recorder at an annual salary of $200, and for several years he chronicled the minutes in the *South Denver Journal (Proceedings of the Board of Trustees, South Denver, Colorado),* often scribbling his notes on Denver Circle Railroad Company stationery provided by Rufus Clark.[5] John Hipp was appointed city attorney, also at $200 per year. A staunch prohibitionist, Hipp was just the man to go after the saloons. He served as president of the Colorado Prohibition party for fifteen years and he was at one time its candidate for governor. Hipp, the University of Denver's first and only graduate in 1884, had been admitted to the bar just weeks earlier.

The first rules made at this historic meeting were to regulate their own meetings. Members were not allowed to speak more than twice on the same question, nor longer than five minutes at any one time; absent members could be fined, but not more than $10 per meeting. Committees were appointed on finance, licenses, streets and bridges, animals running at large, and places of meeting. They then designed a town seal, which had in the center the words "town seal," and around the outer edge the words "South Denver, Arapahoe County, Colorado."

In their second meeting the council designed laws that would in effect run the liquor establishment out of town. They did this by levying absurdly high annual license fees: $3,500 for a wholesale liquor license, and $2,500 for a retail license. Even if the liquor store owner or saloon owner could come up with the money, the applicant would need fifty signatures of nearby residents "showing that the applicant is of good moral character." Alcohol could not be sold on Sundays or between midnight and 6:00 A.M. on any day, and no alcohol could be sold to any minor, apprentice, habitual drunkard, or to any "insane, idiotic, distracted, or intoxicated person." Intoxication in a public *or private* place brought first-time offenders a $10 fine, $25 thereafter, and the marshal could commit offenders to jail as well.

To cover every possible variation of dance hall/roadhouse/saloon/houses of prostitution, the trustees then banned "bawdy and disorderly houses of ill-fame or assignation" and levied $300 fines. Neither could one own a house "to harbor prostitutes or lewd women," or run even so much as a "common, ill-governed or disorderly house." Prostitutes would be punished with a $25 fine for each violation. Dance houses were allowed, but a license from the mayor—at a price of $2,500 per year—was needed and the dance houses were to be closed on Sundays. Fines were stiff: $100 for the first violation, $200 for each offense thereafter. Gambling was banned outright.

The Town of South Denver would be a clean, quiet, and safe town. There would be no dog fights, cock fights, or even fights between people. No person could even invite any other person to fight or quarrel, appear in indecent or lewd dress in public, use vulgar language, fire guns, ride or drive a horse recklessly, or throw stones at people or property. The trustees also banished vagrants, who were described as "any able-bodied person who, not having visible means to maintain himself, and who lives idly without employment, or is found loitering or rambling about, or wandering abroad and lodging in tippling houses, bar-houses and houses of bad repute, sheds, stables, or in wagons or boxes, or in the open air." Suspicious persons "trespassing at night, not giving a good account of himself, begging, or carrying burglary instruments, plus prostitutes and habitual drunkards" also qualified as vagrants. The fine was $15 for each offense. Horses, cattle, swine, sheep, goats, or geese running at large would be taken to the pound at $25 for the first offense, $50 thereafter. Just in case persons or animals managed to wander about in spite of the restrictions, home owners were not to "leave or keep open any cellar door, well, pit or vault, or trench . . . so that passersby will be in danger of falling into same."

By Thanksgiving the council had created 20 of the 129 ordinances they would eventually decree. The law required that all ordinances be published in a newspaper, but because a newspaper had not yet been established in South Denver, the council posted copies of them in public places: the Circle Railway depot on Fleming's property, the Coronado schoolhouse, the ice house at Smith's Lake, and the west ticket office of the exposition building.

As the council met weekly throughout the autumn months to plan their glorious trouble-free town, the opposition had not been idle. On November 27, 1886, a suit was filed in the Arapahoe district court by William and Elizabeth Byers; John and Amalie Gonner; George Clayton; Charles Stebbins; Frederick Keener; David Kline; Margaretta Rice; Alvin Daniels; and Charles, Herman, Luther and Augustus Kountze against Mayor Fleming and trustees Babcock, Johns, Dunlap, Gamage, and Gallup to oust them from office and nullify the town's incorporation. Stating that they objected to, protested against, and questioned the validity and legality of the town's incorporation, the plaintiffs claimed that "the so called town of South Denver has not been legally and constitutionally incorporated under the laws of the State of Colorado,

J. A. Fleming.

James A. Fleming, mayor of South Denver, 1886–1890. *Sketch from the Denver Eye, January 1, 1890*

and is no municipal corporation at all," and that Fleming and the others had "intruded into, usurped and unlawfully held offices in the pretended municipal corporation called South Denver."[6]

They alleged, first, that the power to determine the extent and boundaries of municipal corporations belonged only to a legislative body, such as a board of county commissioners, and could not be delegated to private individuals such as Fleming and the other organizers. Their second point was that before any part of a county could be incorporated into a town it must be *inhabited* as a village or town. Because unoccupied and farming lands constituted about two-thirds of the town's land, leaving only about a third actually inhabited, the property was ineligible for incorporation. The *Denver Republican* suggested that the real reason the suit was brought was because the plaintiffs did not want to pay the increased taxes on the South Denver property that incorporation implied.[7]

South Denver fought back. John Hipp filed a demurrer, claiming insufficient grounds to justify legal action against the town, and a month later, on December 29, 1886, the court sustained Hipp's demurrer and dismissed the case. Enraged, Byers et al. led an appeal the next day. Fleming did not underestimate the threat, but he continued building the town, confident that the council could win a second round too. The trustees retained Charles H. Toll to represent their case for a fee of $85, and they went about their business of building a town.

The trustees had received permission to use Denver's jail on Colfax Avenue until the town could establish one of its own, and a jail committee was appointed to locate a suitable building for it. In January 1887, the trustees rented two rear rooms in the former Makin Brothers saloon on South Logan at about Center Avenue for $10 per month and fitted out their new jail with two cells, cots and blankets, four pairs of handcuffs, and two leg irons. A third cell was added later.

Marshal Alex Miller himself nearly became one of the new jail's first inmates. Miller had used unnecessary force in arresting a suspect, who promptly sued him for assault. The powerful, and outraged, W. A. H. Loveland advised trustee Avery Gallup to fire Miller as marshal. But when Miller tendered his resignation on January 4, Gallup convinced the council to refuse it, and he even

added a deputy marshal, Joseph R. Atkins, to assist him. Loveland insisted on Miller's dismissal, however, and on February 1 the board of trustees unanimously accepted Miller's resignation. Two weeks later Miller was tried in Arapahoe County Criminal Court, found guilty of "assault to injure," and fined $50.[8] As a private citizen, Miller's antics delighted the press, which reported on a fistfight Miller had with his partner, J. J. Putnam. The two men owned the South Denver Brick Manufacturing Company at South Vine Street and Mexico Avenue. One Sunday afternoon Miller accused Putnam of stealing brick to build his own houses. At first, according to the *Denver Republican,* the two "engaged in a war of words," until Putnam attempted to strike Miller on the head with a two-foot iron pipe. Miller dodged and received a blow on the arm, but Miller then knocked Putnam down with his fist. A third employee joined the scrap, on Putnam's side, but "Miller proved a Tartar and . . . knocked them both out and put them to flight."[9] Miller continued to be a force in the community after resigning as marshall, however, and later served on the District 7 school board.

James Fleming was reelected mayor for a second one-year term, to begin April 1, 1887, and Rufus Clark once again served as treasurer. A few days later, on April 5, William and Elizabeth Byers et al. filed their case against the Corporation of South Denver in the Colorado Supreme Court.[10]

The town faced two other court challenges as well. This time the plaintiffs charged that the first twenty ordinances had not been properly published in a Denver newspaper such as the *Denver Republican* or the *Rocky Mountain News* as required by law and were therefore invalid. But in late 1886, Arthur Pierce and hardware merchant John H. Blood had founded a weekly newspaper, the *Denver Eye,* at 130 Broadway, which published the ordinances in their entirety on February 19, 1887. When Pierce produced a notarized statement of proof at the trial in June, the case was dismissed.

Hipp had waged a vigorous campaign against the saloons, especially Pap Wyman, Joe Lowe, and the Lausters, and by April 15 he had eleven cases pending in the criminal court. His arrest of a Mr. Parker for selling liquor without a license and for running a dance house led to a court challenge of the town's liquor ordinances. Parker's attorneys argued that the town's law, which stated that anyone who couldn't pay fines could be jailed one day for each $2 worth of fines, conflicted with the Bill of Rights. Hipp had also denied Parker a jury trial, which also infringed on constitutional rights. The Town of South Denver won this lawsuit too, but by now the atmosphere was so explosive that attorney Hipp, who "cleaned the saloons and roadhouses out of this young town . . . received many anonymous letters threatening his life."[11]

The council kept the pressure on the saloons. By the summer of 1887 Louis York gave up and moved his saloon to Larimer Street downtown. The Lausters stayed but converted their tavern into a restaurant and butcher shop. This left only Pap Wyman and Joe Lowe. By August the town had filed so many suits against Joe Lowe that he was ready to deal. He offered to close Broadway Park and move out if the town would dismiss its suits against him. The authorities agreed, "upon Lowe paying certain costs" before leaving town. Lowe refused, and he bitterly announced that he was going back to Leadville, where "mining would pay him better than running a liquor place in South Denver under such fire as he had been getting."[12] Lowe didn't follow through on his threat, however, and the aggravations continued. Joe had his share of domestic troubles as well as harassment from the law. He and Mollie lived in a small house next to the saloon, and in August 1884 their Swedish servant girl, Lena Larson, gave birth to Joe's child, Thomas Joseph. Mollie filed for divorce on the grounds of cruelty and the divorce was granted on October 20, 1887. Joe and Lena were married on February 11, 1888.

With most of the saloons on the run, the council turned to creating ordinances of a more aesthetic nature. No straw, filth, manure, chips, or rubbish could be henceforth thrown into the street. Dead horses, oxen, and other animals must be removed and buried at once. Candle factories, soap factories, rendering establishments, tanneries, distilleries, breweries, smelters, chemical works, fertilizer works, slaughterhouses, stockyards, foundries, and boiler shops could operate within a mile of the town only with a proper permit signed by at least thirty residents and backed by a "good and sufficient" bond. The Bailey Smelter, erected before the town incorporated but at this point in receivership and idle, was allowed to remain.

In spite of these bans, industrialists tried hard to move factories and businesses into town. In April 1887, Phillip D. Armour of Chicago visited Denver to select a site for a beef slaughterhouse, possibly in South Denver. The trustees quickly put an end to any such speculation. A few months later, however, former governor John Evans bought eighty acres of land between Mississippi and Florida avenues and Logan to Clarkson streets, intending to build mammoth stockyards next to his Texas and Gulf Railroad. The railroad had finally been completed all the way to Galveston, and Evans planned that it would replace the dusty national cattle trail, which was being abandoned as farms and ranches blocked the passage of the huge herds that plodded across the plains each summer. The Texas and Gulf Railroad would become the new cattle highway, the connecting link between cattle raisers of Texas and dealers in the northwest. Evans planned to bring Texas cattle into his South Denver stockyards by rail for distribution to points east, north, and west of Colorado. The enterprise was praised and supported by such strong corporations as the Denver and Rio Grande, Chicago Rock Island and Pacific, and the Missouri Pacific railroads, some of which would construct their tracks to the yards. Because the existence of a stockyard within the Town of South Denver limits clearly violated the town's ordinance, outraged taxpayers immediately petitioned the trustees to stop this unacceptable venture, alleging that outside influences were bent on destroying the quality of the town. Fleming and his southsiders were forced to fight three separate attempts to locate Evans's stockyards in South Denver, but they finally defeated the project.

On December 23, 1887, the Colorado Supreme Court upheld the District Court ruling that dismissed the Byers et al. lawsuit against the town. The court determined that there was no provision expressly prohibiting the delegation of power (to create a municipal corporation) to individuals and that the question of delegating such power to either a governing body or an individual "seems to us to be purely a question of policy or expediency; with which questions courts have nothing to do." As to the claim that only inhabited towns could be incorporated, the court stated, "We do not think the statute should be so construed . . . the interpretation will permit the including of farming and unoccupied lands within the limits of towns to be incorporated." The court then chastised the plaintiffs: "The contention of appellants . . . raises the question of whether the courts can declare an act of the legislature invalid on the sole ground that it is repugnant to natural justice or expediency. . . . The judiciary . . . cannot run a race of opinions upon points of right, reason and expedience with the law-making power. . . . The judgment should be affirmed."[13]

The *Denver Eye,* reflecting later on these turbulent days, justified not only this fight against the nonresident property holders but the other challenges to its existence as well: "These matters of litigation on all points have cost the taxpayers of the town several thousands of dollars, but few have questioned the wisdom of the expenditure, and to-day the taxes are only five mills for general town purposes."[14]

During all this upheaval, Fleming had his own personal problems to contend with. In the spring of 1886 his attorney, George W. Allen, took depositions from witnesses in San Francisco and instructed Julius Heinrich that Fleming planned to visit the city to see his wife Nellie again. At this, poor Julius panicked and offered to leave the county and go anywhere Fleming said in order to avoid a confrontation. Weaseling out of the whole affair, he pledged to "do all in my power to influence his wife to go back to him as I ain't stuck on her although she is very pretty and I make quite a nice little sum of money by having her accompany me." He finished by saying that Nellie "was not the kind of a woman that either Fleming or himself wanted."

In any case, Nellie still would not see her husband when he arrived in San Francisco. James acknowledged defeat, went back to Denver, and filed for divorce on March 18, 1886. The divorce was granted July 19. The sting of rejection may have lessened in the meantime

with his new romance with an older and more reliable woman, Alice Abrams, age twenty-nine, a former Pennsylvanian who had lived in Denver since 1881. James and Alice were married in Denver on September 29. James moved out of the boardinghouse and into his Fleming's Grove mansion with his new wife, where they joined the rest of his family.

Nor did he neglect his mining and real estate interests. Operating from his offices at 271 Seventeenth Street, James offered Fleming's Grove lots "cheap," for part cash and part "on time" at 7 percent interest. By 1887 he owned the Mendota Building on the northwest corner of Fifteenth and Arapahoe downtown (now demolished) and in 1888 he took in William E. Gray as a partner. Fleming and Gray Real Estate and Mines moved their offices into Fleming's Mendota Building and the next year added John T. Donnellan to the partnership. James Fleming began selling the rest of his South Denver real estate between Broadway and Grant streets, for $400 per lot on Grant Street and up to $650 for the choice lots on South Broadway. Taxes were $1.50 per year. He formally platted this property into Fleming's Broadway Addition in November 1889.

The Fleming family moved in and out of the mansion. Thomas had married Minnie A. Voorhees in 1886 and lived in the Fleming's Grove Subdivision nearby. Then in 1887 James moved Alice's mother, Ellen, into the house; his own mother, Susanna, and two of his sisters, teachers Elizabeth and Mattie, moved out, to 428 South Cherokee Street. James's oldest son, Richard, joined his grandmother and aunts a year later. Sadie stayed at the Fleming mansion until her marriage to her cousin, builder Jesse Fleming, in September 1889. Nettie made a career in teaching and never married; Mattie married William Duffies in 1901.

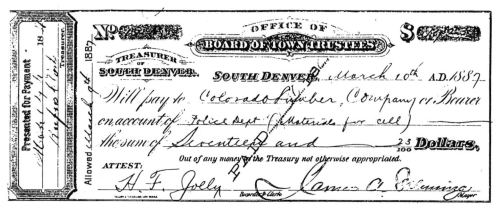

Rufus "Potato" Clark, treasurer, approved this warrant for payment of jail cell materials in 1887. *Colorado State Archives*

Elizabeth taught school until her marriage to *Denver Times* city editor Elias M. Ammons in January 1889. Twenty-four years later Elizabeth became the state's First Lady when Elias was elected governor of Colorado. He served from 1913 to 1915. (Susanna Hill Fleming, mother of James, Thomas, George, Elizabeth, Nettie, Mattie, and Sadie, died December 15, 1912, at the age of eighty-one, just weeks before her son-in-law was inaugurated as governor of Colorado. Her grandson, Teller Ammons, was also elected governor of Colorado in 1937 and served until 1939.)

The town was entering its boom years. In November 1887, Rufus Clark platted part of his campus land (Jewell to Iliff avenues and Race to Downing streets) into Evanston Subdivision. He named the streets Campus (Race), Lightburn (High), Hayes (Williams), Hazen (Gilpin), Center (Franklin), Millington (Humboldt), Prospect (Lafayette), Logan (Marion), and West (Downing), and he fenced in each lot and planted shade trees. Clark stipulated in his deeds that no intoxicating liquors were to be sold or manufactured on the premises, using the same language from Union Colony deeds as University Park developers had. He put the lots up for sale at $100 each and sold the first three (lots 26–28 in block 20) in the 2100 block of South Franklin to Oscar Einarsen on November 11. On November 26, Clark incorporated the Evanston Real Estate and Trust Company with Archie Fisk and Enos Miles, with a capital stock of $180,000, and on November 29 transferred his entire Evanston Subdivision to the company for $140,000. The liquor prohibition remained intact.

With both University Park and Evanston secured for the university, General Robert A. Cameron, Joseph C. Shattuck, John Evans, William E. Pabor, and John Clough called a meeting for April 16, 1888, at Trinity Methodist Episcopal Church, to officially organize the University Park Colonization Society. This meeting was the initial step in forming Evanston and University Park into a formal Methodist prohibition suburb. Bishop Warren, Chancellor Moore, Dean Shattuck, General Cameron, and ex-governor Evans assured the large number of real estate men, Methodist preachers, and prominent citizens and their wives that University Park possessed more advantages than either Evanston, Illinois, or Greeley, Colorado. General Cameron had been Union Colony's first president, Pabor its first clerk

and treasurer, and Joseph Shattuck a principal in its first school. Cameron, who was made president of the University Park Colonization Society, spoke of the struggles and hardships he and the others had encountered firsthand in forming Union Colony eighteen years earlier. Whereas Union Colony had been agricultural, the organizers planned University Park, and later Evanston, as a great educational center of the Rocky Mountain region, where "the dominant and controlling ideas would be conscience and culture, and where these two essential elements to a great civilization shall have a pre-eminent influence over the young in a supremely healthy location, so that in the development of manhood and womanhood from youth, a sound mind may go with a sound body."[15]

Denver citizens were intrigued with this

proposed establishment of a literary suburb closely connected by frequent railroad communications with an important and progressive city, in a locality the healthiest that the world knows. Sequestered from intrusive mundane concerns, both students and teachers will be able to devote themselves to the study of the most all-embracing range of knowledge. It sounds like a revival of the middle-age idea of a university, a sort of philosophic monasticism, tempered (for the teachers) by marriage."[16]

Evans built a little depot at Fillmore Street on the south side of his Texas and Gulf Railroad tracks. He met potential buyers at the depot with his carriage and drove them about the empty countryside selling lots. Visitors stepping off the train at this depot would have seen nothing on the empty prairie in early 1888 except John Clough's home in the distance, but Evans no doubt persuaded them to visualize the future Chamberlin Observatory straight south of the depot, and to imagine the university building to the right.

Rosedale Subdivision was also platted in 1887, and named in honor of Amanda Ellis Field, who came to Colorado in 1864 with her husband, Thomas M. Field, a civil engineer, from Missouri. Thomas became involved in constructing the Denver Pacific, Kansas Pacific, and Denver and Rio Grande railroads, and with a partner he established Field and Hill general merchandise trading posts all along the railroad lines. Thomas Field served as Denver's city treasurer from 1874 to 1876; in 1878 he was the democratic candidate for lieutenant governor but was defeated by H.A.W. Tabor.

In 1871 Field bought eighty acres from Clarkson to Broadway streets and Iliff to Harvard avenues and in 1880 built a small frame house at about South Grant Street and Wesley Avenue in what is now Rosedale Park. The family moved into it in 1883, when son John and his sister Pattie were already in high school. The two walked to Jewell Avenue and Broadway to ride the Circle Railroad train to school downtown. A younger sister, Lizzie, may have attended District 6 schools south of their home. The Fields planted apple trees east of the house and Mrs. Field grew such an abundance of yellow roses around the frame house that legend says that when Arthur Eads and George W. Timmerman platted a subdivision between Sherman and Broadway in 1887, they named it Rosedale in her honor.

The family moved from Rosedale to a two-story brick business building at 265 Broadway, in which they used the second floor for community meetings and parties as before, when it was known as Killie's Hall. While the family lived at what became known as Field's Hall, Thomas Field farmed the forty acres at Clarkson and Iliff while building an 8,500-square-foot house just east of the small frame cottage, for $40,000. John stated that the family moved into the mansion, which became known as the Thomas M. Field House, in 1890 and planted the first Russian olive trees in Colorado around the house. Thomas Field died either about the same time the house was completed or shortly thereafter. His wife, Amanda, and children, John and Lizzie, continued to live there until 1895, when they sold it to the Joel W. Shackleford family. (Pattie had married Isaac Cunningham Van Meter in 1892.) David Moffat's First National Bank came into possession of the forty acres, and in 1902 Moffat sold the property to the State of Colorado for development as a State Home for Dependent Children. The Thomas M. Field House was renamed Campbell Hall. Additional buildings were constructed and some 115 children were moved into it from the North Denver state home. By 1938, twenty-five buildings existed, including dairy and horse barns and sheds for hogs, calves, and chickens on a 58.6-acre site. Twenty of these acres were farmland and eighteen were reserved for playgrounds and an athletic field.

Infants were cared for at Babyland, and after the babies learned to walk they were moved to another building called Toddlerland. Later, girls were housed in Campbell Hall (the Thomas M. Field House), and the boys in dormitories. At its peak in the 1940s and 1950s, the home had over 250 children and adolescents. The children were educated at the Dora Reynolds School at 2305 South Washington until it was closed in 1957. Louise A. Merrill, a pioneer in the area of junior high school education, was its principal for more than ten years.

The State of Colorado phased out the children's home during the 1960s and closed it in 1971. The Thomas M. Field House (Campbell Hall) and other State Home buildings and property were sold to the City and County of Denver in 1978. The Thomas M. Field House was placed on the National Register of Historic Places August 10, 1979, but the mansion was neglected for several years and a fire in 1987 destroyed the interior. The building was torn down in 1989.

Three buildings remain on the grounds today, on the edge of Harvard Park. The City Civil Service Commission occupies Babyland, and the Denver Police Department uses Edbrooke Gymnasium. The powerhouse and laundry, with its twin chimneys, is being renovated by the Department of Parks and Recreation.

Across Broadway, next to Rufus Clark's homestead, Mary H. Mechling platted the West Broadway Subdivision in December 1887 (Louisiana to Mississippi and the river to the railroad tracks), naming the north-south streets Platte River (Elati), River Street (Delaware), Mechling Avenue (Cherokee) and Richmond Avenue (Bannock). A few homes had been built in the area earlier; the house at 1199 South Bannock dates from 1880, 1148 and 1150 South Cherokee were built in 1885, as were 1417, 1526, 1536, 1559, 1566, and 1610 South Acoma. A beautifully restored house near Alameda Avenue, at 337 South Bannock, was built in 1888.

For many of the special events at nearby Jewell Park, people watched from carriages and wagons parked on South Broadway instead of paying admission. For this reason and because the Denver Circle Railroad charged only five cents per ride, the company's chronic financial trouble continued. In 1885 the Farmers' Loan and Trust Company of New York, which held the loan, had sued the Denver Circle Railroad for $125,000, claiming that it was insolvent, and the railroad went into the receivership of Charles McIntosh. Loveland remained its president.[17] The

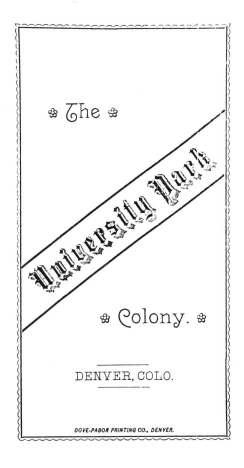

UNIVERSITY PARK
COLONY.

Plans and Purposes.

DESIROUS of forming a community where the dominant and controlling ideas shall be conscience and culture, and where these two essential elements to a great civilization shall have a pre-eminent influence over the young in a supremely healthy location, so that in the development of manhood and womanhood from youth, a sound mind may go with a sound body, a number of gentlemen have banded themselves together and assumed the name of The University Park Colony.

University Park Colony brochure. *University of Denver Archives*

railroad continued to operate its daily trains, but in January 1887 the Denver Circle Railroad Company and Jewell Park were sold to "a syndicate of New York Capitalists" for $750,000 and the name changed to the Denver Terminal Company.

But McIntosh was not ready to give up Jewell Park. With several others, he incorporated the Overland Racing Association on May 27, 1887, with himself as director, and bought the park and renamed it Overland because of its considerable distance from the city. Despite the town's ban on alcohol and general rowdiness, the park had earned a bad reputation, so the association promised to abolish the present "liquor-selling and dance-house system, and ladies and children can go there as freely as to Central Park in New York."[18] Ed Chase, who operated his beer and betting stand openly without a license in spite of repeated arrests, was largely reponsible for the park's deteriorating reputation. Many citizens complained that

because of his prominence in Denver, his influential friends kept him from suffering the fate of other, smaller liquor sellers who paid fines and were sometimes jailed. In one case the South Denver police magistrate issued a warrant for Chase's arrest, but the marshal never served it, "for the reason that certain officials in the town instructed him not to."[19] At least two witnesses were ready to swear that they had bought beer from Chase and drank it on the premises, but when the police magistrate fined Chase for selling the liquor, the case was appealed to the County Court and never went to trial. (The Overland Racing Association could do nothing about the entrenched Ed Chase, either; he kept his stand at the track well into the 1890s.)

The syndicate that had purchased the Denver Circle Railroad Company soon defaulted, and on June 1, 1887, the railroad was sold under foreclosure to the Atchison, Topeka & Santa Fe Railroad. The popular train continued to run in South Denver for two more years under the new management.

The Denver Circle Real Estate Company was not involved in the Denver Circle Railroad Company sale, in spite of the fact that some of the same individuals were involved in both enterprises. But Loveland and Henry's Denver Circle Real Estate Company had its own difficulties, which ended in a lawsuit against Rufus Clark that was finally settled by Judge Hallett in the U.S. Circuit Court.

When Rufus Clark and Loveland and Henry drew up their contract in November 1881, the values of their jointly held real estate were largely speculative, depending almost wholly upon the success of the Circle Railroad through the lands. But three years later, although tracks were in use in South Denver, none had yet been constructed on the rest of the planned beltway around the city. The company's precarious

financial condition threatened its continuance. Clark was convinced that the railroad would soon go into receivership (it did the next year) and the market value of the property would be depressed and the lands unsalable. In May 1884 Clark and W. A. H. Loveland and T. C. Henry canceled their November 1881 contract, and Clark deeded 270 acres that they had held jointly to Loveland and Henry for $250 per acre, or just under $70,000. Loveland and Henry paid about $10,000 down and executed a deed of trust to Colorado National Bank president Charles B. Kountze and his cashier, John Hanna, for promissory notes on the balance, the final payment to be paid in May 1886. Loveland and Henry conveyed the properties, which included part of Sherman Subdivision (Louisiana to Florida avenues), what is now Rosedale, eighty acres between Jewell and Mexico and Broadway and Clarkson, and a 120-acre strip between Delaware and

Thomas Field House. *Photo courtesy of Denver Landmark Preservation Commission*

Broadway (less fifty acres set aside for school land, rights-of-way, and so on) to their sons Stuart Henry and Frank Loveland, who became the sole owners. But after two more years of struggling, Loveland and Henry, holders of the notes, defaulted on their payments to Rufus Clark in March 1886. Clark immediately contracted with Charles McIntosh, who had incorporated the South Denver Real Estate Company but also remained as a director of the Denver Circle Real Estate Company, to take the land off Clark's hands in case Clark was "forced to buy it back." That settled, Clark, claiming that Loveland and Henry had paid only $135 on the principal and $844.51 in interest, advertised the entire 270 acres for sale at a public auction.

At this news, Horace Tabor, alarmed at the precarious state of his investment in the Denver Circle Real Estate Company, filed an injunction against Rufus Clark in an attempt to prevent the foreclosure of the property and to protect his shares.[20] Tabor testified that he had never attended a company meeting and did not know that the company was struggling for existence. He charged that Clark conspired with Henry and Loveland to cancel the contract in order that the three of them could obtain the land and deprive the stockholders from all interest therein.

Clark denied that Tabor ever owned any shares at all. In the Tabor vs. Clark trial, it was revealed that Tabor had in fact paid $5,000 to buy 100 shares from another stockholder, Thomas M. Nichol, who had purchased them from T. C. Henry. Henry's name remained on the certificates and Tabor had no proof whatsoever that he had ever purchased a single share. Clark, protesting Tabor's charge of collusion with Loveland and Henry, accused the two men of using Tabor as "a mere volunteer, for the purpose of getting time for said Henry and Loveland and to harass and oppress this defendant," and even paying Tabor's court fees for him.

The injunction was dismissed on August 10, and the property was released for sale. The auction was held on the Tremont Street side of the Denver Court House on August 3, 1886, and Rufus Clark bought the entire 270 acres back for $76,800. The next day he sold them to McIntosh's South Denver Real Estate Company. In February 1887, McIntosh sold forty acres of it to George W. Timmerman and Arthur Eads, who platted it into Rosedale and sold Broadway front lots for $75 each and all others for $30 each. The company sold another large tract in Sherman Subdivision to S. Vinson Farnum. Farnum in turn sold his lots to private parties.

On May 12, 1887, Frank Loveland and Stuart Henry sued Rufus Clark, the South Denver Real Estate Company, George W. Timmerman, Arthur B. Eads, S. Vinson Farnum, John R. Hanna, and banker Charles B. Kountze for $250,000 in damages.[21] The two men claimed that this amount was the worth of the land had it been sold in blocks or lots and not in quarter sections and bought by Rufus Clark. They also claimed that they were the true owners of it and that Rufus Clark had acted fraudulently.

By this time the Sherman Subdivision land was considered prime real estate estimated to be worth $800 per acre. Loveland testified to its potential:

The Denver Circle Railway runs through the center of it, the property is well watered—gets the first water from the city ditch. The city cars are extended out, and the city has extended out. Artesian wells have been sunk on Mr. Fleming's property—one of the best artesian wells in the state; the soil is good; it is a beautiful location; it has got good communications—more so than any property in the city; it faces on Broadway, which is the great drive of the city, and there is no day or evening you go there but you can see so many carriages going backwards and forwards, which brings the property in sight of everybody. That advertises it, and anybody, a judge of property, cannot but see that the future of that property must be of immense value. The Denver University is located some two miles beyond that."[22]

The district court ruled for Clark et al. on August 5, 1887, and on December 7 Loveland and Henry appealed to the Colorado Supreme Court.[23] But on April 19, 1888, the Supreme Court ruling went against them. Because by this time the land was worth over half a million dollars, Loveland and Henry continued their fight in the U. S. Circuit Court. But Judge Hallett overruled their pleas and dismissed the case on December 20, 1888.

In the spring of 1888 the whole city geared up for special races at Overland Park. For twelve days in May the public went to the horse races, picnicked, and enjoyed music and special events for a small fee. To draw crowds, the promoters had to sell alcohol, and in March the Town of South Denver council granted a special license for sale of liquors "in view of the great benefits resulting to the town of South Denver from the advertisements given out." A more practical reason may have been behind the town council's decision to temporarily reverse its hard-line liquor policies: during the races the town arrested several people for drunkenness and received $50 in fines, "with many more cases to be tried." By 1889 Overland Park Club had built a clubhouse. "No tips, no dogs allowed, and no wagers except twenty-five cents per rubber point at whist, one cent per point at bridge whist, and ten cents per heart at hearts."[24]

A major industry moved to South Broadway near Overland Park in 1889. The Woeber Carriage Works, a prosperous factory that had operated at 236 Eleventh Street since 1867, built a new factory just across Jewell Avenue from Overland Park, west of the county road (Santa Fe Drive). The company had manufactured carriages, but after 1883 it converted to manufacturing mostly streetcars. The South Denver plant became a major employer, with 120 men on its payroll, producing cable and electric cars for the Denver Tramway Company and filling orders from Pueblo and Salt Lake City at the rate of fifty per week. In the summer of 1890 a violent hail and windstorm destroyed a nearly completed construction house, reducing it to its foundation. But the company recovered and added another warehouse and more employees. Nearby, J. W. Dasher built two stores and three houses on the corner of Iowa Avenue and Evans in 1890. The Edward W. Robinson Lumber and Coal Company moved into the two brick buildings in 1893, and the Denver Lumber Company has occupied them since the early 1950s.

The first streetcar appeared in South Denver in December 1888. Up until 1887, southsiders had been happy with their little brown horse car, which traveled from Alameda Avenue down South Broadway and along Sixteenth Street, downtown's major retail strip. Then the horsecar company manager, a Colonel Randolph, made a fatal mistake that planted the first germ of the idea for a cable system. Randolph tried to switch them from the brown car on Sixteenth Street to the green car on Eighteenth Street. "This did not suit our people even a little bit. The Eighteenth Street line took most people right where they didn't want to go, and left them there with the privilege of walking to any desired destination within the city."[25] Their plea to not have the "little brown jug" taken away from them was

ignored, and the colonel told them that they could accept the situation or walk. At that, the angry southsiders told him they would build a cable system, "at which he laughed." In their "righteous indignation, a community of enterprising men from the South Side, always foremost in every progressive movement, arose as one man and said: 'This insult is unendurable. We will resent it, and in a manner that will be felt.'"[26] They quickly took action on their threat.

Governor Evans, William Byers, and others had incorporated the Denver Tramway Company in 1885 and were experimenting with a system of operating its downtown cars by underground current designed by Sidney H. Short, professor of physics and chemistry at the university. Short began his project in 1884, to the derision of many because of the amount of time it took. On April 11, 1885, the *Rocky Mountain News* speculated that "Professor Short will have to put a snow plow on the electrical railroad before he can use it." Short's "experiment in electric traction" sent a 2,000-volt current through an underground conduit, but the difficulties of insulation resulted in the failure of the system. Horses reared as they felt electric shocks, and pedestrians complained that they suffered a severe shock if they happened to make simultaneous contact with the mid-track slotway and one of the rails when crossing the street.[27] A committee from the south side paid Governor Evans and William Byers a visit and convinced them to stop sinking money ($200,000 by then) into Short's futile electric system in favor of a cable system down Broadway. In the end the southsiders agreed to raise a $50,000 subsidy to build the cable road as well as rebuild the Cherry Creek bridge to accommodate the heavy cars. The city council granted them a franchise for a cable road (franchises also went to North and East Denver at the same time), and the southsiders decided to apportion the money to be raised among lot owners at so much per front foot, grading back from Broadway east and west. "It was a hard pull. . . . Concessions were made by the Tramway people; the hard-worked, but never discouraged committee kept at it until finally the day came when the last dollar was subscribed, the subscriptions turned into the bank, the compact signed."[28] Mayor James Fleming donated considerable personal funds to the enterprise, and his cousins, lumber company owners and builders Jesse and Calvin, were instrumental in the drive to accumulate the remaining subscriptions.

Colonel Randolph was shocked into action. "One fine, bright morning the bobtail horse car company awoke to a full realization of the fact that a cable railway was in actual course of construction. Then was the horse car company aroused from its Rip Van Winkle sleep and went out and kicked itself. It realized that it must at once get a move on itself or be left."[29] Colonel Randolph's horsecar company began to convert to cable.

The cable road was built on Broadway first, and on December 19, 1888, the first cable car in Denver was sent over the South Broadway line toward Alameda, crowded with enthusiastic citizens. The tracks swung around a loop between Alaska and Dakota avenues for the return trip. Patterson wrote,

> The bridge over Cherry Creek was fully occupied by the horse car line, so the cable company built two wings, one on each side. We all patronized it, and it was considered almost a disgrace to be seen riding in the horse car. [Horsecars] kept up their service, however, a long time afterward. The cable company finally compromised with the horse car company, who had been turning their lines into cable ones, and agreed to district the city, each having their own streets. Then up came the horse car track on Broadway.[30]

On June 20, 1889, the town council authorized the South Denver Cable Railroad Company to lay a single- or double-track street railway down Broadway as far as Jewell Avenue, and it floated a $10,000 bond to finance

Overland Park Clubhouse, 1889. *Denver Public Library, Western History Department*

it. Cable lines were giving way to electric, "the electric road being cheaper to build, cheaper to run, can make better speed and is less liable to accidents causing temporary stoppage of cars and consequent annoyance and inconvenience to the public."[31] The company decided on electric, and the South Broadway Electric Road was completed December 25, 1889. A powerhouse and depot were built west of Broadway on Colorado Avenue, near the Woeber Carriage Works, which manufactured the car bodies for the line. The track itself was built by Sprague Electric Company and was the first electric line to be built in Denver. Cars ran at a speed of twenty miles per hour on a "center line" system composed of a single line of poles, which held brackets that extended to the center of the track and carried the trolley wires. The powerhouse was closed in 1892 and the current supplied thereafter from the Grand Avenue station in north Denver.

The Denver Tramway Company opened a transfer depot and car repair barn on the Alameda Loop at 405 South Broadway in 1890. During the depot's construction, excited South Denver residents got the idea that the Denver Tramway Company would also conduct a summer theater in it, but president Rodney Curtis quickly assured the community that there was not the slightest foundation for such a belief. The most they might do would be to plant grass and flowers in front of it. The depot contained two waiting rooms, one for gentlemen and one for ladies, a conductors' room, and a well-appointed club room for its employees. Passengers for both electric and cable cars were transferred under cover. Few families had their own transportation, so they used public transportation to go to Elitch's Zoological Gardens, Manhattan Beach (at Sloan's Lake), and other parks for recreation and picnics. As Denver grew, trailer cars were used during rush hours. Sometimes fifty of these trailers would be backed in to Alaska Place and other nearby streets, waiting for the switch engines that would push up and hook a trailer onto each tram as it came along South Broadway. An average of 1,500 people transferred there on weekdays, and up to 5,000 on Sundays and holidays.

To serve the university campus, its founder John Evans, now owner of the Denver Tramway Company, extended a line south on Pearl Street, east on Alameda, south on Franklin, east on Virginia, and south again on

University Boulevard to Evans Avenue. The first car came out on this track, later referred to as the line to "Tramway Tech" (as the university became known), on February 3, 1890. Two years later the South Pearl line was extended from Alameda to Jewell avenues. Property owners along the line subsidized it with $10,000 and stipulated fifteen-minute service and five-cent fares. On its first day, June 22, 1893, 139 passengers rode the cars before 9:30 A.M. Still later, the University Park Railway and Electric Company built an electric trolley line down Evans Avenue to Milwaukee, alongside the Circle railroad tracks.

The Denver Circle Railroad removed its night trains in the face of such competition, but faithful passengers complained that this did them a great injustice and the cars were restored. The little railroad continued to run two more years after the streetcars arrived, but it could not compete with them. William Austin Hamilton Loveland's dream to encircle the entire city of Denver with a beltway of narrow gauge track disappeared altogether when the Santa Fe Railroad Company dismantled the Denver Circle Railroad tracks about 1893. "One of its engines, the 7, was destined to lead a far more adventurous life in Colorado than it ever did in the tame reaches of South Denver. It was sold to the newly-built Rio Grande Southern and spent the rest of its useful life hauling trains over the high trestles at Ophir and the breath-taking country at Lizard Head Pass, Dallas Divide, and elsewhere in the La Plata mountains."[32]

The Washington Park line came into South Denver at Downing and Alameda, turned south on Franklin, east on Kentucky, south again on Gaylord, west on Louisiana, north on Downing, and west on Ohio to connect with the Pearl Street line.[33] Electric trolleys provided suburbs with excellent transportation for decades, but as ridership fell in favor of automobiles, the Denver Tramway ran its last trolleys in the summer of 1950 and replaced them with buses.

For all their foresight and hard work, southsiders were properly acknowledged by the local press. "The South Side," the *Denver Times* wrote, "must in all fairness be accorded the credit for having first set in motion the ball that, rapidly gathering force as it moved along, has so revolutionized the transit system of our entire city and suburbs."[34]

Even before the first streetcar track was laid in South Denver, developers had divided their land along the projected routes into saleable lots. Peter H. Bunch, president of the Breenlow Land Company, platted Breenlow Subdivision from Warren to Harvard avenues and South Broadway to the railroad tracks in March 1888. Richard T. Root of Des Moines, Iowa, platted Jewell to Iliff avenues and South Downing to South Clarkson streets into Mountain View Place on June 11, 1888. He named the internal streets in this little tract Harrison (South Corona), Mountain View (South Ogden), and Highland (South Emerson). City Ditch made a wide loop through what are now the 1900 and 2000 (south) blocks of this subdivision, providing

Electric trolley enters the tramway car barn and depot at South Broadway and West Dakota Avenue.
Denver Public Library, Western History Department

plentiful water within close reach of most lots.

Now that Fleming's Grove had a school, the residents began to build churches as well. Methodist officials appointed circuit-riding preacher John Collins to serve South Denver in 1888. Collins had pastored small congregations around Cañon City, Castle Rock, Morrison, Platteville, Fort Lupton, Breckenridge, and Rocky Ford, traveling between his charges on horseback, since 1880. He met with Fleming's Grove residents Eliza Milner, Mr. and Mrs. J. F. Sanders, and Mr. and Mrs. Webster Daniels, and in April the little group started the Fleming's Grove Union Sunday School, meeting each Sunday afternoon at the Fleming's Grove schoolhouse. On September 30, 1888, they organized the Fleming's Grove Methodist Episcopal Church, incorporated on February 4, 1889, and erected its first church building at Iowa Avenue and South Washington Street at a cost of $3,000. Bishop Henry White Warren dedicated the church in 1890, and the next month its name was changed to Cameron Memorial Methodist Episcopal Church, in commemoration of a $250 gift, perhaps from General Robert Cameron.

John Collins served this church, South Denver's first, for $700 per year until it secured its own pastor, Reverend A. K. Stabler, in 1892. More families moved into Fleming's Grove and the church flourished, not only in numbers but in quality. "Cameron Memorial is one of the best churches in this world," a 1903 report to the annual conference boasted. "There are larger and richer churches, but none where the spirit of Christ is more manifest. . . . The pastor, Rev. A. L. Chase, has been greeted all year with large and zealous congregations, and our great need is for a larger building."[35] By 1909 Cameron Memorial built a new 800-capacity church across the alley, on Iowa Avenue and Pearl Street, at a cost of $35,000. The congregation held its first service in the east wing in 1911, laid the cornerstone March 9, 1913, and dedicated the church on July 11, 1913. This lovely church has three-foot-thick concrete walls, a corner bell tower, Corinthian pilasters, a three-story stained glass dome crowning the worship area, and numerous other stained glass windows. Its perfect acoustics make the church a favorite choice for neighborhood concerts. The original church building was sold to a Swedish Methodist congregation, then to a moving company for use as a warehouse. Cameron repurchased the building in 1920 for $2,650, named it Wesley Hall, and used it for Sunday school rooms and a basketball court. In 1989 Cameron once again sold it to a private party.

As the 1880s drew to a close, the University, too, was on the move. With plans for campus buildings well under way, Rufus Clark's Evanston Real Estate and Trust Company began to promote Evanston as an adjunct to the University Park Colony: "As stands the famous Evanston of Illinois in its relation to the great central metropolis of the Union [Chicago], so stands the thrifty Evanston of Colorado in its position to the grand metropolis of the Rocky Mountain Region. . . . For a long time the owners of this superb tract held it in reserve, awaiting the thorough improvement of University Park, now so far advanced that Evanston has finally been placed on the market." Plans were to build twenty-five handsome residences ranging in value from $2,000 to $7,500 each. An arrangement with a "wealthy Kansas Colony" had been made whereby it would spend perhaps $150,000 in improvements to help found the Evanston Colony. Prices for this grand development went from $100 per lot in November 1887 to $250 per lot in 1888.[36]

Real estate tycoon and amateur astronomer Humphrey Barker Chamberlin donated a first-class observatory to the university, to be built between Grey Gables and the university buildings. Ground-breaking ceremonies were held in what is now Observatory Park in early 1888. Denver's well-known architect of mostly institutional structures, Robert Roeschlaub, designed both the main Colorado sandstone observatory and a smaller students' observatory next to it. The project was directed by University of Denver professor of mathematics and astronomer Herbert A. Howe, a genius who had earned his master's degree when he was eighteen and began teaching at the university at age twenty.

The thick walls of the observatory were designed to maintain a constant temperature, sustaining a greater accuracy in the time-recording apparatus of the $11,000 telescope. The foundation was constructed independently of the deep piers that supported the telescope to eliminate structural vibrations that might influence the instruments. Installation of the telescope itself, a twenty-inch equatorial refractor made by Alvan G. Clark of Massachusetts, was delayed until 1894

The Reverend John Collins organized three Methodist churches in South Denver. *Iliff School of Theology Archives*

because it had been on display at the 1893 World's Columbian Exposition in Chicago. The students' observatory contains a six-inch equatorial refractor and other instruments.

Two years after the observatories were completed in 1891, Chamberlin lost all his money in the Panic of 1893. "All I have left is what I gave away," he said. His marvelous $40,000 observatories, which played a key role in broadening popular understanding of astronomy in the West, were named to National Historic Landmark status on March 27, 1980.

In April 1888, the town reelected James Fleming as mayor, and the council appropriated a $5,500 budget for the fiscal year 1888–89. The town had finally convicted Pap Wyman for liquor violations and rejoiced when in June the court indicted their old enemy Joe Lowe as well. That summer Joe closed down Broadway Park and moved to a new "beer garden" on the northwest corner of Broadway and Dartmouth Avenue.

Joe's new Cottage Grove roadhouse, patronized by "sports and women," soon became as notorious as Broadway Park had been. But Joe had not moved quite far enough south; although Cottage Grove was closer to the town of Sheridan than to South Denver, South Denver considered Cottage Grove within its one-mile jurisdiction and kept the pressure on.

Town administrators turned their attention to improving the water situation for its 1,500 residents, who were dependent on artesian wells for their water. In the fall of 1888 South Denver voters approved financing the $160,000 expense by issuing fifteen-year water bonds through the Chemical National Bank of New York at 6 percent interest per annum.

Fleming picked a site on the two-mile-long Petersburg Ditch above the town and commissioned Walter P. Miller, G. B. Coulter, John Babcock, and Avery Gallup to oversee the construction of the wells, pumps, conduits, reservoirs, dams, fences, and bridges that such a project entailed. The commissioners reported back that the ditch, about four feet deep and varying from ten to twenty feet wide, was too narrow for carrying water to the entire community of South Denver or for providing enough waterpower to move the waterworks machinery. The ditch would need to be widened by fifty feet.

The trustees proceeded to negotiate for the land and water rights, and the first purchases went smoothly enough. During the summer of 1888 the town made a $50 payment to Norman Failing, who had once operated a flour mill on the ditch, for a lot in Petersburg and his 385 shares of stock in the Petersburg Ditch Company for a total of $2,500, making the final payment in December. The trustees then bought twenty adjacent acres from Bertha Magnes, who also granted the right to enlarge the Petersburg Ditch.

Bertha's husband, Peter Magnes, and Sam and Joseph Brown had dug the ditch from the South Platte River in 1861 for irrigation of lands, domestic uses, and for waterpower for Failing's now abandoned flour mill. While the Magnes's were ready to sell, Sam and Joseph Brown refused to agree to sell their ditch or the twenty-five feet on either side of the entire length of the ditch for the purpose of widening it, which the Town of South Denver wanted them to do. The town then brought suit against the Browns in an attempt to acquire it by condemning the property. The case went

The Town of South Denver

South Denver's first church was the Fleming's Grove Methodist Episcopal Church, erected in 1888 at Iowa Avenue and South Washington Street. It was renamed Cameron Memorial Methodist Episcopal in 1890. *Iliff School of Theology Archives*

to trial in June 1889, with John Hipp arguing the town's case. The Browns claimed that the ditch had been dug for domestic irrigation purposes, to water their farms, and that even though it was true that the flour mill ran on waterpower from the ditch, it was never meant for pumping water via mechanical means. They believed also that they would be deprived of ditch water for their own lands and that the whole project would "lead to vexations and expensive litigation" over their right to use the ditch, maintenance of a dam, and so on, and that their land would depreciate in value. The town won the right to proceed with its plans and was ordered to pay $5,443 to the defendants for the four acres of land taken by the town. Sam Brown accepted his share and conveyed his acre and a half the next month, but Joseph and his wife Anna still refused to cooperate. Without Joseph Brown's land, the Petersburg Ditch could be widened only as far south as his property line (about Oxford Avenue) at this time.

Nevertheless, the town built a fine stone powerhouse equipped with the latest approved pumping apparatus and with engines of sufficient power to supply water to a city of 50,000 people. The contract to place the pumps and lay the pipes was awarded to Charles P. Allen and seventy-five men were put to work laying the twenty-one miles of twelve-inch pipe. By the summer of 1889, a pump costing $20,000 pumped two million gallons of water per day into the parched town. By the middle of November, South Denver, the *Denver Eye* bragged, had "as fine a system of water works as there is west of the Missouri River, considering the size." Rates were "never more than half those of the city of Denver, and a South Denver lot could be irrigated for $5 for a season of six months, including the grass borders and trees on the sidewalk lines in front. Ordinary dwelling house water rentals for the year are only $2 to $3 and $5 per year."

With a superb water system, public transportation, and two schools, South Denver began to be noticed as a desirable place to live. "There has never been any especial boom and no wild excitement in real estate in South Denver," the *Denver Eye* remarked, but "a steady growth has always been apparent." Near Smith's Lake lay Bryn Mawr, an unpretentious fifty-acre tract selling lots at $200 to $250 each. Bryn Mawr, some of which was now owned by Charlotte Gallup, boasted that it was three miles nearer downtown than University Park and was the "cheapest in the city and remote from the smoke and dust of smelter and factory walls and stacks." Avery Gallup's thirty-acre Broadway Highlands adjoined Rosedale to the south, and its 288 lots were available for $75 to $350 each. This addition's boundaries were Harvard to Vassar avenues and Broadway to Pearl streets. Gallup, property owner, town trustee, horticulturist, and promoter, advertised a unique advantage of this addition—people watching: "Broadway is beyond question the one leading thoroughfare and great driveway of the city. Every afternoon or evening can be seen all of the fine turnouts of the city, and the scenes are as lively as in the parks of our eastern cities."

Charles McIntosh's South Denver Real Estate Company, owner also of the Sherman Subdivision, laid out the Overland Park Subdivision (Jewell to Louisiana avenues and Bannock to Broadway) and the Grant Subdivision (Mexico to Jewell avenues and Broadway to Clarkson streets) in the fall of 1889. McIntosh offered brick and stone residences in Grant and Sherman subdivisions costing from $2,500 to $5,500 each and would "give you a long time to pay for it," or vacant lots from $150 to $600 each. The company's 1889 advertisements stated that from 50 to 100 families already resided in these two subdivisions. The Electric Heights Land Company, George J. Boal, president, platted Electric Heights Subdivision October 1889, from Mississippi to Florida avenues and University Boulevard to Clayton. Streets were appropriately named with electric connections: Sprague (Josephine), Edison (Columbine), Westinghouse (Elizabeth), and Julien (Clayton). The *Denver Eye* claimed, in its January 1, 1890, issue, that nearly 100 houses were built in the Town of South Denver in 1889.

Chamberlin Observatory. *University of Denver Archives*

Under New Management

By 1890 Fleming's town had gained such a fine reputation that landowners to the south approached the town council about annexing their three sections, from Yale to Hampden avenues and the South Platte River to Colorado Boulevard (presently Englewood), to the Town of South Denver. The council agreed to put the issue on the May election ballot for the people to decide. Privately, Mayor Fleming believed that the Town of South Denver would itself be annexed by the city of Denver in the very near future. In fact, when the citizens along South Broadway asked for a post office of their own, Fleming and his council petitioned the U.S. government to refuse it. In a revealing resolution addressed to First Assistant Postmaster General J. S. Clarkson in Washington, D.C., the board of trustees stated that they "look upon the establishing of any post office in our town with disfavor, as . . . our town adjoins the city of Denver, and *in all probability will some day be taken in as part of the city of Denver*" (italics added).

Convinced that the Town of South Denver as he knew it would soon cease to exist, Fleming decided to move on. In early 1890 he announced he would not consider a fifth term but would instead support John S. Babcock as candidate for mayor in the April 1890 election. Fleming himself had decided to run for Colorado state senate on the Democratic ticket.

Accolades for James Fleming's contributions to the town were quickly forthcoming. Fleming, the *Denver Eye* noted, was

> as splendid a citizen as Denver can boast, a man who took an active interest in all early developments and a liberal giver to every enterprise intended to advance the interests of South Broadway. It was Fleming who dug a well for the free use of Fleming's Grove citizens, was responsible for building the South Denver Water Works, and donated the energy, enterprise, untiring zeal and more than $5,000 to building the cable and electric roads in South Denver. . . . When his shoulder is once at the wheel he knows no such word as fail."[1]

Fleming and his trustees had brought a town into being, had written its laws, and had defeated the powerful William Byers and Charles Kountze to keep it. They had run out most of the saloons and had kept John Evans and the railroad giants from establishing stockyards in the town. They had helped bring in Denver Circle Railroad trains, the streetcar system, water, a church, and two schools. Thousands visited Overland Park for horseraces and picnics, a fine university was in the making, and more industries like the Woeber Carriage Works were moving in.

The four-term mayor had made enemies, too, among them the influential banker Charles McIntosh. Fleming had removed the town's accounts from McIntosh's bank, alleging that McIntosh allowed the town's bank warrants to lie unpaid in his safe while drawing 10 percent interest. Fleming had also refused to buy land from McIntosh to build another school, which angered not only the banker but also many constituents who needed additional classroom space for the Fleming's Grove schoolchildren. The town was still without firehouses, a proper jail, a town hall, a post office, banks, parks, and electric lights, all of which the growing populace demanded. Fleming was accused of personal violations as well, in particular that he had helped himself to special water privileges during the Petersburg waterworks installation. He had had underground pipes laid from the City Ditch, beginning at Corona Street and Colorado Avenue, to his own property at Florida and Logan, prompting one critic to suggest that the mayor "was too good to himself in the distribution of water pipes."

But most serious of all, Fleming had angered the lucrative liquor industry by prohibiting saloons, and he intended to keep it that way. So long as only prohibition trustees were elected, the laws were strictly enforced, but in 1889 John L. Russell, who opposed the strict enforcement of the liquor ordinances, was elected to the board as a voice for the liquor "gang." Fleming regarded Russell's election as a great mistake and the beginning of an attempt to reintroduce saloons to South Denver. "We tried to reform him," Fleming said, "but he was beyond reforming, and from the first tried to turn the board into a political machine for the benefit of the Gang."[2]

John S. Babcock, Fleming's friend and trustee, ran for mayor on the Progressive ticket, even though he represented Mayor Fleming's "old element," which was criticized for not being progressive enough. Because many people saw the Fleming-Babcock party as controlled by the Denver Tramway Company (which needed a friendly mayor for the advancement of its streetcar system), the Progressive ticket was usually referred to simply as the Tramway Ticket.

Banker McIntosh and John L. Russell (the "new element") chose a carpenter by the name of Simeon M. Vaughn for their Citizens' party's candidate for mayor. Vaughn and William Lawson owned a contracting firm, and Vaughn lived at 1508 South Sherman Street, a block from Fleming's own house. Fleming knew Vaughn well and believed that the wily Russell had set up the honest, competent, easy-going—and naive—Vaughn for his own political ends.

With the political lines drawn, liquor dealers met with Fleming and offered to support Babcock if his administration would grant them some concessions, perhaps by lowering the license fee. But Fleming flatly refused to consider any such proposal and the liquor element joined with the McIntosh-Russell-Vaughn group to defeat Babcock, earning their party the label of Gang Ticket. The campaign quickly turned into a battle between Fleming's anti-saloon and Russell's pro-saloon factions and ended in violence at the polls.

On election day, both sides brought their backers to the polling place on South Logan at about Center Avenue, perhaps in the former Makin Brothers saloon the town used for a jail. When voters appeared at the polls early on the morning of April 1, they found themselves facing Russell's "gang" of liquor supporters, free-flowing whiskey, crowds of strange working-class men (brought in to vote illegally), and ballots that revealed how they voted. "Ruffians, thugs, tin horn gamblers and general rounders" with names like G. W. "Galvanized Whiskey" Bell, "Poker Jake," and "Whipsaw Bill" crowded around the polling window and terrified the voters. Bell, who ran a "gentlemen's club" in the 400 block on South Broadway, had been arrested by Fleming's marshal for selling whiskey without a license the day before, but his friends posted bond, and Bell spent the day "throwing whiskey into the voters and the increasing crowd."

Fleming's behavior was no less outrageous. He had had the ballots printed in "different forms and papers, so that it was not possible for anyone to cast his vote [for mayor] without its character being well known," the *Denver Republican* claimed. Both the Fleming-Babcock-Tramway faction and the McIntosh-Russell-Vaughn Gang imported nonresident employees to vote. These men worked in South Denver brickyards and grading camps but lived outside the limits. These voters were challenged and at least one man was arrested and jailed.

The deputy sheriffs hired to keep order were, the *Denver Republican* said, "cheek by jowl with the Russell bummers" and used their "blustering terrorism" on reputable voters to such an extent that as the day progressed many of the 600 registered voters refused to venture to the polls at all. At 5:30 in the afternoon the whiskey-induced tension spilled over into violence when someone stole the pollbook. Fleming swore that John L. Russell had it last, but a Russell deputy tried to arrest an innocent bystander by the name of Brown, who reached for his pistol. An inebriated Joe Lowe, who "had no more right to vote or be seen near the polls than a resident of Kansas," joined Johnny Kerwin in beating and kicking Brown before the victim was "rolled off the platform and fairly carried by three or four men" to a waiting sheriff. At this, the dispirited Babcock-Fleming delegation left.

That day South Denver voters elected Simeon Vaughn to be their next mayor, on the saloon-license ticket.[3] Benjamin Niesz, Avery Gallup, and Samuel Seccombe were elected trustees. The voters also approved annexation of the three sections to the south. For reasons unknown, the annexation never happened; the neighbors across Yale Avenue changed their minds, reapplied a second time, and backed out again. The town remained as originally incorporated.

When Vaughn took office in April 1890, the town council had grown to fifteen members: the mayor, six trustees, a clerk, a treasurer, an attorney, a police magistrate, a marshal, a town engineer, a street commissioner, and a water commissioner.[4] De Witt C. Webber, a University of Denver graduate, replaced John Hipp as town attorney.

South Denver's need for more schools was by now acute, so in August the board decided to build a nine-room schoolhouse at Exposition and South Pearl in District 2. Lincoln School was designed by architect T. D. Robinson and completed in 1891 at a cost of $4,185 for the land and $33,525 for the building. Mr. J. H. Dodds was its first principal. Eight more rooms were added in 1904 and in 1929 twenty lots were bought at $59,580 for another addition. Architect George W. Williamson and general contractor William Tamminga constructed this addition at a cost of $152,000, and the 1890 section was torn down.

Excited anticipation preceded the selection of a site for a second school, to be called Grant. "Plans for a $30,000 school house to be erected somewhere on the hill, the exact site has not been fixed yet, are progressing as rapidly as the architects can turn them out. Its progress is being noted by everybody, for when completed no handsomer structure of the same kind can be found anywhere." This prediction proved true, for Grant, "one of the more finely finished school structures in the city,"[5] was built also in 1890 at Colorado Avenue, between South Pearl and Washington streets, just three blocks from Fleming School. Ira C. Adams was the first principal. James Fleming's brother, Thomas (also the town's water commissioner), and his wife, Minnie, were its first janitors.

Grant School was not ready for occupation by September, however, and an exploding population of 280 pupils arrived for classes at Fleming's Grove School, a building designed for fifty. To house the additional 230 children until Grant could be finished, the District 7 school board leased a vacant hotel on South Broadway and held classes there as well as at Fleming's Grove. For three years Grant was an elementary school. The town's first high school was established in two rooms of the building in 1893, but it remained small until 1907, when student enrollment grew to 125 and a faculty of seven. John J. Cory was its principal. An addition was built onto the high school rooms in 1907, and the high school became known as South Side High. A separate junior high was added in 1919, with Rufus H. Palmer its first principal, and elementary children were moved out.

The Fleming's Grove schoolhouse at Colorado Avenue and South Grant Street had been used an an annex to Grant in 1890; then it had been sold to a church congregation in 1892, when its pupils were transferred temporarily to Lincoln. It had been bought back in 1894 and used for elementary classes for many years afterward. In 1920, the building was torn down and a handsome brick building was erected on the site. The new school was named Thatcher School, in honor of Puebloan Joseph A. Thatcher, president of the Denver National Bank in the 1880s. (Thatcher School closed in 1978 and was converted into private condominiums.)

Grant elementary children were transferred to Thatcher, and Grant became a junior and senior high school. Another addition was built in 1923. When the senior high students moved to the present South High School at 1700 East Louisiana in 1926, Grant became Grant Junior High. This building was torn down in 1953 and the present school built at 1751 South Washington.

Another acutely felt need in 1890 was for a town hall. The council had been meeting at Fleming's Grove School ever since the Exposition Building, their prior meeting place, had been torn down. The council had hoped to convert the Fleming's Grove School property into a town hall once all the pupils were moved to Grant School. The school had a large yard that could be used as the town pound, and there was room on the grounds to build a hose house (firehouse). But the school was still in use. Another possibility was the magnificent new forty- by sixty-foot two-story building of pressed brick and stone being erected on the northwest corner of Colorado Avenue and South Broadway.

The Vaughn administration tried to secure a $60,000 bond to finance the building of a new town hall, a jail, and two or more hose houses, but the bond proposal failed to pass, and the projects were tabled until the next fiscal year.

The Broadway and Colorado building instead became home to the Independent Order of Odd Fellows (I.O.O.F.) Silver State Lodge #97.[6] Almost immediately, the spacious two-story hall became a popular neighborhood social center for dances, concerts, club meetings, and church services. The excitement and activity that went on inside the building

are hinted at by the grand staircase leading to the second-floor ballroom, the original board for posting upcoming events on the front door, and a ticket window with hinged shutters on the original north wall.

A small group of South Denver Presbyterians—George Crosby, Elizabeth G. Snedaker and her daughters Emma B. Carlson and Elizabeth Snedaker, and others—had been meeting at Fleming's Grove School since perhaps 1889. On November 25, 1890, about forty Presbyterians met at the Odd Fellows Hall with Rev. Clarence Eddy, a minister from Keyport, New Jersey, to begin organizing a church and Sunday school; they completed the process on January 25, 1891. Town trustees Benjamin Niesz and Samuel Seccombe were charter members of the South Denver Presbyterian Church. Niesz, also a trustee of the church, had commissioned architects William A. Lang and Marshall R. Pugh to build his home at 1800 South Sherman Street in 1889; this lovely home was later owned by Frank Byers. Samuel H. Seccombe, a former school principal, was appointed deputy clerk of the

Lincoln School. *Courtesy Denver Public Schools*

district court in 1890. His wife taught at Fleming's Grove and Grant schools, and the couple lived at 1574 South Pennsylvania Street in Fleming's Grove.

The South Denver Presbyterian congregation met at the Odd Fellows Hall for the next four years, using an organ lent by J. R. Hicks not only for services but also for concerts and Sunday school programs. Mr. J. A. Chain left the congregation $5,000 in his will, and with this generous gift they purchased two lots in Grant Subdivision from town clerk Charles H. Peters on June 11, 1894, for $840. By October they had constructed a two-story chapel along the alley between South Grant and South Logan streets, on Mexico Avenue. A new building, incorporating the chapel, was erected and first occupied on March 27, 1910, and an addition was built on to that in 1927. The present sanctuary was completed at 1700 South Grant Street in 1965. All the old buildings have been torn down.

The town also lacked a bank in 1890, so Mayor Vaughn, trustee Niesz, and clerk Peters teamed up with banker McIntosh to organize a cooperative building and loan association where working-class residents who seldom visited "the city" could deposit their wages every Saturday night. Unfortunately, no more was heard of this enterprise; the first bank did not appear in South Denver for another twenty years.

The working-class newcomers needed simple, affordable frame houses even more than a bank, but Fleming's administration had passed an ordinance in 1886 that restricted the erection of frame buildings for fire reasons. Although anyone could build a brick house anywhere without any permit whatsoever, no frame buildings could be built without a permit from the mayor himself. Because these permits were difficult to obtain, many builders erected modest frame houses in open defiance of the law.

The arrest of building contractor J. H. Jack for violating the building ordinance brought the matter to a head. Jack sued the town, claiming that the ordinance was invalid because it had not been properly published in a newspaper, as was required by law. Former mayor Fleming was furious. Recalling that the town had beaten a similar charge before, in 1887, he explained—again—that because there was no newspaper in South

Grant School. *Courtesy Denver Public Schools*

Thatcher School. *Courtesy Denver Public Schools*

South High School. *Courtesy Denver Public Schools*

South Denver Presbyterian Church. *Denver Public Library, Western History Department*

Denver at the time, every ordinance had been posted in a public place according to law. "The plea that they should have been published in a Denver paper is nonsensical. They might just as well say Colorado Springs ought to publish its ordinances in a Denver paper," he protested.[7]

Jack won the lawsuit, and the ordinance against building frame houses was invalidated. A group of residents who had been arrested, fined, and even jailed for this offense then demanded restitution: whereas "the present town board of this town have by their high-handed action in throwing some of our most respected citizens in jail and forcing them to pay tribute to them in the shape of fees and fines for the enormous crime of home building, therefore be it resolved that we demand of the officers of the town of South Denver that they immediately return all the moneys that they have forced from us."[8] Whether they got their money back or not is not recorded.

But more was at stake than a few disgruntled home builders. Jack's lawsuit had invalidated all of the ordinances that had been written before the *Denver Eye* existed. Indeed, a few days later a man by the name of Sherwin was arrested for discharging firearms in the town limits. His trial had not proceeded far when it

was discovered that the pertinent ordinance had been struck down. The magistrate was compelled to discharge his prisoner.

More important was the canceling out of the liquor ordinances. Although the council warned that anyone who attempted to open a saloon would be jailed under the old ordinance, they had no power to stop it and they knew it. The council gathered together and resubmitted the ordinances and by August 16 had reinstated most of them. These new ordinances stood unchallenged and the town laws were saved.

Two more items on the council's agenda that summer were plans for a city park and electric lights. They passed a $10,000 bond to grant a contract to Ludolph P. Martin to construct electric light works at a cost not to exceed 1 percent per hour for sixteen-candle power. Eighty-foot iron towers that were constructed with six or eight electric lamps on top threw light for many blocks around. A man had to climb to the top of this tower every day to replace the carbons and clean the lamps.

The news that the trustees were negotiating to buy two park sites—one near Alameda Avenue and Franklin Street (Smith's Lake) and the other at Louisiana Avenue and Franklin (the opposite end of what is now

Washington Park)—excited the residents as nothing else had. With little money to work with, the trustees negotiated with property owners Mrs. Henry M. Porter (John W. Smith's daughter Laura) and a Mrs. Clark for the Alameda acreage, but they wanted $3,000 an acre or $60,000 total and would not consider less. To complicate matters, the city of Denver claimed to hold John W. Smith's 1875 lease on Laura's lake property and was still paying rent on it, even though the lease itself had apparently disappeared.

The board of trustees then tried hard to convince Charles W. Stebbins to donate a piece of land in between the two sites (the present meadow of Washington Park) that sloped down from the present Franklin Street between Arizona to Mississippi avenues. This prime site was on a hill facing the mountains, with City Ditch flowing in a graceful curve at its feet. Stebbins, who with Henry Porter had hauled freight from Atchison, Kansas, to their mercantile business in Denver in ox wagons for the past thirty years, had platted 320 acres extending from Mississippi to Jewell avenues and Clarkson to Franklin streets (which included the choice land coveted by the town for a park) into Stebbins Heights in February 1890. But four years earlier, Stebbins had joined Byers et al. in the lawsuit to protest the existence of the Corporation of South Denver. Therefore, it was thought that "there would be some hesitancy" on Mr. Stebbins's part to contribute his best piece of land to the Town of South Denver for a park or anything else. Stebbins, who now lived in New York, did authorize his agents, Buchanan and Kirk, to sell four pieces of one block each of less valuable ground at undisclosed locations to be used for four different parks, but the town deemed this land unsuitable.

The council then approached Richard Root, whose land included a shallow lake in a bowl between Ogden and Clarkson streets and Harvard and Wesley avenues—a lovely setting for a park. The town tried hard to obtain possession of it, but Root refused to sell, saying he planned to convert the lake area into a pleasure resort along the lines of a popular Highlands family resort on the south side of Berkeley Lake. The resort never developed, probably because of public opposition to his plan to serve alcohol. The little pond is now part of Harvard Park and Golf Course.

Then trustee Niesz made what seemed to be a delightful discovery. While examining some early records of the town, he claimed to have discovered that several owners of property had each given the town a block of land for parks. Two gentlemen, he said, had donated a strip of land 25 by 600 feet near Broadway and Alameda; he found another of five acres; two more tracts of two and a half acres each; and one ten-acre block in University Park—Simpson Park, extending from Evans to Warren avenues and Monroe to Jackson streets. The town board was ecstatic; they merely needed to develop land that was already theirs. By the end of August they announced plans to start work on the "main parks" in the fall to be ready for the public by the following spring.

The revelation that the Town of South Denver lay claim to Colorado Seminary's Simpson Park shocked university trustees and adjacent property owners into action. An examination of the 1886 University Park plat revealed the loophole: the seminary had granted use of all parks to the general public rather than reserving them for the colony. Niesz took that to mean that "the public" could develop them as well as "use" them.

The seminary's only option was to redraw the plat and clarify its language, and they set about the task of reviewing and revising the document. The town backed off and the trustees filed an amended plat the next summer, on August 31, 1891, whereby Colorado Seminary "reserved to itself . . . all parks shown on said plat." They also added an entire additional block to its main park on Evans and Milwaukee, extending it south to Iliff Avenue. The new section, between Warren and Iliff avenues where the new observatories stood, was widened to 580 feet. Because the north half of the park remained at 320 feet wide, Fillmore and Milwaukee streets curve at Warren Avenue. Supposedly these two jogs in the road were designed to protect the delicate telescopes in Chamberlin's observatories from being shaken by the passage of large, rumbling delivery drays. The curves forced the vehicles to reduce speed and slip slowly and gently around the observatories without causing damage. The new two-block-long park was named Observatory Park on the new plat.

Neither Simpson nor Asbury parks were ever developed, and the university finally platted Simpson Park into lots on January 23, 1923, under the signature of William Gray Evans, president of the board of trustees (1905–1924) and son of founder John Evans.

Asbury Park became the location of Wycliffe Cottage for Young Ladies, the university's dormitory for girls, and other college buildings.

The town's excited pursuit of parks in 1890 was abandoned as Niesz's discovery of "free" park sites proved to be unfounded. Youngsters shed their clothes in whatever swimming holes they could find on hot summer days, however. Scandalized owners and neighbors demanded the arrest of the "gay young men who insisted on showing their anatomy in the waters of Smith's lake. The nuisance has become so great that ladies refuse to go on the elegant and beautiful drive in that vicinity," the *Denver Republican* said.[9] The town marshal did arrest the boys—repeatedly—for indecent exposure and fined them about $11 for each indulgence.

Although the public was unaware of it, the town was about to acquire a park they had not even considered. In the spring of 1891, James Fleming decided to leave South Denver. Vaughn and Russell's relaxation of his hard-won liquor laws, which had already resulted in the return of saloons and roadhouses, coupled with the fact that he had lost the 1890 election for state senator by only 121 votes, may have convinced Fleming to leave.[10] He may have made a deal with Vaughn (as was alleged later) to support his neighbor in a bid for a second mayoral term if Vaughn's administration would buy Fleming's stone mansion and lovely grounds at 1500 South Grant Street, an entire block, for a town hall and park. To assure Vaughn of his commitment to the deal, Fleming did a most surprising thing; he switched to Russell and Vaughn's Citizens' party—the Gang Ticket he had so vigorously opposed in the 1890 elections the year before—and even served as a teller in the balloting for mayor and trustees during its caucus meeting.

The 1891 mayoral election was considerably quieter than the previous year's had been and was a walkover for the Russell ticket. On April 8, 1891, 404 of the 930 registered voters reelected Simeon Vaughn as mayor and John L. Russell, John S. Babcock, and August Gamage as trustees.[11] The voters also approved the expenditure of $60,000 to build a town hall, a jail, and two hose houses.

Almost immediately, Fleming proposed to sell his house and grounds to the town and buy $40,000 worth of bonds the town would then issue. Fleming would give the town his check for $15,000 and his property. If the bonds sold at par, Fleming would receive $55,000, but the board claimed that they were worth only ninety-five cents and the purchase would end up costing the town only $32,000.

Only trustee Benjamin Niesz objected to this proposal and fought it vigorously. During Fleming's administration, Niesz, owner and proprietor of Niesz & Company Boots and Shoes downtown, had offered to sell a valuable tract of land he owned at Broadway and Louisiana Avenue in Overland for a town hall site but had been rejected. Niesz placed the blame squarely on Fleming.

On May 5, 1891, the council agreed to print the bonds, with only Niesz dissenting. After the meeting, an outraged Niesz rounded up his supporters outside the board, including Harry M. Banks, who lived at Bannock and Louisiana near the property Niesz had tried to sell to the town for a town hall site, and flew into action. He had a sympathethic attorney, J. E. Harper (who later served as police magistrate for the town), draw up the necessary legal papers that would enjoin James Fleming from receiving the bonds from the town or from negotiating them, in case he had received them. After being worked on all night, the document was taken to district court judge Alvin Marsh at five o'clock the next morning in an attempt to complete the legalities before the bonds could be delivered to Fleming. "Unless the bonds were delivered to Fleming before the meeting, or between the hours of 10 Tuesday night and 5:00 the next morning, our injunction will catch them. I think they will be balked in the scheme," Niesz said.

Claiming that Fleming himself had declared that the property was worth no more than $31,100, Niesz wondered who was to get the surplus of $20,000. He called the purchase a steal and a robbery, and charged the board with squandering the people's money. "Since the price paid for the property is high beyond reason," he told reporters, "there must be something crooked in the sale." He alleged that Fleming and Vaughn had cooked up the deal before the last election and then forced the "outrageous business" on the new administration. Besides, Niesz contended, the town had been authorized to build, not buy, a town hall.

Mayor Vaughn told the *Denver Times* that "Niesz is trying to pose as an apostle of reform, and as heroically

Fleming mansion as town hall. *Photo by Millie Van Wyke*

defending the people" and instructed his attorney to defend the town.[12] Niesz and Banks managed to stay the transfer for a short time, but popular sentiment was against them. The property contained everything the town needed—a house for use as a town hall: a Circle Railway depot, a barn that could be converted into a hose house, piped-in water, and most important, lovely grounds for a park. Since his retirement as mayor, Fleming had added more fruit trees to his already attractive lawns, gardens, orchards, and flower beds, and Fleming's Grove flourished as never before. Included in the deal was Fleming's wonderful ditch and the artesian well in Fleming's Grove. But a $10,000 encumbrance also came with it; the balance of this note, at 6 percent interest, was due July 1, 1893. Mayor Vaughn insisted that the property was worth every cent, and that Niesz was comparing improved with unimproved property. Vaughn said he himself could do the carpentry work necessary to convert the mansion into a town hall for $500. The taxpayers were pleased with the board's action and supported the mayor.

Judge Marsh did in fact "balk the scheme" by issuing a temporary injunction against the trustees' disposing of the bonds. In the meantime, Niesz gathered signatures from 162 men who protested the purchase. The fight lasted for three months, but by

mid-July the injunction was removed and the sale went through. Rumor had it that Fleming planned to file a $5,000 damage suit against Niesz and Banks for their efforts, and Niesz countered by proposing "to make music at the next board meeting," which, of course, he did, his main contention now being that the board disallow the $95 fee paid to town attorney Webber for defending Vaughn et al. in Niesz's injunction suit. There is no record of this board meeting, its likely raucous proceedings, or who won this round.

Meanwhile, James and Alice Fleming, Alice's mother (Ellen), and James's sons moved from Fleming's mansion into the Luray Hotel downtown, not far from his offices in the Mendota Building. Fleming divested himself of business partners and now ran his mining and real estate company alone. He had won a seat on the 1892 Denver Chamber of Commerce and Board of Public Trade, but he missed active politics. In late 1892 he spent some months at the Democratic party's New York headquarters, where he worked toward getting Democrats elected to national office in the 1893 election. During this time, Fleming made some important political connections with Arizona Territory candidates and decided to leave Colorado. He moved his wife, Alice, his son Richard, and Alice's mother, Ellen, to Phoenix, Arizona, and went into banking while he waited for a summons to participate in the territorial government.[13]

In 1893 the newly elected Arizona governor Louis C. Hughes of Tucson appointed James A. Fleming, age forty-three, to the post of treasurer of Arizona Territory. Because Fleming was virtually unknown to the Arizona populace, some objected to his appointment, but the *Arizona Republican* embellished his accomplishments, stating that Fleming "is regarded as among the foremost financiers not only of Arizona but of all that wide region west of the Rocky Mountains. Before coming to Arizona he lived in Denver where he had become second to none of the famous financiers of Colorado in influence."[14]

Fleming took office April 13, 1893, and found Hughes in agreement with his own causes of prohibition and the suppression of gambling. Fleming's hand can clearly be seen in the passing of a new election law that prohibited candidates from asking any person or persons, directly or indirectly, to drink beer or other intoxicating drinks. Governor Hughes, obviously pleased with Fleming, also appointed him a colonel of the Arizona Rangers. The Hughes administration was under constant attack by its enemies, however, and Hughes was removed from office in March 1896 on charges of using undue influence in the Arizona legislature to secure the passage of acts that he favored. James Fleming presumably was ousted with him.[15]

During his years in Phoenix politics, Fleming also founded the Phoenix National Bank and was its president. In 1895 he constructed the Fleming Building, which housed his bank; this building was demolished in 1970. After his removal from the office of territorial treasurer, Fleming relocated his family to the thriving copper mines near Globe, Arizona, and once more Fleming seems to have struck riches. By 1903 James and Alice were back in Phoenix. Fleming apparently married a fourth time, about 1912, and lived for brief periods in Kansas City, Missouri, and Philadelphia with his new wife, Edna. Fleming died in Phoenix on January 26, 1917, at the age of sixty-seven.[16]

The South Denver town council held its first meeting in its new town hall July 21, 1891. They turned Fleming's barn into a firehouse and named it Vaughn Hose House in honor of the mayor. Twelve men formed a volunteer fire department, which included James Fleming on its list of honorary members. The firefighters wasted no time gearing up for their main business, next to fighting fires—a lively social life. The *Denver Times* reported on its first annual ball, held at the Odd Fellows Hall.

> There were sounds of revelry by night. . . . The "halle de danse" was decorated in a most tasteful and artistic manner, while about 80 or more of the most prominent residents whiled away the fleeting hours to the inspiring strains of music from Warren's Orchestra. About 12 o'clock the doors of the supper room were thrown open and those present partook of a bounteous and elegant repast. The pleasant occasion will be a long-remembered one as the event of the season."[17]

A second and more elaborate hose house, a two-story red brick and stone building, was erected in 1892 on the old Exposition Building site, at the corner of South Broadway and Center Avenue. The lower floor of this firehouse had room for three fire companies and sleeping and reading rooms above. In a concession to the trustee who put Mayor Vaughn into office, this building was named the Russell Hose House. Almost immediately, citizens in the south end of town complained that the northern residents got a hose house and grounds costing nearly $9,000, whereas they had to make do with Fleming's old barn. The council placated them by expanding and remodeling their firehouse at a cost of $600. The Vaughn Hose House was torn down in 1895, when the city of Denver acquired the property and named it Platt Park, but the Russell Hose House at Broadway and Center still stands; the letters S.D.F.D. (South Denver Fire Department) stand out boldly above its two sets of double doors. The building is now privately owned.

The Russell Hose House, a mile north of the Odd Fellows Hall, also quickly became a meeting place, and it was the site of the beginning of St. Frances de Sales Catholic Church. Shortly after the fire station was built, Pastor James N. Brown held Catholic worship services there until the congregation built a small, temporary chapel called St. James at Lincoln Street and Alameda Avenue. Father James J. Gibbons replaced Father Brown in 1893 and built a parish hall next to the chapel a few years later. In 1906 the parish built a two-story school at 320 South Sherman Street, which served as the parish church until the current structure was built in 1911 next door. This beautiful church has a

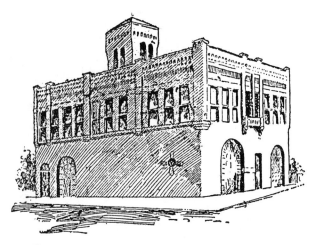

Russell Hose House. Sketch from the *Denver Times*, August 16, 1895. *Courtesy Denver Public Library, Western History Department*

single soaring spire and large stained glass windows. The window along Alameda Avenue is in memory of Monsignor John J. Donnelly, its fourth pastor, who led this working-class parish for thirty-seven years. A $39,000 high school was completed at 235 South Sherman, and a convent at 301 South Grant Street, in 1924. The grade school was expanded in 1948 and the high school in 1960. During the 1950s and 1960s as many as twenty-eight Sisters of St. Joseph, who lived at 200 South Sherman, taught 650 grade school students and 750 high school students. The high school closed in 1973, when it consolidated with Central Catholic High School.

The First Reformed Presbyterian Church may also have had its beginnings at the Russell Hose House in 1892, with Rev. J. Milligan Wylie as its first pastor. The next year they erected an architecturally unusual brick church building with beautiful pastel stained glass windows and a pitched floor at 501 South Pearl Street, laying its cornerstone on March 10, 1893. The church retains its original pews and pulpit, but a few of the stained glass windows have been stolen and replaced with plain glass. The building now houses the Christian Indian Center, a mission under the auspices of the Christian Reformed Church of Grand Rapids, Michigan.

Residents now came to the newly converted town hall at 1500 South Grant Street to present grievances of varying degrees of importance to the town council. In one instance seventeen home owners complained

about the evils of playing baseball on Sundays by "noisy, rough characters such a place naturally calls around." Mr. J. S. Van Dusen had built several houses near the baseball field at the corner of Broadway and Center, built by the Denver Circle Railroad Company in 1882, and was losing sales on account of this annoyance. The petitioners cited Ordinance 72 of August 1890 that prohibited persons from collecting together for any purpose to the annoyance or disturbance of the citizens thereof.[18] Mayor Vaughn gravely received the petition and placed it "on file."

Another problem involved the animal pound. Time after time cows and horses were impounded for running loose, only to be liberated in the dark of night by their owners. One angry citizen pulled a pistol on a deputy attempting to impound his horses and took them home. Unclaimed impounded cattle were yet another problem. In one such instance, John Babcock purchased several horses from the pound, only to be sued by their owner several weeks later.

These were minor, even amusing, problems compared to the ongoing saloon dilemma. The full impact of the Vaughn-Russell administration's concessions to the liquor establishment in 1890 had manifested itself with a vengeance. Saloons and roadhouses operated more freely, and new ones had moved in. Violence had broken out among the saloon proprietors themselves, who tried to eliminate each

First Reformed Presbyterian Church. *Photo by Corinne Hunt*

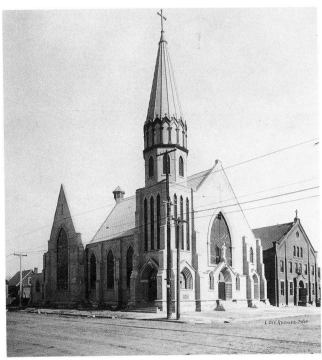

St. Frances de Sales Catholic Church. *Denver Public Library, Western History Department*

other by beatings or by reporting their competitors to the marshal for violations. Beer wagons roamed the streets as well. Mr. S. V. R. Van Duzer, who operated such a wagon between Denver and Fort Logan, was severely beaten as he traveled down South Broadway. The public felt threatened by this dangerous turn of events and by the summer of 1891, they demanded arrests. Vaughn assured them that he intended to close the saloons. But the Russell-Vaughn Gang had cast their lot with the saloon element in the 1890 election and now found themselves at their mercy.

Vaughn had the marshal make a show of arrests and fines and even claimed that two liquor violators pleaded guilty, threw themselves on the mercy of the court, and declared their intention to retire from the business. When the public learned that Vaughn had in fact suspended the lawbreakers' fines, there was talk of holding a mass meeting to protest.

The marshal had also closed Joe Lowe's Cottage Grove three times, but it simply opened the next day, Lowe insisting that his place was outside South Denver's one-mile limit and therefore the town had no

jurisdiction. Cottage Grove was actually closer to Sheridan than to South Denver, and when angry South Denver citizens called again for its closure, exasperated town attorney De Witt Webber maintained that South Denver had its hands full with resorts inside the limits and should clean them up before it talked about those outside. "Some over-zealous people blame me for not prosecuting those places," he stated, "but the fact is I cannot get a single man to testify against them. In my opinion the best thing to do is to reduce the $3,500 license to about $500 and get something out of them. They run anyhow, so we might as well get some revenue from them." In response to this outburst, a South Denver citizen suggested that Webber resign. "It seems strange that men who have been driven out of Denver come to our city, a temperance town, and open a 'gentlemen's club' and the town attorney confesses his inability to prosecute them. . . . By acknowledging his inability to make convictions, does he not invite the worst class of saloon-keepers to open their groggeries in our midst?"[19] Sheridan's sympathetic attorney expressed a willingness to help out by also trying to close up Lowe's place but had no more luck than Webber had.

The public also demanded verification of rumors that Philip Zang, a successful brewer, had offered the board of trustees $100,000 for the town hall and grounds in order to establish a large resort where liquor could be sold. The trustees denied knowledge of such a possibility and the property remained with the town.

Throughout Mayor Vaughn's second term, trustee Benjamin Niesz and his vocal outside supporters, notably Harry M. Banks, bedeviled the mayor and the other five trustees. The trouble had started with the purchase of the Fleming mansion and since then, nearly every item on the council's agenda became an issue for argument. The *Rocky Mountain News* took sides, referring to South Denver's leadership as Mayor Vaughn and his henchmen, "Mayor Vaughn & Co. having five pairs of lungs to Niesz's one, drowning the latter out. Yet the latter succeeded in staying in sight, and doubtless held the board in check on a number of occasions. Mr. Niesz claims that the Vaughn crowd were in for boodle. . . . So it has been for months, the wards fighting among themselves over alleged grievances, which the one claims to have against the other." The public's patience was wearing thin. Nearly 130 citizens, fed up with the constant "wrangling" in the council chambers, organized the Independent Club of South Denver to not only "wipe out the Vaughn faction, but to completely obliterate the Niesz-Banks faction also."[20] They outfitted three club rooms in the Sans Souci building, which Sister Eliza had vacated, and laid plans.

In the spring of 1892, this group chose Joseph C. Shattuck, the University of Denver's financial manager, as their candidate on a People's Convention ticket. Shattuck had served as vice-president and general manager of Union Colony in early 1870, was elected to the territorial legislature in 1874, and in 1876 became superintendent of public instruction for the state public school system, a post he held until 1885. In these two capacities, Shattuck helped write the state's first water and irrigation laws, and its first education laws. He was professor of pedagogics and dean of the Faculty of Liberal Arts at the University of Denver from 1885 to 1887, and at times he acted as director of the university during Chancellor Moore's frequent absences. Shattuck, his wife Hattie (Harriet), daughter Francine, and two sons, Hubert and Orville, lived at 1812 South Lincoln Street, but Shattuck had been a driving force in organizing the University Park Colonization Society, and in 1895 he built a residence on the northwest corner of York and Asbury in University Park. His cow pasture later became the site for the university's athletic complex.

The People's Convention and Joseph Shattuck won the election, and Shattuck became South Denver's third mayor in April 1892.[21] Shattuck came down hard on liquor violators. He instructed Marshal Reed to notify Joe Lowe and other saloon owners to close up their places or face arrest. The new town attorney, E. J. Short, promised he would vigorously prosecute all the saloon cases now in the courts and any other complaints that might be brought.

The town had closed down G. W. ("Galvanized Whiskey") Bell's "Gentlemen's Club" in the 400 block of South Broadway, but Mike Ryan immediately established his own roadhouse in the building. Marshal Reed closed this club, too, and the large, two-story wooden building of notorious repute stood empty for several months. But in early December 1892, residents were scandalized to find that a Madame Mitchell had

Mayor Joseph C. Shattuck. *Denver Public Library, Western History Department*

rented it, moved in, and planned to open yet another roadhouse in it. "Madame Mitchell, late of 1108 15th Street, who has an unsavory reputation, . . . immediately erected a high board fence around the place, put up alluring signs which read 'Refreshments,' 'Hot and Cold Drinks,' etc., and rented a part of the building to one Professor Von Deo, a shadowy personage, who was announced to give dancing lessons from seven to twelve o'clock every night," the *Daily News* reported.[22]

Reaction was swift. On December 4, clergy of all denominations and "citizens interested in preserving law and order in the town" were invited to a meeting for the purpose of taking steps to drive Madame Mitchell out of town. "The announcement that the madame had rented the old Gentlemen's Club and moved out there has stirred South Denver to its center. The people are determined that such a house as she proposes to run will not be tolerated," said the *Denver Republican*.[23] That Sunday the Reformed Presbyterian Church's minister, Rev. J. Milligan Wylie, delivered a blistering sermon against the madame, and other ministers of the town hurled anathemas from their pulpits as well, as this "sudden invasion of modern Goths and vandals stirred up the good people to a high pitch of wrath and excitement."[24]

Outraged citizens held an Indignation Meeting in the old Sans Souci building on December 6, presided over by Mayor Shattuck. Reverend Wylie again thundered his objection, as did Rev. J. M. Grace, pastor of the South Denver Presbyterian Church, and Rev. D. M. Hopkins of a neighboring church, who acted as secretary of the meeting. It was Reverend Hopkins who suggested that the mayor appoint a secret vigilance committee of twelve to watch Madame Mitchell's place to get evidence of violation of the law if possible. Shattuck agreed to an elaborate scheme of secrecy in which he would appoint a committee of one individual, who in turn would appoint a vigilance committee of twelve. No one was to know who composed the committee but the one who appointed them and he in turn would not be known to any but the twelve and Mayor Shattuck.

But a party or parties of overly stimulated and impatient bona fide vigilantes apparently decided not to wait for the vigilance committee to act. The very next evening, Madame Mitchell's building became enveloped in a sudden sheet of flame. The Russell Hose House responded immediately but could do little, and they called for two more fire companies from the city of Denver. But the building burned to the ground. The "inmates" escaped with only the clothes they were wearing, but they lost all household effects. There was no stove in the building, and the circumstances pointed to the origin of the fire as the work of an incendiary. Madame Mitchell was not heard from again.

Marshal Reed arrested other colorful characters, which the Denver newspapers followed with delight. "As the result of an all-around scrap at Wilderson's place in Whiskey Hollow, South Denver, Police

Magistrate Harper had a batch of cases to attend to. Wilderson is still laid up from the effects of the row." Another man was fined $5 and costs, and two others bound over to keep the peace.[25] "Whiskey Hollow" may have been a nickname for clusters of saloons along either South Broadway or South Santa Fe Drive. The town's case against Ed Chase, charging him with selling liquor without a license at Overland Park, was pending.

But Joe Lowe managed to escape the town's clutches. His Cottage Grove roadhouse resort flourished until Joe was killed by former policeman Emmanuel A. Kimmel in a brawl at George Walker's saloon on Curtis Street downtown on February 11, 1899. In the process of the sensational trial before District Judge George W. Allen, who had provided legal services in the incorporation of South Denver, Kimmel's attorney, Thomas Ward, tried to produce former South Denver attorney De Witt Webber to testify that Lowe had said he would one day kill Kimmel, and that he had warned Kimmel of this threat. Webber's statements were regarded as hearsay, however, and were denied.

Cottage Grove was finally eradicated, but several of its neighbors, saloons as bad as Lowe's or worse, that congregated at Orchard Place (now Englewood) remained, and problems arose when gamblers and carousers took over the streetcars on their way to Orchard Place, especially on weekends. "South Broadway cars on Sundays are rendered unfit for decent people, owing to drunken and lewd men and girls using them on their way to and from that sink of inequity, Orchard Place," the *South Denver Eye* complained. The active southside Women's Temperance Union went after Orchard Place, a "disgrace to South Denver; a foul resort . . . and an abomination too great to be longer borne." Another women's group, the Civic Federation, called for a special organization of all clubs "to abolish the dishonor and disgrace of it."[26] Eventually the angry women succeeded, and in 1906 the gambling area was transformed into La Tuileries Gardens, an amusement park that prospered only about a dozen years before it too closed.

Shattuck's board dealt with more mundane things as well, such as the pollution of the South Platte River—in particular, complaints of a dead horse not being buried deep enough, so that its bones lay exposed. The town thrived, despite a general economic depression gaining speed throughout the country, and the 1892 assessed value rose a bit, to $3,835,495.

Family-owned grocery, drug, and other neighborhood stores anchored the corners of residential blocks up and down South Broadway, Pearl, Logan, Acoma, and Cherokee streets. The population had grown from 150 at the time of incorporation in 1886 to nearly 5,000 by January 1892, and over 250 residences had been built. Mrs. May L. Jefferson built the three-story brick Jefferson Block still standing at 430–436 South Broadway, across from the tramway depot on the site of the unfortunate Madame Mitchell's place. The Bush and Soetje Drug Store and the South Denver Printing Company, printers and publishers of *The South Denver Eye,* inhabited part of the first floor. Arthur Pierce and John Blood had sold the newspaper to J. G. Garrison in 1891, and the paper continued to inform South Denver residents of community events into the 1920s. Several Jeffersons lived in the apartments above, one a dairyman, another a tramway motorman, and another in real estate.

The South Denver Post Office was also established in the Jefferson Building in early 1892. A Mr. Webb was the first South Denver postmaster until he mysteriously disappeared a few months later. He was last seen boarding a Broadway streetcar without his overcoat on a Saturday evening. All his clothes were in his room and his post office accounts were in order. When detectives found no trace of Mr. Webb, Miss Nettie Culver of Wray, Colorado, was appointed deputy postmistress to fill this vacancy.

In August 1892, Joe Lowe's old Broadway Park roadhouse on the southeast corner of South Broadway and Jewell Avenue, vacant since Lowe's departure in 1888, became South Denver's first hospital, the Broadway Park Sanitarium. Owner Dr. R. N. Pool of New York City planned to specialize in "cataplasmia treatment of cancers, abdominal tumors, lungs, and catarrhal affections.[27] The city watched the transformation from raucous saloon to quiet sanitarium with interest as 150-foot two-story wings of fifty rooms each were added to each side and the grounds were prepared for croquet and tennis, flower beds, and fountains.

Pool's corporation soon ran out of money and the twenty contractors and subcontractors refused to continue work until satisfactory financial arrangements could be made. In December the Broadway Park Sanitarium corporation was again placed on a sound financial basis. Its liabilities were $16,000, but when the present improvements were completed, the estimated assets totaled $17,400. An attorney deemed the company solvent, but the creditors insisted that Dr. Pool distribute $10,000 worth of nonassessable, paid-up stock among the creditors. Pool also agreed to give his services free to the company until the last creditor was paid and to "teach the officers of the company how to prepare his formula for the cure of disease, so that in case death or any other cause should remove him from the superintendence of the institution, the work will not be interfered with."[28] The sanitarium opened its doors in early 1893 but was unprofitable and closed a few years later. For a time the Broadway Rabbitry and Poultry Yards filled its lovely building and beautifully landscaped grounds with the clamor and squawk of hundreds of chickens and rabbits, and still later the building was occupied by a dog kennel.

Nearby, South Denver Baptists organized their first congregation in 1892, meeting at S. B. Cunningham's home, the present 1824 South Logan Street, and then at Fleming's Grove School. Rev. George Eaves was the first pastor in 1892 at a salary of $400 plus a supplemental allowance from the State Home Missionary Society. Organist Julie Batchelor received sixty cents per week. The little congregation purchased Fleming's Grove School on May 18, 1892, from the District 7 school board, when the students were temporarily transferred to Lincoln School. To finance part of the purchase, the congregation borrowed $2,000 at 8 percent interest, with payments of $40 per quarter for the next five years. But the little congregation was unable to meet these payments and sold the schoolhouse back to District 7 on August 14, 1894, for $3,000. Fleming's Grove once again became an annex to Grant School.

The Bethel Baptist congregation then erected their own building on the corner of Logan Street and Colorado Avenue, their present site, with a membership of sixty-four. An addition and remodeling were completed in 1915 and this structure was used until 1954, when a new auditorium was built. An education building had been completed in late 1948.

To serve the Rosedale and Overland neighbor-

Bethel Baptist Church.
Denver Public Library,
Western History Department

hoods, the District 7 school board purchased eleven lots at South Lincoln Street and Vassar Avenue and built Vassar School in 1892 at a cost of $12,000 for both land and building. The two-story building had two rooms on each floor and was heated by coal stoves. However, it boasted a marble-topped washbowl and running water to each floor, ending the "pail-and-dipper era of refreshing thirsty children."[29] Miss Fanny Richardson both taught and served as principal. Ada B. Gibbs and Margaret Ogden were teachers, and Lewis Keys was custodian. Vassar School was closed in 1924 and the students transferred to the beautiful new Rosedale School, an English Tudor building designed by Jacques Benedict at 2330 South Sherman Street.

Two years later, in 1894, the District 7 school board added Milton School, erected on the north side of Myrtle (Evans) Avenue between Bannock and Cherokee streets, also at a cost of $12,000 for land and building. One former student who lived on South Santa Fe Drive jumped onto the back step of a Fort Logan army supply wagon each morning as it made its daily run into Denver for supplies, hopped off at Milton, and caught the wagon again in the afternoon for a ride home across the open prairie. The four-room brick school served the Overland community for sixty-five years, until it was discontinued in 1959. The building was torn down in 1966.

University Park schoolchildren attended Coronado School at South Jackson Street and Florida Avenue, but by 1890 crowded conditions there forced District 35 board members to construct a second school. They erected a business building on the northeast corner of Asbury Avenue and York Street in 1890 and held temporary primary school classes there for two years.[30] This two-story building was then purchased by Mrs. Mary Lowe Dickinson, the first woman to be named a full professor (English Literature) and the first woman to hold an endowed chair, the Mary Lowe Dickinson Chair of Belles-Lettres, at the University of Denver.

But the residents wanted a permanent elementary school, and John S. Babcock, who had successfully launched District 35 and erected Coronado School, now made it possible. In 1892, Babcock donated seven lots on South St. Paul Street and Iliff Avenue for District 35's University Park Elementary, a red brick structure with four classrooms and a lunchroom, erected in 1893. In 1924, a Spanish-style addition designed by architect Lester Varian, who also designed the Phipps mansion, was constructed for $90,000 and the old building was no longer used for classes. University Park School became the training school for student teachers from the University of Denver and many of these student teachers became teachers in the Denver public schools. Still another section was added in June 1949, by

Rosedale School. *Courtesy Denver Public Schools*

architects Dudley Smith, Casper F. Hegner, and Thomas F. Moore. This addition included an auditorium, eighteen classrooms, two kindergarten rooms, a cafeteria, a PTA kitchen, a visual aid room, and a library, built at a cost of $675,000. The original 1893 building, just west of the present building, has been torn down. Babcock himself had built a lovely home with a handsome corner tower at 2300 South Cook Street in 1892.

Three years earlier, when water became available in 1889, Bishop and Elizabeth Warren moved into Grey Gables on Warren Avenue and South Milwaukee to begin settling University Park and to help with construction of the university itself. Their children felt terribly isolated living so far out in the country. "A trip out from Denver and back by horse and buggy took the better part of a day. Louise and her sister traveled by morning train to Denver to attend high school and returned home on the evening train."[31] When the cornerstone for University Hall was laid April 3, 1890, the occasion provided "cheap advertisement for realty dealers holding land in that locality. Some of the crowd

The Town of South Denver

Milton School. *Courtesy Denver Public Schools*

present at the ceremony were greatly struck with the locality and they invaded the real estate offices with the result that many sales were consummated," the *Denver Republican* reported.[32] But even with the Warren's leadership, sales in University Park had not gone well and the future of the colony was threatened. Evans admitted that some of the lots had been sold too soon to yield the best financial results to the university, and that they had been forced to dispose of the fifteen lots donated by John Babcock "indiscreetly." In desperation, John Evans, Elizabeth Warren, and the

university's secretary of the board of trustees, Arthur C. Peck, bought a large plot of land from the university and convinced half a dozen prospective buyers to build "beautiful and imposing edifices" on the lots during the summer. Many other homes followed, in the 1900–2200 blocks of St. Paul, Milwaukee, Fillmore, Clayton, Columbine, and Josephine streets in 1890–1892, most built by university professors and their families. A row of fine houses referred to as Professors Row sprang up along Milwaukee street between Grey Gables and Evans Avenue. Chamberlin Observatory's architect,

The original University Park School. *Courtesy Denver Public Schools*

Robert S. Roeschlaub, built a house for the observatory's director, Professor Herbert Howe (who married Dr. Joseph Shattuck's daughter, Francine) at 2201 South Fillmore; the professor could be seen dashing back and forth to the observatory at all hours of the night to observe his beloved heavens. During the 1890s, Dr. Howe served concurrently as the observatory director, dean of the College of Liberal Arts and dean of the Graduate College, and as acting chancellor when Dr. William F. McDowell resigned in 1899. "He had little time for sleep. In fact he drove himself so relentlessly in preparing for the appearance of Haley's comet in 1910 that he inadvertently fell asleep just as the comet crossed the eye of his telescope; he felt he had betrayed his trust and he wept bitterly when recalling the incident."[33]

Residents of early University Park got their fuel from a coal yard that had joined Gallup's nursery along the Texas and Gulf Railroad tracks, and their groceries and mail from the store on the corner of Milwaukee Street and Evans Avenue, built by William and Sarah Evans. The University Park Post Office was established in this building in 1890, the mail being brought out on the Texas and Gulf railroad. Sarah Evans was the first postmaster. University Park became so prestigious (even though unaffordable for most buyers) that

unscrupulous real estate brokers sold "University Park" lots to misinformed clients, when the properties were in fact as much as two miles or more from the park.

Architect Roeschlaub completed University Hall on the university's campus in 1892. The three-and-a-half-story University Hall was set on the high point of land on the prairie, overlooking the city of Denver and the Platte Valley and the mountains for miles around. Built of rose Colorado stone, the large, imposing building was intended to be the center of the university; multiple entrances enabled students to enter from any part of campus, and all components were housed within its walls. To the right of the main entrance were large and elegantly furnished parlors for the reception of visitors. Opposite these were the offices of the chancellor and dean of the faculty. Directly across the hall from the main entrance was a chapel with a slanted floor of seats. Broad stairwells in the towers at both ends led to the floors above. The second floor held "recitation rooms" for math, science, and languages classes, and the third floor held the laboratories and "society halls," including the Evans Literary Club and the Phi Alpha Society.

University Hall was dedicated on February 22, 1892. The hall was festooned with the American flag and the university's red and gold colors, and every residence in University Park was decorated in red, white, blue, and gold for this gala occasion. The Circle

The Evans corner grocery and post office, built in 1890 at Milwaukee Street and Evans Avenue, served the University Park community for several decades. *Denver Public Library, Western History Department*

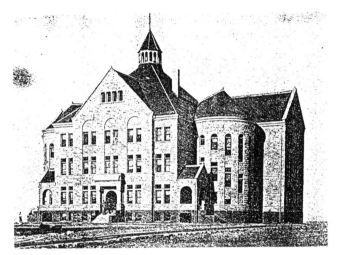

University Hall, University of Denver campus. *Sketch from The Coloradan, December 1892*

railway brought in a large trainload of spectators and the electric line added extra cars. The ceremony was held in the small chapel, which was decorated with flowers and entwined with the university colors. "Three thousand people assembled in front of the main entrance, where they joined in several songs and were addressed by a number of speakers after they had finished within."[34]

The thirty College of Liberal Arts students moved into University Hall for classes the same week; the women entered on one side and men on the other, a relic of "old fogey restrictions" from another age, as one student complained. "All who wear hats must enter on one side, all who wear bonnets the other. Those horrid boys must not go up the same stairs as the innocent maids. Co-lunching is an unpardonable sin."[35] Total enrollment in all of the university's departments and schools in 1890–1891 was 848; all but the Liberal Arts section remained in downtown buildings for the time being.

Shortly after University Hall was dedicated in 1892, the Iliff School of Theology began to take shape across the circle. John Iliff had often expressed the desire that his wealth might someday help endow both a school for training in mechanical arts and another for educating young men for the Methodist ministry. In 1887 Jacob Haish gave $50,000 to establish the Haish Manual Training School as part of the university, and Bishop Warren raised an additional $50,000, part of

which may have been contributed by Elizabeth in John Iliff's memory. In 1889 Elizabeth Iliff Warren fulfilled her promise to give $100,000 to endow the Iliff School of Theology. At the same time, her stepson, William Seward Iliff, announced that he would donate $50,000 in his father's memory to pay in full for the construction of the school. The Warrens engaged the services of Fuller and Wheeler, architects, of Albany, New York, but their plans for this distinguished building have been lost, except for some of the architects' drawings showing detail for interior wood trim for Iliff Hall. The school contained spacious halls, lecture rooms, offices, and a chapel. Total cost by the time the building was finished was $62,250. Its first class, of six full-time and five part-time students, enrolled in September 1892, and two faculty members were hired. The Iliff School of Theology building is still in excellent condition.

Students at the university had little financial aid in the 1890s, and about 60 percent of them worked their way through the university by caring for furnaces, horses, cows and lawns, by delivering newspapers, washing dishes in restaurants, and keeping house. As South Denver's population increased, the Denver Tramway Company hooked trailers to the trolley cars to handle the rush-hour commuter traffic during peak periods. For the next thirty years, University of Denver students collected nickels morning and afternoon as "trailer hounds" on the South Pearl line between downtown Denver and the university, which became tagged "Tramway Tech." But all was not serene on the ride to Tramway Tech. No conductor wanted to take

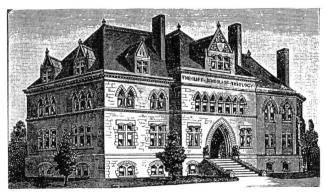

Iliff School of Theology. *Sketch from The Coloradan, December 1892*

the particular car that the students boarded for the trip because "a gang of students would shout, laugh, yell, ring the bell, pound on the floor, and behave in a manner that was noisier than it was decorous."[36] On one occasion a student was thrown bodily from the car, a car window going with him (the students paid for the damage). When the Denver Tramway Company sued the University of Denver and threatened a number of students with arrest, Dean Shattuck promised that there would be no more trouble and the suit was dropped.

The students were fond of pranks. Dr. Russell was a popular teacher at the university, and the Russell's backyard at 2163 South Fillmore, like those of many residents, was really a small farm. The Russell's black cow proved to be subject to Halloween escapades for years to come. She once was discovered with white stripes painted on her, and twice she was found on the third floor of University Hall. Several years later another of Professor Russell's unfortunate cows was led up the front stairs of Old Main and tied to the bannister. Professor Russell, the story goes, chased the cow up and down the hall during the night trying to retrieve the frightened animal, but she could not be coaxed down the stairs. The next morning a student brought up an armload of hay and milked her in the second-floor hallway. She was finally hog-tied and slid down the stairs on a mat.

The university erected an athletic field on the Gallup Nursery's former site at the railroad tracks and Fillmore Street, across from the Texas and Gulf Railroad depot. "Special passenger trains would bring in teams and spectators for games. The entire set-up consisted of wooden bleachers, a running track, football-baseball field and a small frame building for showers and lockers. Game day was an exciting experience and always brought crowds to the Park," Robert Shattuck wrote.[37] This field was used until the old baseball field at South Broadway and Center Avenue was developed into Union Park in 1901, and eventually the structure was torn down.

Other campus and dormitory buildings joined the flagship University Hall and the seminary. Robert S. Roeschlaub erected Wycliffe Cottage for Young Ladies, a three-story university dormitory with a wraparound front porch and wide front steps, on the northeast corner of Asbury Avenue and Columbine Street about 1891. Roeschlaub later proposed and attempted to

create a comprehensive campus plan for the university, but only one building, Carnegie Library, was completed. Andrew Carnegie granted the university $30,000 for the library, contingent on its raising matching funds for an endowment for the building and its collection. The library was to be the centerpiece of the north campus, facing Evans Avenue. "It is essentially a pavilion, its prototype buildings like the French classical garden pavilions at Versailles. A key feature is the predominance of the long French windows over all other design features."[38] Both Wycliffe Cottage and the Carnegie Library, which for some time served as the campus bookstore, have been demolished.

The science hall on the west—still in use—and the Buchtel Chapel on the east were both eventually built, but not by Roeschlaub. Thomas Barber designed the "Moorish Baroque" chapel but is reported to have denied designing it. The chapel was gutted by fire in the 1980s, and only the bell tower was saved. This section has been restored and surrounded with beautifully landscaped grounds.

A final architectural landmark, Evans Chapel, a sandstone structure built by John Evans in 1878 as a memorial to his daughter Josephine, was moved from Thirteenth and Bannock streets to the university campus in 1960. Each stone of this exquisite chapel was carefully disassembled and numbered for reconstruction on the campus. Evans Chapel was placed on the National Register of Historic Places on February 10, 1975.

On April 23, 1892, Henry and Elizabeth Warren bought a full block of land from Colorado Seminary and built a stone residence on it. Elizabeth called the house, at 2160 South Cook, Fitzroy Place in honor of her birthplace of Fitzroy, Ontario. "One would expect both these buildings of Lyons red sandstone, built simultaneously, to be designed by the same architects and they were, for William S. Iliff paid Fuller and Wheeler $1,750 for the architectural design on June 10, 1892."[39] The style is Richardsonian Romanesque, and it included windows of varying sizes, shapes, and positions, Queen Anne towers, and a massive roof in the two-and-a-half-story, thirteen-room house. The house contained an elevator and a central vacuum system, as well as an air-cooling system. In the basement was a well-insulated room that could be

Evans Chapel.
*Photo by Millie
Van Wyke*

Fitzroy
Place. *Photo
by Millie
Van Wyke*

Buchtel Chapel, University of Denver campus. The University Park Methodist Episcopal Church congregation, which originated in the Evans store in 1891, met here until building their own church across from the campus in 1927. *University of Denver Archives*

filled with ice by way of a chute extending up to the north driveway. The cold from this could flow by narrow openings into two adjoining rooms, one for meat and the other for perishable provisions. The house was large enough to accommodate the Warrens and five of their six children; it was beautifully furnished with fine paintings and other art objects collected in their travels all over the world. The dining room could seat thirty, and the Warrens entertained frequently.

A small gardener's cottage and a two-story stone and shingle gambrel roof carriage house with cupola and rear porte cochere were erected as well. The Warrens kept horses, a cow, chickens, and a garden on the Evans side of the grounds, and Mrs. Warren had playground equipment set up for the neighborhood children and laid a sandstone walk.

In the 1890s the Warren children married and left home. Ellen married John Robert Van Pelt, Edna married the Iliff School of Theology dean Arthur Briggs, and Carrie married Methodist minister J. Wellington Frizzelle. William Seward Iliff married Alberta Bloom and built a home at 2145 South Adams Street. The athletic Will had been captain of the university football team in 1884 and was the force behind building the university's Hilltop Stadium on the campus (now destroyed) in 1925.

By 1900, only Louise, who never married, was left

with her parents in the big house. Dr. Robert Shattuck, grandson of Dr. Joseph C. Shattuck, grew up at 2180 South Clayton and married Elizabeth's granddaughter Alberta Iliff. He remembers Elizabeth and Louise driving about the neighborhood in their electrical car, "very properly and stylishly dressed always with hat and gloves . . . Miss Louise in later years would go calling and send in a gift of eggs and/or milk by her chauffeur. Always these gifts were a visible sign of her regard and friendship."[40]

In 1910, a fire broke out following one of the Warren's parties; it damaged the house and the bishop's library and destroyed many of the beautiful furnishings and art objects. A surge of electricity had gone out over the wires, causing the basement wires to become so hot that piñon wood stored under the dining room ignited. The dining room was gutted and the table silver laid out on the table to be put away the next day became a molten mass. The family moved to 857 Grant Street for two years while Fitzroy Place was restored.

Bishop Henry White Warren died at Fitzroy Place in 1912. After his death both Elizabeth and Louise continued to contribute financially to the Iliff School of Theology and both served on the board of trustees, as did William Seward Iliff. Elizabeth died in 1920 and Louise lived at Fitzroy Place until her death in 1966. She willed the home and property, valued at about $175,000, to the Iliff School of Theology, which sold it to a private party. It is now a private school. Fitzroy Place was added to the National Register of Historic Places on February 20, 1975.

The corner grocery and post office at Milwaukee and Evans became a focal point for the University Park community in the early 1890s. It had a waiting room for the Circle Railroad train and later the tramway cars; it was the end of the line for both. Dairymen, ranchmen, and gardeners came for their mail and to do their trading. For decades mail time was about 11:00 A.M., and in later years Judge Hubert Shattuck (son of Dr. Joseph Shattuck) maintained that "all he had to do to see and exchange pleasantries with his neighbors was to be out on his south lawn at the midmorning mailtime and in due time all the people would stream by."[41] As the community grew, tourists and sightseers toured University Park on the tramway's "scenic line," and trolley car parties were popular as fund-raisers or

just for fun.

The little corner store bustled even on Sundays. Postmistress Ann Augustus (Mrs. W. W.) Evans operated a Methodist Sunday school there as early as 1891 and by 1894 it had grown so that the people requested that a "church society" be formed. Fifty-six charter members organized the University Park Methodist Episcopal Church on September 16 and moved its Sunday worship services and Sunday school to the chapel of University Hall. Prayer meetings were held at Mrs. Lyle Waterbury's house every Wednesday evening. Professor Ammi B. Hyde, already seventy years old, was its first minister and served for two years. A brilliant man, Dr. Hyde was a professor of languages (specializing in Greek), a librarian, and a counselor of students as well as a minister for the university for another seventeen years before he retired in 1911. Several ministers conducted services over the next few years until Edward E. Bean was appointed the first full-time minister in 1900.

During Reverend Bean's pastorate, the congregation absorbed a fledgling congregation begun by William C. Johnston in the Coronado schoolhouse in 1894, with Reverend Marvin Rader pastor. An average congregation of twelve, mostly young people, attended the Coronado Mission's Sunday evening services, and this little group supported and educated a girl in India as its mission project. Coronado Mission did not flourish, however, even though in 1896 the Methodists made it part of the city missions network and helped fund it. The University Park Methodist Church took it under its wing in 1902 and tried to keep it going. But the next year a Methodist conference report stated that although the mission board had worked hard and even spent some money on it, "the neighborhood does not grow and the gardeners, in the summer time especially, are somewhat indifferent to help."[42] By the next year the mission was incorporated into the University Park Methodist Episcopal Church.

The University Park Church met in University Hall and later Buchtel Chapel on the university's campus until 1927, when they built a church on Warren Avenue, between University Boulevard and Josephine Street. This portion of the present structure is known as Wasser Chapel, in honor of Dr. William Campbell Wasser, pastor at that time and active participant in all phases of church life until his death in 1966 at the age

Myrtle Hill School, South Race Street and Mississippi Avenue. Erected in 1906, it later was renamed Washington Park School. *Courtesy Denver Public Schools*

of ninety-nine.

North of the university, the Myrtle Hill Subdivision, one block long (Mississippi to Tennessee) and six blocks wide (Gilpin to University, then known as East Broadway), developed to the point that the residents needed a church, a school, and stores. Miss Carrie E. Bartels had purchased the plot from a professional German gardener, John Gonner, who raised abundant crops on South Vine Street. Carrie, "who declares herself to be single and unmarried," platted Myrtle Hill

on August 9, 1888. She then married Frank Bailey and the couple raised alfalfa and operated a nursery on several adjoining acres. They offered lots in Myrtle Hill, "a bright suburban beauty spot," at $200 to $250 each and became deeply involved in community affairs. Frank served as a trustee on the town council and later as an alderman to the city of Denver. Carrie worked closer to home, enabling the construction of both a school and a church.

The school came first. Carrie Bailey donated land at

the corner of South Race Street and Tennessee Avenue for a two-room District 2 schoolhouse, completed in January 1893 at a cost of $3,396. George McMeen and Etta Bradshaw were the first teachers of Myrtle Hill School's grades one through four. In 1901 McMeen was appointed principal of Myrtle Hill School at a salary of $75 for the first three months and $80 per school year after that if his performance proved satisfactory. McMeen did well enough so that within five years he had three full-time teachers at Myrtle Hill. In 1906 a five-room structure was erected a block away on South Race and Mississippi, and the original building was sold and torn down. In 1922 the first addition was built at a cost of $80,203 for eight classrooms and a gymnasium. The next year its name was changed from Myrtle Hill to Washington Park School, and seven classrooms and an auditorium were added in 1928 at $103,233. The building was sold in 1982 and is now a private academy.

A church followed shortly after. Hattie Lort, a teacher from Maryland who moved to 725 South High Street in 1891 with her sister Ella to seek a cure for her asthma, met with Reverend John Collins the next year about organizing a church in Myrtle Hill, but Reverend Collins felt that it was not yet time to start a church. So the sisters started a Sunday School in their home. When Reverend Collins heard about this, he joined them and led the adults in worship one Sunday morning in 1892 while the Lort sisters took the children into the kitchen and bedroom for Sunday School. The Myrtle Hill Methodist Episcopal Church was formed that day, and Carrie Bailey gave them the land at South High Street and Tennessee Avenue for a building site.

The little Myrtle Hill Methodist Church was formally dedicated by University of Denver chancellor William F. McDowell on September 3, 1893. Founder John Collins was the minister for the first year, until G. F. Mead succeeded him in 1894. W. D. Phifer took the post in 1895. The church building cost $2,265 and the little congregation of twenty-seven members carried a debt of $400 for the next five years, through the Panic of 1893, and finally paid it off in 1898. A popular method of fund-raising was to hold a streetcar party. The Denver Tramway Company illuminated and decorated a special car for this purpose and made it available to churches, lodges, and other organizations. "It could be chartered for a flat rate, and tickets could

be sold. The merry car full toured from Myrtle Hill to University Park, to Cherrelyn, to North Denver and City Park, with everyone on board singing Stephen Foster songs."[43] Myrtle Hill Methodist Episcopal was renamed Washington Park Methodist Church in 1911, and a new church was built in 1917, when John Evans II, grandson of governor John Evans, gave six lots on the corner of South Race Street and Arizona Avenue for it. University of Denver's Chancellor Henry A. Buchtel laid the cornerstone. A branch of the Denver Public Library was housed in the church, and the neighborhood children also enjoyed Saturday night movies there for ten cents. The west wing annex was added in 1950.

Hattie and Ella Lort's love for children also led them to start a private kindergarten in their home. In 1893 they bought a milk wagon and a white horse and had their brothers Frank and Tom Lort build seats in it. Each morning Hattie set out to pick up the children to bring to the new school established in their now enlarged house. This may have been the first kindergarten in South Denver. By 1898 three other schools—Milton, Vassar, and Fleming's Grove—also had kindergartens. Bertha M. Goodfellow was the teacher at Fleming's Grove.

As Myrtle Hill grew, stores and shops opened along South Gaylord Street; the William Reed family opened the first grocery. This section has been revitalized as Old South Gaylord District.

Reverend John Collins also led a Methodist congregation in Rosedale as early as 1889, when the church had thirty-three members and 120 Sunday school enrollees. The congregation incorporated on February 14, 1893, as the Warren Avenue Methodist Church and met in a small frame building on the corner of Warren Avenue and South Bannock Street. This church was dedicated by Bishop Warren on December 17, 1893. In 1897 its name changed to Collins Chapel when John Collins, who had served as minister from its beginning, was appointed assistant minister at Trinity Church downtown. When membership reached fifty in 1900, the congregation constructed the John Collins Methodist Episcopal Church on South Bannock Street and Iliff Avenue. The historic building is now called the John Collins United Methodist, Home of the Olde Methodist Church.

Reverend John Collins was purposeful, dedicated, and a dynamic fund-raiser for all the churches he started, even though his own salary was barely adequate. Once, a member of the John Collins Methodist Episcopal Church pleaded for more money; while the man was still speaking, John Collins nabbed the nearest parishioner, "took the man by the collar and demanded a subscription. By his volcanic methods he has created such public admiration in the city and county of Denver that it would have been easy for him to have raised every church debt in the district."[44] Historian John Templin stated, "But for his organizing ability, three or four of the strongest South Denver Methodist Churches might not have been organized at their strategic times, and perhaps the over-all picture of Methodism in Denver would have been quite different."[45] Reverend John Collins and his wife built the house at 2219 South Sherman in 1901, and Collins died September 30, 1932, at the age of eighty-four.

In all these early Methodist Episcopal churches, Iliff School of Theology students served as ministers half-time or less, helping to lay the groundwork for these congregations.

John Collins Methodist Church. *Iliff School of Theology Archives*

Turning Points

South Denver's boom years began to fade as the country's economy began a downward slide. The city of Denver was hard hit as well. By 1892, the city needed new revenue and this meant adding more taxable property. It turned its eyes toward the suburbs. South Denver was second only to Highlands in growth of wealth and population. It had a university, Broadway Park Sanitarium, Overland Park, and adequate water and transportation. The town's close proximity to the prosperous industrial districts of Overland and Manchester with their huge paper and cotton mills was also seen as an attraction.

Mayor Shattuck fought back with all the resources he could muster, convinced that the town's liquor ordinances would be repealed and his administration's vigorous efforts to restore the town to its pre-Vaughn and Russell days of total prohibition would be threatened. In a stirring speech at one of the December 1892 "indignation meetings" over the Madame Mitchell affair, he "gave the annexation question a knock-out blow, stating that the city of Denver would license saloons and South Broadway would soon be lined with dives of the worst order."[1] He could not let that happen.

Shattuck circulated a petition against annexation and gathered enough support to prompt sarcasm from annexation supporter Alex Miller. Disgusted with the "housewives and newcomers" who signed Shattuck's petition, Miller complained that "the only people of South Denver who opposed the [annexation] plan were those in office and a few strangers in the place. The petition being circulated was largely signed by ladies in the absence of their husbands, and the husbands on hearing of it had caused their names to go on record in an entirely different light."[2]

Stephen R. Pratt, president of Brinkhaus Investment Company, who lived at 836 South Logan Street, presented South Denver's case against annexation at a meeting with Denver's mayor on February 16, 1893, where he warned both the city of Denver and the state legislators not to take away their rights and property and give it to another: "We have a good water plant and other properties and it would be violating the laws of the state to take it away. . . . You won't get that consent under the present measure, and should you attempt to annex us against our will there will be started litigation that will be unending and will cost more than all the benefits to be derived can repay in ten years," he said.[3] Pratt's pleas and threats landed on deaf ears. The next day, the *Denver Republican,* siding with the city, reported that those suburban property owners against annexation were interested only in protecting their personal interests: "Not an idea or an objection was advanced beyond the hackneyed cry of heavy taxes and neglect. No look was taken beyond that short vision, and no attention was paid to the future of Denver and its widening possibilities. It was a wailing protest against taxation."[4]

Three days later, Shattuck and his trustees drafted a formal protest against

> the seizure of our property without allowing our people a voice in the matter, as one of the most unjust and uncalled-for measures ever proposed in an American legislative body. We renounce the claim to superior wisdom of the framers . . . and hold that the citizens of South Denver know as well what is for their own good . . . than any coterie of city hall officials. . . . We appeal for protection against the bill, which would turn us over without defense to excessive taxation to swell the millions which the city hall gang of Denver wish to stand, since it is admitted that the principal reason for this annexation is to secure property to raise money, the city of Denver being incumbered to near its bonding capacity.[5]

South Denver elected two Republicans to the General Assembly of the Colorado State Legislature in March 1893—John Babcock to the House of Representatives and De Witt Webber to the Senate. Senator Webber was simultaneously serving his third term as South Denver's town attorney, had served as president of School District 7, and at age twenty-seven was the youngest man in the Senate. Representative Babcock served as chairman of the House Committee on Agriculture and Irrigation. That spring the legislators decided that any town could be dissolved and annexed if twenty-five residents signed a petition for such annexation and an election of the town's inhabitants followed.

With this news, pro- and anti-annexation forces immediately geared up for the April mayoral election. Mayor Shattuck ran for a second term on the Workingmen's Citizens ticket, which represented the anti-annexation position. The 200 members of the South Denver Working People's Club, backed by incumbent trustees Benjamin Niesz and William Lawson, chose as their candidate for mayor Solomon Barcus, a fifty-eight-year-old bricklayer and contractor. Barcus and his wife, Margaret, lived at 425 South Pennsylvania Street and had two grown sons, Adelbert and Arthur. The "People's ticket" adopted a resolution that *"whenever Denver makes a fair and businesslike proposition on the annexation question the town of South Denver will be ready to receive it, and with good chance of consummating the consolidation* (italics

added). . . . The resolution protests against any attempt at forcible annexation."[6] President Paul Gregory divided the town into no fewer than nine districts—Fleming's Grove, Overland Park, Smith's Lake, University Park, the Broadway and Virginia area, the south end, the west side, Myrtle Hill, and Corona Street—and assigned five men to campaign in each.

The two political parties opposed each other on the liquor issue as well as on annexation; it was the saloon problem that led to a highly charged election race. Shattuck's administration had tried hard to eradicate the saloon-infested Whiskey Hollow neighborhood by arresting illegal liquor sellers. But Whiskey Hollow remained alive and well and in late March its inhabitants became associated with Barcus's party. As the campaign became more lively and desperate, Barcus himself was referred to as the gang candidate for mayor (as Simeon Vaughn had been in the 1890 election) and his more radical supporters were openly called gangsters.

Two weeks before the election, Shattuck's Citizens party debated Barcus's Working People's Club before 250 people at the Odd Fellows Hall. Before the meeting had progressed very far, Niesz, one of Shattuck's own trustees, accused the Citizens party of being a "kid-gloved aristocracy" and told the crowd that Shattuck, a University of Denver official, had granted University Park the lion's share of town funds for improvements. Niesz was shouted down and the subject turned to saloons. Mayor Shattuck's representative "held up the gang leaders as a rapacious and mendacious pack" working hard among the disreputable element of Whiskey Hollow for votes. Mayor Shattuck himself charged Barcus's party with failing to include in its platform an attack on Whiskey Hollow, "an eyesore where liquor is sold surreptitiously, a place that defies the laws and has to be watched with the greatest vigilance." Barcus's gang party, he charged, "will never make an attack upon the hollow except with kegs of beer, and that will be upon election day." Niesz then tried a different tack; he jumped to his feet once more, this time to charge that Shattuck was controlled by the powerful Denver Tramway Company and held its interests foremost. When Shattuck's other trustees "rose at him" and pronounced such a statement a slander and untruth, Niesz "made an unctuous half apology and sat down amid jeers." A little later Niesz wanted to make another speech but the chair ignored him. After the meeting was adjourned, tension erupted into a fistfight between extremists of both parties. Only a few stiff punches were delivered, however, before the gangsters, who were charged with starting the fight, were hustled from the hall.[7]

On April 4, 1893, the electorate cast 426 votes for Barcus and 387 for Shattuck, a clear victory for the gang candidate and the saloon element. But the voters also chose three trustees from Shattuck's Citizens party to keep the new mayor in check. Walter P. Miller received 402 votes and Daniel H. Pike received 415; these votes were uncontested. But the third elected trustee from the Citizens party, Albert E. Riddle, beat out the People's party candidate, a Mr. Brown, by only one vote: 398 to 397. Because Riddle's victory meant that the 1893–1894 council was weighted by four prohibition trustees against Barcus and his supporters, Niesz and Lawson, the future of the town's politics depended on which of the two men sat on the council. The People's party hoped to balance the council evenly; they asked for a recount of votes on the grounds that many of the voters were not residents of South Denver. They lost the case, however, and Riddle was seated on the board of trustees. The anti-saloon contingent had the majority.

The hapless mayor found himself conducting the first council meeting at the town hall on April 11 with a board that was stacked against him. Mayor Barcus, Benjamin Niesz, and William Lawson opposed "kid-gloved aristocrats" Frank A. Bailey, Walter P. Miller, Albert E. Riddle, and Daniel H. Pike. Barcus tried to recover from his humiliating defeat on the board of trustees by placing his supporters in the office of attorney, in the police department, and as commissioners. When trustees Bailey and Miller nominated Senator De Witt Webber for a fourth term as town attorney, Barcus refused to accept the nomination, stating that it was illegal for a man to serve simultaneously as state senator and town attorney.

As the meeting wore on, Barcus, whose choices were unacceptable to the board, refused to appoint *any* officers at this meeting. Miller countered with a proposal to oust Barcus and elect Frank Bailey mayor pro tem in his place. Barcus denied the existence of any such office as mayor pro tem.

During these proceedings, Fleming's stone mansion was crowded with noisy and boisterous supporters of the mayor and his two allies. Several times these "political friends of Barcus and Niesz created noise and confusion to drown the voices of members . . . and yelled and hooted insulting cries and epithets, and the mayor failed, refused and neglected to keep decent order and decorum to the great injury and insult of the majority of the Board of Trustees and to the good name and fame of the Town of South Denver," stated former mayor Simeon Vaughn in a five-page written protest the next day. Barcus retaliated by stripping Vaughn's and Russell's names from the hose houses and renaming them simply Numbers 1 and 2.

In the end, De Witt Webber won the position of town attorney, but his appointment rankled "certain repudiated politicians and ex-town officers," who continued to protest his appointment throughout the summer. To appease the opposition, Webber appointed law student Hubert Shattuck, son of the former mayor, to represent him at trials, a move that apparently pacified everyone.[8] Hubert's father, Joseph, went back to his office at the university, where he served several more years. When Joseph Shattuck died in 1921 at the age of eighty-six, he had spent fifty years in Colorado education.

Meanwhile, the economic condition worsened, and in the summer of 1893 the silver market collapsed when Congress repealed the Sherman Silver Purchase Act of 1890, which required the Treasury to buy silver. With no market for silver, Colorado dived into a full-scale depression. The silver crash bankrupted many of Denver's land owners and business leaders, and silver kings lost their fortunes overnight. By mid-July, 45,000 Colorado workers were out of jobs, multitudes of businessmen declared themselves penniless, mines shut down, and at least ten banks closed their doors. At Overland Park the city ran a soup line for the unemployed, who were mostly miners. Mattie Silks, one of Denver's well-known madams, supposedly contributed a large circus tent for shelter.[9]

The Town of South Denver became financially strapped as well. The July 1 deadline for paying off Fleming's $10,000 note was approaching and they had no money to pay it. Apparently they had been paying only the interest, as the entire principal was still unpaid. On June 20, 1893, the board negotiated a three-year extension of payment with the Philadelphia Mortgage and Trust Company and paid a $300 commission for the privilege. The new note was now due July 1, 1896. A major project facing South Denver had to do with building a sewerage system, which they still did not have. Forbidden to discharge its sewerage into the South Platte River, the town would have to build its sewer lines to a point below the city, all the way from South Denver to Riverside Cemetery several miles north of Denver, which would bankrupt the town. The alternative was to connect with the city of Denver through annexation.

In June the *Denver Republican* had urged suburbs to unite with the city "to which they owe their existence" to bring Denver the prestige to which the newspaper believed it was justly entitled and that the contiguous towns "would exhibit anything but a patriotic and enterprising spirit" to refuse to become a part of it.[10] Perhaps seeing the handwriting on the wall, the university trustees, clinging to their cherished ideal, moved to exempt University Park and the campus from annexation so that they could still establish their independent, Methodist, and most important, prohibitionist, colony.

Barcus, whose party platform had included a willingness to entertain any *reasonable and businesslike* annexation proposal, wanted assurances that once the Town of South Denver became annexed, its services would not be curtailed nor its ordinances repealed. His four anti-saloon trustees were particularly concerned with the possibility of losing the right to control saloons. The town watched closely the progress of a lawsuit filed in Arapahoe County Court by the nearby town of Valverde against the city on this issue. The case went to the Colorado Supreme Court, which ruled that in the case of annexation, water and light services were not to be curtailed and that the town's liquor ordinances were to continue in force unless repealed by a vote of its own electorate.[11]

With these assurances in place, the Town of South Denver could at least entertain the possibility of annexation. On December 5, 1893, the Arapahoe County Court authorized Mayor Solomon Barcus and his trustees to provide for an election of South Denver voters on whether the town should be dissolved and the territory included therein annexed to the city of Denver.[12] The trustees immediately passed Ordinance

No. 129 that set the election date for January 30, 1894. On that day voters in all five precincts turned out to vote at Hose House No. 1 at Center and Broadway, the town hall, Mrs. Coffren's store near Jewell on Broadway, the store and post office at Milwaukee and Evans, and Frank Bailey's barn in Myrtle Hill. By an almost three-to-one margin, South Denver men and women (women had won the right to vote only two months earlier) chose to dissolve their town and become part of the city of Denver: 288 voted for annexation and 100 voted against it.

Two days later, Barcus and his council met to wind up the town's business. They considered a University of Denver request to prohibit the sale of intoxicating liquors within one mile of the campus, and a petition from University Park citizens who wished to form a volunteer fire company. The group had already picked out their officers, nozzlemen, and plugmen and merely requested that the town provide all necessary equipment. (Both University Park and Overland organized volunteer fire companies but no firehouses were ever built.) The council approved requests to repair fire hydrants, to sell the town plow for $15, to lease electric poles for one year for a fire alarm system, and to grant a property owner free water for one year. The council also passed an ordinance that changed the numbers and names of all the streets and avenues in the Town of South Denver to those we know today.

On February 7, 1894, the Town of South Denver was formally dissolved and the city of Denver took over all nine sections, including the university. Montana City, too, which was so promising in 1858 as a challenger to Auraria and St. Charles/Denver City, disappeared for good into the metropolis its old rivals had become.

Denver's mayor, Marion D. Van Horn, was eager to see exactly what the city had gained from the annexation and ordered William H. Young to assess the financial affairs of "the late Corporation of South Denver." Young quickly realized it would be nearly impossible for an accurate idea of the situation to be gathered: records and papers were unintelligible, the books inaccurate, and important documents missing altogether. Young found, among various other illegal transfers of funds and unpaid warrants, that $400 was missing from the water rents. The town had allowed thirty-three of its prominent citizens to use the

(Form 8.)

Canvass of Vote.

South Denver Colorado, _February 1,_ 189_4_

The Board of _Trustees_ of the Town _____ of _South Denver_

met this day for the purpose of canvassing the returns of the special election held on the _Thirtieth_ day of _January_, A. D. 189_4_, in pursuance of the ordinance of the said _Town_, adopted on the _Fourteenth_ day of _December_, A. D. 1893, submitting the question whether the Town _____ of _South Denver_ should be dissolved, and the territory included therein annexed to the City of Denver.

Present the following members : Mayor, _Solomon Barens_

and the following _Trustees_ namely : _Frank A. Bailey_ _William Lawson_ , _Walter P. Miller_ _Daniel H. Pike_ , _Albert E. Riddle_ _Benjamin I. Nies_

The meeting was called to order by the Mayor. The _Town_ Clerk and Recorder produced the ballot-boxes, poll-books and returns delivered to him by the judges and clerks of said election, and the returns were thereupon opened by him in the presence of the Mayor and Board of Trustees _____ , whereupon said returns were canvassed by the Board of Trustees _____ aforesaid, showing the following vote at said election, to wit :

	FOR ANNEXATION.	AGAINST ANNEXATION.
Precinct No. 1,	86	4
Precinct No. 2,	67	33
Precinct No. 3,	78	37 Returns not certifia
Precinct No. 4,	11	17
Precinct No. 5,	46	9
Precinct No. 6,		
Precinct No. 7,		
Precinct No. 8,		
Precinct No. 9,		
Precinct No. 10,		
Precinct No. 11,		
Precinct No. 12,		
Total,	288	100

Whereupon Trustee _B. I. Nies_ moved, and Trustee _F. A. Bailey_ seconded the adoption of the following resolution:

"WHEREAS, In pursuance of the ordinance of the Town _____ of _South Denver_ entitled "An ordinance to provide for the submission and determination of the question whether the Town _____ of _South Denver_ shall be dissolved, and the territory included therein annexed to the City of Denver," adopted on the _Fourteenth day_ of _December_, A. D. 1893, a special election was held in each of the precincts of said Town _____ on the _Thirtieth_ day of _January_, A. D. 189_4_ the official returns of which election in each of said precincts have been duly certified and are now exhibited to and canvassed by the Board of Trustees _____ of the Town _____ of _South Denver_ ;

This official election return shows the balloting results for and against annexation to the city of Denver. _Colorado State Archives_

municipal water supply at no cost. Young meticulously noted names, addresses, and amounts and recommended that the city of Denver conduct a house-to-house canvass in order to obtain a correct record of the "number of lots to be irrigated, number of rooms in house, bath and closet connections."[13] His recommendation was accepted and the city's water representatives visited every house in South Denver. It is not known whether the city collected its money.

Young's final report showed that as of February 8, 1894, Denver, which had hoped to profit from the annexation of the Town of South Denver, inherited a deficit of $15,331.79. Projected to January 1, 1895, the deficit grew to $19,083.98. On the bright side, Denver acquired taxable property amounting to $4,043,115.

Annexation did not solve South Denver's water problems, however, partly because two powerful water companies were fighting for control of the entire city of Denver's water contracts, including South Denver's. In 1891, before annexation, the Town of South Denver had finally settled the lawsuit with Joseph and Anna Brown by agreeing to maintain a dam that would force enough water into the Petersburg Ditch so that the Browns could get water into their own lateral canals. The town widened the ditch through the Brown's property, which greatly increased the water capacity and allowed the town to add twenty-five miles of pipe to reach houses that had been previously forced to depend on artesian wells. John Babcock and several other owners of ditches and canals within South Denver had also deeded their water rights to the town. But South Denver's Petersburg waterworks, installed by Mayor Fleming in 1889, had not been properly maintained and now, in 1894, required expensive repairs and updating. The water had become contaminated and the plant needed a new $4,500 charcoal filter.

The night before the annexation election took place, the trustees had granted a ten-year contract to the American Water Company, which would use the contaminated Petersburg plant, even though a verbal agreement was already in effect with Citizens Water Company, which could assure the town pure water from sources other than the Petersburg works. This decision was unacceptable to attorney De Witt Webber and two other trustees who had been absent when the town had granted the water contract to American Water

Company. Webber and his two colleagues successfully contested the contract, and two weeks after the town was annexed, district judge George Allen issued an order restraining the American Water Company from taking possession of South Denver's Petersburg waterworks. The Denver Board of Public Works appointed a caretaker to protect the machinery from freezing and "other possible damages." The matter was finally settled in November, when the Denver Union Water Company, successor to the American and Citizens companies, took over the lease. Southsiders complained to the bitter end, objecting strenuously to the water rates, which were much higher than they had been before annexation. The city of Denver operated the water system at a loss for several years until the Petersburg pumping works were disconnected about 1910.

The Panic of 1893 devastated many South Denver investors. Horace Tabor had invested in South Denver on two occasions, both with disastrous results. After his real estate deals with Loveland and Henry had gone bad, Tabor decided in 1890 to try a new cyanide smeltering process to save his already failing silver mines.

Tabor organized the Gold and Silver Extraction Mining and Milling Company with Saguache rancher and miner Edward Werner and shipbuilder and industrialist Leonard Gow of Glasgow, Scotland. The company purchased the Bailey smelter at the "Foot of Virginia Avenue, near Broadway Electric Depot, South Denver" from Tritch's German National Bank and spent $14,500 to equip it for the McArthur-Forrest Cyanogen Process.[14]

By July the mill was testing ore samples sent from all sections of the country to its assay house. T. L. Wiswell, treasurer of Tabor's investment company and general manager of the new mill, felt they would be doing a "large and laborious business" if the numerous letters of inquiry about the new cyanide experiment were any indication. In the first days of full operation in the spring of 1891, the tanks leaked when the cyanide reached them, but by May the heartening "thunder of the stamps" could be heard. Gow assured the investors that "several men who have seen our mill say it is a very fine one and everything certainly works beautifully." By October, he reported that the Denver mill "has provided good results, working at first very slow and offering obstacles with regard to filtration drawing off of the solutions. The working has improved very much, till now very satisfactory results can be obtained." But as time went on, the experiment with the cyanide process proved only mildly successful. There were problems, too, in getting the ores from the mines into Denver.

By the spring of 1892 money became tight; the Glasgow investors withdrew their support, stock value declined, and Tabor found himself unable to finance the still uncompleted mill by himself.[15] The Silver Panic of 1893 ended any hopes the already crippled Gold and Silver Extraction Mining and Milling Company had, and the property reverted to Tritch's bank for the second time. The buildings remained empty until 1899, when William K. Burchinell and Thomas Wygant began experimental reduction work in the plant, perhaps using the cyanide process, which was ultimately successful and was now in general use. But their efforts in the history of a smelter "remarkable for its failure to succeed"[16] also faltered and the German National Bank, recognizing the hopelessness of operating a permanent smelter on the site, set its sale for January 8, 1901. But an arsonist set fire to the smelter the night before the proposed sale, and the structure burned to the ground. The fire department, which dealt with a broken steamer, scarce water hydrants, and a "great building of dry wood," fought the blaze for seven hours before the fire was contained. The smelter was worth only about $3,000 at the time of the fire and was insured for $2,700. The loss on the machinery was heavy, however, estimated at from $10,000 to $15,000. This historic industrial site would later house a radium processing plant and the Robinson Brick Company.

Humphrey Barker Chamberlin, donor of the Chamberlin Observatory, was also a victim of the depression; John Babcock, whose seat in the legislature could not protect him, another. Both lost all their property and money, and both were grateful they had the sense to donate the observatories and University Park school, safely protected from the crash. These wonderful institutions, which they had given away, were all they had left. As fortunes fell, John Babcock sold off his many properties and became a custodian at University Park School, the very school for which he had donated the land. The Babcocks lost their lovely home on the corner of South Cook Street and Iliff

Avenue and lived in an apartment in the basement of the school, next to the lunchroom. Salary was $30 per month plus free rent, coal, and lights. Babcock later worked as a custodian at South High School and retired afterward. He died in 1947 at age ninety-six. The Babcock's daughter, Katherine, now eighty-six, still lives in the modest house her parents built in the 1930s across from University Park school.

The Silver Panic had ravished the University of Denver, too, and for the next six years the university floundered. At the beginning of the 1890s, the university had ten departments and 848 students in its two locations, with assets of over a million dollars, most of it in pledges backed by unproductive land in University Park, which could not now be sold. "It would have been well had the university possessed less land and more money," history and economics professor James Edward Le Rossignol wrote later. "It would also have been well had there been more concentration of effort and less expansion. Nobody was to blame. It was a mistake. The boom did not continue. Land values fell. The prospective million dollars [anticipated on the sale of University Park land] could not be realized. Many friends of the university became poor."[17]

A $160,000 debt hung over the school in 1894. Chancellor William F. McDowell (1890–1899), faced with calamity, reorganized or dropped whole departments and paid professors' salaries only at irregular intervals. When cash was unavailable, the university simply gave some of its unsold land in lieu of a paycheck. Ira E. Cutler, for example, a science professor at the university and also a painter, choir director, and horticulturist, was given two lots to the south of his house at 2122 South Clayton Street in lieu of salary. In 1896 the trustees granted tuition-free education to the College of Liberal Arts students as an experiment, but it is not known whether this successful practice was continued beyond that year. By 1898 student enrollment, which had dropped to a low of 282 in 1893–1894, was back up to 607.

"[The depression] was not a swift and sudden storm that came and went, leaving devastation in its wake," Chancellor McDowell said later. "It was sudden enough in its coming, but showed no haste in its departing." Still, the university hung on through the hard times, surviving a court challenge to tax its unused and formerly tax-exempt land, an action that would have destroyed the university.

Rufus Clark once again came to its rescue. For a decade he had tried to develop Evanston through his own Evanston Real Estate and Trust Company and use its profits to help finance the university. But in spite of the company's efforts the property had few if any buyers. In May 1899 Clark sold part of his Evanston property (from Iliff to Yale and Downing to University Boulevard, excepting the campus property) to William C. Johnston of Colorado Springs for $60,000, using a portion of the profits to help rescue the university from its perilous debts. He also "devoted considerable money realized from this sale" to rebuilding the Rufus Clark and Wife Theological Training School and church in Shangay, Sierra Leone, West Africa, which they had established in 1886 and which had recently been partially burned during a riot.

Johnston moved to Denver and tried to revive the Evanston Colony concept. "It is his intention to establish an aristocratic Methodist village near the university," the *Times* reported, "and he will endeavor to induce some of his wealthy Methodist friends to build out there. He fully anticipates that this summer and fall will witness the erection of some magnificent suburban homes."[18] But Johnston must have soon realized the futility of this, for in July he sold Evanston's 2,000 lots, with 4,000 shade trees, irrigation ditches, and street improvements, to Colorado Realty and Securities. Johnston stayed on as manager but there was no longer any hope of establishing an elite, cultured university town with elegant houses in Evanston, either. Evanston as a Methodist colony died aborning.

In June 1899 Chancellor McDowell resigned, marveling that the university had not fallen apart during the terrible financial crisis; in 1904 he became the Methodist Episcopal resident bishop in Chicago. Dr. Herbert A. Howe became acting administrator while the trustees talked Henry Augustus Buchtel (pronounced "Book-tel") into rescuing the floundering institution, which was trying to deal with debts that had grown to $170,000. Buchtel had pastored Trinity Methodist Church downtown and was known to the Denver community as a seasoned preacher, exceptional fund-raiser, and visionary. He was installed as the university's third chancellor on February 5, 1900, and

stayed for twenty years. When he arrived, he found the university mortgaged, faculty salaries in arrears, and a debt of approximately $200,000. Buchtel plunged in, doing what he did best—orating and working the crowds who came to hear him. He gave talks on every conceivable topic to any group willing to listen and reaped a considerable amount of money in return. By April he had raised $50,000. But despite Buchtel's diligent efforts over the summer, the trustees faced the prospect of foreclosure of the mortgage on University Hall, and the sale of the hall was set for November 25. The only bidder was an industrialist who wanted to turn the building into a glue factory. Somehow, this horror was staved off. Buchtel and his board wiped out the $200,000 debt in three years.

Shortly after his inauguration, Buchtel lost the Iliff School of Theology, then still a part of the university. Buchtel believed himself to be head of both schools and apparently challenged some policies or administrative moves made by Bishop Warren and Iliff's president A. H. Briggs, who accused Buchtel of trying to devour the Iliff School of Theology and subordinate Briggs's administration to his.[19] The Iliff School of Theology closed in 1900. When it reopened in 1910, while Buchtel was still chancellor, it was as a separate institution.

In 1906 Republican legislators approached Chancellor Buchtel about his running for governor of Colorado. Buchtel accepted the challenge on condition that he would be a one-term governor only. He campaigned on a platform of corruption-free government and promised his audiences that he would be under no commitment, obligation, or pledge to any individual, organization, or corporation of any kind. On November 6, he won the election by 20,000 votes. At mid-morning the student body and faculty descended on his house; two men lifted him to their shoulders and carried him away to the chapel, where a throng of jubilant well-wishers waited to congratulate him. Afterward the young women students "tied long ropes to a dogcart and hauled the governor-elect all over the campus at a breakneck speed. When the girls tired, the faculty unexpectedly took hold of the ropes and gave the dignified Chancellor another ride over the campus. Then the whole crowd took a long trolley ride over the city. College adjourned until the next Monday."[20] Buchtel remained chancellor of the university but

Buchtel Bungalow, University of Denver chancellor's residence and, for two years, Colorado's "governor's mansion." *Photo by Millie Van Wyke*

appointed Reverend Charles F. Senter to act as field secretary in his place while he was governor.

Buchtel took office as governor January 8, 1907, at Trinity Church, which he had built twenty years before. The question soon arose as to whether Buchtel would leave University Park and move downtown in order to be closer to the state house, but he and Mrs. Buchtel decided to remain in the University Park bungalow they had just completed. Thus, their home at 2100 South Columbine became the state of Colorado's "governor's mansion" from 1907 to 1909. Political figures were frequent visitors, bringing the little town of University Park close to the major events of the day.

Reverend Buchtel's health began to fail in 1917, and in 1920 he resigned as chancellor. He died poor and in debt on October 22, 1924, but he had said earlier, "If I had the privilege of living my life over I do not see how I could make it better. . . . I have done my best and I have no regrets." Mrs. Buchtel sold the house to the university and the Buchtel Bungalow was placed on the National Register of Historic Places in November 1988.

From South Denver's earliest days, the people insisted on having parks and were disappointed when Mayor Vaughn's administration failed to provide them

with more of them. Nevertheless, Jewell Park, which evolved into Overland Park, filled the demand for horseracing and large events, and the Fleming's Grove grounds at the town hall met the need for a smaller neighborhood park. In 1895, after the town was annexed, the city of Denver tore down the hose house (Fleming's old barn) and renamed the park in memory of James H. Platt, a well-known industrialist (founder of Equitable Accident Insurance Company and the Denver Paper Mills Company) who had drowned in a fishing accident in June 1894. Reinhardt Schuetz, Denver's first landscape architect, formally designed Platt Park into one of Denver's finest small parks around a bandstand the Barcus administration had built for $118. Fleming's wonderful trees, the *Denver Times* claimed, "would be giants of the forest if there were any forests here. Nothing more lovely could be imagined than their grouping and the arrangement of shrubbery and lawn in this park. It is claimed to surpass in its smaller territory anything that can be seen at City Park. . . . Platt Park is very popular and is surrounded by enough people to keep it thronged every summer day. Children gather there to play and women wheel babies into its shade." But its very smallness caused it to be sometimes overlooked by the city, and its flower beds

Sarah Platt Decker Library.
Photo by Millie Van Wyke

were planted with leftovers from larger parks.[21] For many years Temple D. Kuykendall, the Town of South Denver's parks commissioner from 1891 to 1893, was custodian of Platt Park. Kuykendall, a favorite with the children of the neighborhood, moved into the former Fleming mansion and town hall with his wife and son Arthur and cared for his beloved park until his death in 1900.

The Fleming mansion was then occupied by the South Side Woman's Club, organized April 17, 1897, as a branch of Sarah Platt Decker's Woman's Club of Denver. Louise K. Salcer was the South Side branch's first president. The club's primary goal was to establish a library in South Denver, and the women immediately began a book drive. Once a week they carried donated books, coal, and kindling to the mansion. They would then start a fire in the fireplace and gather around it to sort books and set up their library in one of the rooms.

In 1913, the Denver Public Library built a branch in Platt Park and fittingly named it the Sarah Platt Decker Library in honor of the widow of James Platt, who had remarried Westbrook Decker. A well-known suffragette, clubwoman, and lecturer, Sarah Platt Decker had died just the year before, in 1912. She was the first woman to lie in state at the Colorado State Capitol for her contributions to the city as the first president of the Woman's Club of Denver, first woman on the Colorado Civil Service Commission, president of the State Board of Charities, and a past president of the National Federation of Women's Clubs.[22]

The South Side Woman's Club happily transferred all the books they had collected for sixteen years from their library into the new building. Built with Carnegie funds at a cost of $22,000, Decker Library was the third branch library erected in Denver and the only one out of eleven built between 1913 and 1929 to be faithfully preserved. Decker Library was patterned after the home of Anne Hathaway, William Shakespeare's wife, in Stratford-Upon-Avon, England. Architects Willis Marean and Albert Norton designed a V-shaped English cottage with flower beds and a raised grassy courtyard in front of the gabled entry. English touches included tapestry brickwork adorned with woodbine, massive brick chimneys, and a gabled green tile roof. Inside, the English cottage theme was reinforced by a large fireplace, leaded glass windows, and a vaulted ceiling with heavy oak beams.[23] Two large paintings, "Lady of the Lake and the Sword Excalibur" and "The Pied Piper of Hamelin," are by Dudley Carpenter. The Sarah Platt Decker Branch Library became a municipal landmark

The Town of South Denver

in 1985.

In 1914 the Denver Parks Department formally turned the Fleming mansion over to the South Side Woman's Club as custodians of the building and remodeled it into a civic building for use by the neighborhood. The club furnished the house, and only the president was authorized to schedule community events. The South Side Woman's Club used the Fleming mansion as its headquarters for fifty-seven years and "developed quite a proprietary feeling" toward the structure. At one point this resulted in an argument with the city of Denver, who had ordered the building condemned. The plan was to tear the building down and erect a more modern structure. But the club was adamant about keeping the historic building and "after much bitterness" the city remodeled it to include restroom facilities.[24] In the mid-1950s the South Side Woman's Club purchased a former church building at 2026 South Williams for $10,000 and converted it into their present clubhouse. For more than ninety years the club had served the community by granting scholarships to college students, sponsoring Red Cross classes, and furnishing Christmas baskets to the impoverished. In the past the club provided milk to babies of needy families and made clothing and supplies for two world wars.

After the South Side Woman's Club vacated the Fleming mansion, it stood empty for a few years until the city converted it into a neighborhood recreation center in 1957. Today Platt Park's community center and mansion are reserved for residents aged fifty and over. Pool tables fill what was once the Fleming family's living room and later the office where mayors Vaughn, Shattuck, and Barcus received the town's citizens. The 107-year-old Fleming mansion was designated a Denver Landmark on November 26, 1973. Its original fireplace is still there. Terracotta details around the chandeliers are original, and some of the windows still have original Belgian glass. The handmade wrought-iron jail door was given to the scrap iron drive during World War II.

Platt and Overland parks weren't enough for the fun-loving people of South Denver in the late 1890s. They wanted a large, central park, and much discussion and argument went on about choosing its location. Once again, the Vaughn administration's original choice, Smith's Lake, was chosen for what was to

become Washington Park, this time by park commissioner Henry Young, who lived in South Denver; Charlotte Gallup's son Perry, a member of the board of park commissioners; and Alderman Frank Bailey, owner of Myrtle Hill, which adjoined the site.

Laura Smith Porter had inherited Smith's Lake and supposedly its lease from her father, John W. Smith, but still the lease could not be found. By 1897, the city had paid practically the value of the lease and wanted the land. As early as August 1890, the *Denver Republican,* reporting on the Vaughn administration's efforts to secure land for parks, warned that "if the South Denver Board of Trustees do not secure the Smith lake property, that sheet of water, with its surroundings, will be turned into a resort. . . . It is a matter of much surprise to all residents of South Denver that Smith's lake has never been improved. It is situated nearer the business center of Denver than any other."[25] Rumors had resurfaced that someone with "plenty of capital" was trying to lease or buy the Smith Lake property to build a pleasure resort rather than the neighborhood park the residents wanted, and the park commissioners did not want this to happen.

Frustrated and hindered because of the ongoing problem in clearing the title, Mayor Thomas S. McMurray instructed city attorney George C. Norris to begin proceedings in October 1897 to condemn not only the twenty Smith acres in question but an additional forty more to the south. Perry Gallup anticipated that this transaction would bring the property into city hands quickly. The commissioners hoped "to have the dirt flying by the first of December, and wonderful changes will be made before spring. Trees, bushes, flower beds, and grass will work a wonderful transformation in this now barren land by summer," the *Daily News* reported.[26] But still the matter could not be resolved, and the park site remained bound up in legal difficulties until the summer of 1899.

Not all residents considered the Smith's Lake location ideal. It was "too much on one side of the residence portion, . . . on no prominent street or thoroughfare, and it would be hard to find," said "old resident" Mr. T. B. Aldridge in a letter to the *Denver Eye* in June 1899.[27] The editor agreed and suggested that the old Broadway Park Sanitarium grounds at Broadway and Jewell would be much more desirable. Here were twenty acres ideal for a park: it had never been subdivided, it had a lateral canal cut from City Ditch, and it had a number of large trees. Workers from the Woeber Carriage Works as well as the paper and cotton mills west of the South Platte River would be able to enjoy the park, and it was close to Grant, Milton, and Vassar schools. The greatest advantage, of course, was that it lay on South Broadway, the greatest thoroughfare in the state.

The city had its mind set on Smith's Lake, however, and dismissed the suggestion. Shortly after Aldridge's argument surfaced in the *Denver Eye,* the park commissioners finally acquired the coveted Smith's Lake property. A few weeks later, in July, the city purchased thirty additional acres from Kentucky to Mississippi avenues and Marion to Franklin streets, for $25,500. The *Denver Eye,* which had accused both the McMurray and the new Johnson administration of corruption and working some sort of graft scheme in the affair, considered this purchase a result of a political deal in which the creditors would take all the profits. Still fighting for the Broadway Park Sanitarium site, the *Denver Eye* deplored the Smith's Lake property:

> Thirty acres of bare land, lying above the city ditch, with no tree or even shrub upon it, and when they knew a lake cannot be made unless it is provided with a copper bottom, and when nothing resembling a park can be made in the next ten years; and at the same time abandoning the prettiest natural park site anywhere in Denver, are things the people of South Denver would like to know about and we will inform them. [28]

But Johnson's park commissioners formalized the park purchase, picked Washington as its name from a list that included Broadview, Sylvan, Ramona, and Ouray, and began landscaping in August. The *Denver Eye* graciously capitulated, noting that the name chosen for the park was in honor of our first president, George Washington. The editor decided that "the cherries having all been picked and the tree cut down it is time to bury the hatchet." Washington Park, just fifty acres then, became a reality.

Reinhardt Schuetz, who had designed Platt Park, also designed Washington Park, assisted by John B. Lang, its first superintendent. The Lang family moved into the Whitehead farmhouse on the property and Lang and Schuetz began the exciting task of creating a new park.

Lang, born and educated in greenhouse, landscape, and nursery culture in Germany, worked ten hours a day for $50 per month supervising workmen who made $40 per month. They graded the grounds with teams of horses pulling scrapers. Lang drove his horse-drawn wagon into the mountains to get evergreen trees and chokecherry and currant bushes and planted young maple, red oak, horse chestnut, Kentucky coffee, and golden rain saplings. Lang's son John, a boy at the time, enjoyed every minute of it. "Mr. Schuetz pedaled through the park on his bicycle, checking on the progress. He carried his lunch of walnuts in his pockets and would sit on a bench and crack them open as he watched the beginning of the transformation from barren prairie to green urban park," he recalled. [29]

Lang supervised the landscaping and planting as well as construction of children's playgrounds and built a toolhouse and barn near the Whitehead farmhouse. Although Lang was "making improvements as fast as he can and is bringing the park into line as an attractive pleasure resort," by 1902 the park was not frequented much because it was outside of the center of population "and somewhat difficult to access." The city continued to add more acreage over the next few years, and the *Denver Times* predicted that since new houses were being built nearer and nearer to it every year, the park will "soon be in the center of a thickly populated district." [30] Lang moved to City Park in 1906 and Adam Kohankie took over as superintendent of Washington Park.

Kohankie was a longtime resident of South Denver. He had voted in the 1886 incorporation election, had been a volunteer fireman with the Russell Hose House, and worked as a florist for John L. Russell at Broadway and Lincoln. As Washington Park superintendent, he oversaw the digging of Grasmere Lake in 1906 and surrounded it with willow trees. Over the next several years, he guided the construction of tennis courts, a bathhouse and bathing beach, a boat house and pavilion, and a lily pond and rock garden in the northeast corner.

Denver's first bathing beach opened on the north end of Smith Lake in 1911, but only men and boys could use it that first summer. Women had to wait until their half of the bathhouse was completed the next year. For two years a rope was strung down the center

Swimming at Washington Park. *Denver Public Library, Western History Department*

Wynken, Blynken, and Nod statue with the Eugene Field House in the background. *Photo by Millie Van Wyke*

of the beach, dividing it in half for separate use by males and females; each sex had its own pier as well. But in 1914 a new rule allowed men who wanted to swim with their dates to slip underneath the barrier to the women's side. This rule was of course immediately abused, and "mashers" took advantage of the rule to "make advances and fresh remarks." Mothers of teenage girls demanded privacy for their daughters and wanted the total separation of men and women reinstated. Instead, the park commissioners abandoned separate bathing altogether; that summer the commissioners opened the lake to mixed bathing and females were instructed to don skirted costumes and stockings. For thirty years, South Denver youth spent lazy summer days swimming in Smith's Lake and playing in the sand. A polio epidemic in the 1940s closed it down; it never reopened.

In 1917 the Daughters of the American Revolution brought to the park a cutting from the tree under which George Washington had taken command of the Continental Army in 1775 in Cambridge, Massachusetts. They planted this scion of the Washington elm next to the flagpole and surrounded it with a wrought-iron fence. To further pay tribute to George and Martha Washington, in 1926 city planner Saco R. De Boer designed a replica of the formal Martha Washington gardens at Mount Vernon, Virginia. Superintendant Kohankie laid out this garden on the north edge of Grasmere Lake, across the road from the Washington elm. The elm tree flourished for sixty-six years; when it died in 1983, the Peace Pipe Chapter replaced it with an oak tree.

The park once contained Denver's smallest branch library, located in the 1875 Eugene Field House just inside the east entrance at Exposition Avenue. Field was managing editor of the *Denver Tribune* from 1881 to 1883 and wrote verse and a column called "The Old Gossip." He lived in the frame house at 307 West Colfax Avenue for only a few months and never owned it. But he was well known, and when the city threatened to demolish the house in the late 1920s, Mrs. J. J. ("The Unsinkable") Molly Brown raised funds, bought the cottage, and moved it to Washington Park in 1930. It served the Washington Park community as a library until 1970, when it became too small and was vacated. The house is presently used for park-related meetings. The Eugene Field House, "noteworthy as the residence of a well-known poet and journalist with style and wit," was named a Denver Landmark in 1973 and placed on the National Register of Historic Places in 1979.[31]

One of the children's verses Field wrote was "The Dutch Lullaby," known by its first lines: "Wynken, Blynken, and Nod one night, Sailed off in a wooden shoe." Twenty years after its publication, Denver's Mayor Speer saw a statuette of the three children depicted in this poem in a Chicago art gallery, and discovered that it had been fashioned by Mabel Landrum Torry of Sterling, Colorado. The mayor commissioned her to make a life-sized copy in marble, and when it was finished in 1919, the Wynken, Blynken, and Nod statue was placed in the center of a small pool in the park. Years later it was moved to a grassy spot next to the Eugene Field House, where it remains.[32]

The historic Smith's Ditch in Washington Park remains an open channel, as it was originally designed and constructed in 1867, the only segment of the ditch that is still visible and not buried underground. Because of this and because Smith's Ditch "has character, interest and value as part of the cultural, economic, social, developmental and historic heritage, is associated with persons and historical events significant to the development and heritage of the City, portrays an era of Denver's earliest history, and constitutes an established and familiar feature of Washington Park and the surrounding neighborhood," the ditch from Virginia to Louisiana avenues was designated a National Historic Landmark in April 1977. The commemorative plaque can be found west of the Washington Park Community Center. In 1986 Washington Park itself was included in the National Register of Historic Places as part of the Denver Park and Parkway System.

The Washington Park Recreation Center, built in 1971 for $550,000, counts 200,000 visitors each year, and children adore the state-of-the-art playground equipment that was installed near the community center in 1989. To accommodate everyone safely, walkers and joggers navigate the parkway roads in a clockwise direction while bicyclists zoom around the mile-long park the opposite way. Picnickers, volleyball and tennis players, fishermen, lawn bowlers, sun worshipers, and flower lovers alike enjoy this beautiful

156-acre park, once considered so remote that no one would ever use it.

Athletic parks were also popular in South Denver as early as 1883 when exposition visitors watched baseball games at Broadway and Center Avenue near the hall. In 1901 John R. Crabb built a permanent baseball diamond, a bicycle track, and a 2,500-seat grandstand on the grounds and named the new field Union Athletic Park. Denver's six city league baseball teams used Union Park for their home field and the University of Denver teams practiced there. Exhibition games were popular; nearly 4,000 people came to watch the Boston Bloomer girls play an exhibition softball game that first summer. Union Park also hosted Denver's Western League for six games that season, four because of a fire at the team's own field at Sixth Avenue and Broadway, and two because it was too wet.

A dispute over training quarters in March 1903 closed Union Park for a few months, but when it reopened that summer it sported new tents and a dance pavilion. The owners brought band concerts and vaudeville shows to the park as well as athletic events. For two decades circuses and bicycle races drew huge crowds.[33] Later, as Merchants Park, high school and collegiate football and baseball games and track and field events took place on its fields. At one time in its history the park was converted into an airdome ice skating rink, and for two unusual days, was used for auto polo.

As the community continued to grow in the first years of the new century, residents added still more schools and churches to meet educational and religious needs. Students in the Platt Park area attended McKinley School on the corner of South Logan Street and East Louisiana Avenue. This five-room "handsome new school for the South side" opened in March 1903 and accommodated 250 pupils.[34] At one time, two rooms on the second floor were used for open-air classes. The present structure at 1230 South Grant replaced the original building in 1979 and absorbed Thatcher students as well when that school closed. The contemporary, tri-level McKinley-Thatcher building, designed by James Sudler and Associates and constructed by R. G. Fisher Company, uses 122 solar panels on its south side to convert solar energy to heating and cooling functions.

Two other elementary schools were built later to accommodate west Washington Park students. The present brick Asbury School was built on South Marion Street and Evans Avenue in 1925 to replace a portable frame classroom building erected earlier near Evans and South Lafayette. After this school quickly became overcrowded, the sixth grade students were sent to Reynolds School and the kindergartners used a house where the custodian later lived until an addition could be erected in 1927. Asbury expanded again in 1947.

Steele School was built at 320 South Marion Street Parkway in 1913 and opened with 223 pupils and six teachers. This building replaced the original Lake View School that may have existed as early as the mid-1880s. The new school was named for Colorado Supreme Court judge and former governor Robert Wilbur Steele, "a model, an inspiration, a friend, and helper to young men in Colorado."[35] Steele School was remodeled in 1929; when this addition was completed, the school had eighteen classrooms, a library, an auditorium, a gymnasium, and a kindergarten, and 535 pupils and fifteen teachers.

The Rocky Mountain region's first major Catholic seminary, St. Thomas, was founded in South Denver in 1907 under the auspices of the Society of the Congregation of the Mission of St. Louis, Missouri, known as the Vincetians. St. Thomas Seminary's original four-story red brick building at 1300 South Steele Street was designed by Denver architect John J. Huddart. All aspects of the seminary were housed there, including living quarters for its first rector, Father Thomas Levan, four faculty members, and the students.

Twelve students arrived in the fall of 1908 for a six-year program of philosophy and theology. After classes the seminarians helped grow alfalfa and potatoes and tended to pigs and cattle on this huge chunk of prairie bounded by Steele and Monroe streets and Arizona and Florida avenues. This little "farm" served them well for eighteen years. In 1926 architect Jacques Benedict, who had designed Rosedale School the year before, built the 138-foot-high Tihen Memorial Tower. Sculptor Enrico Licari topped it with twelve-foot-high angels on each corner. In 1930 Benedict used over 200 different shapes, sizes, and colors of brick in designing the Renaissance revival St. Thomas Seminary Chapel next to the tower. Seventeen of its stained glass windows came from the world-renowned Franz Meyer studio in

McKinley School. *Courtesy Denver Public Schools*

Asbury School. *Courtesy Denver Public Schools*

Steele School. *Courtesy Denver Public Schools*

Munich. A Botticino marble altar, a $15,000 gift of Paul Mayo, was hand-carved in Italy from eighth-century designs.[36]

The seminary became licensed to award Bachelor of Arts and Master of Arts degrees in the 1920s, and it began producing most of Colorado's priests. During the 1940s and 1950s Bishop Urban J. Vehr created forty-three new parishes and hoped to staff them with St. Thomas graduates. This increase in enrollment strained the facilities of the seminary. Designed for 140 students, the seminary housed 220 in 1953 and was forced to turn students away. To alleviate the overcrowding, a recreation center, a three-story

Theology Building designed by Benedict's protégé John K. Monroe, and a 150,000 volume library were constructed in the 1950s. Enrollment dwindled to thirteen in 1988, however, so the seminary welcomed the general public as tuition-paying students. It also sold off part of its land to a private developer. St. Thomas Seminary was named to the National Register of Historic Places in 1989.

Denver's climate, described in St. Thomas's first catalog as "high, dry mountain air, bracing and invigorating" was blatantly used to entice "young priests broken in health" to its school. This practice of exploiting Denver's location as a cure for all sorts of respiratory problems in order to settle the empty prairies had been going on for some time. As early as 1868 Denver's board of trade (the chamber of commerce of the 1860s) and real estate developers attracted thousands of pulmonary disease sufferers to the city in this way. By the 1880s so many of these "consumptives" had found Denver that the city began discouraging such heavy influxes of "weak, dependent people." But Denver's reputation as a cure-all could not be shaken, and the "one-lunged army" grew to 30,000 by 1893.

Few advertisements for South Denver failed to mention that the pure air of Myrtle Hill and University Park, away from the smoke and smelters and dust and noise of Denver, was beneficial to people with weak lungs. Because most of the tuberculosis sufferers were poor, they could not afford private sanitariums, and until 1899 when the National Jewish Hospital for Consumptives opened its doors to needy patients in the general public, patients were cared for at home. After the turn of the century, two ethnic groups, the Swedish and the Dutch, opened their own private sanitariums on the south side.

By 1880 there were 4,000 people of Swedish extraction living in Denver. A small group of them organized the First Methodist Episcopal Church at Twenty-second and Court Place downtown. In the 1890s this little congregation sponsored the South Denver Swedish Methodist Episcopal Church, which met for many years in the Odd Fellows Hall. In 1913, Carl Eklund purchased the original Cameron Methodist Episcopal Church building on Washington Street and Iowa Avenue for $1,000 and renamed it St. Peter's Methodist Episcopal Church. The Swedish people worshiped here until 1917, when they sold it to a private party and went back to their mother church in the city. (This downtown congregation eventually grew into Emmanuel Methodist Episcopal Church and moved to Yale Avenue and Downing Street in 1945.)

Another group, the Scandinavian Club, was also active in South Denver by 1892 and also held regular meetings in the Odd Fellows Hall. The club evolved into the Scandinavian Methodist Episcopal Mission a few years later, and for a time, around 1907, both the church and the mission met in the same building but as two separate entities. The mission disappeared from record in 1910.

In 1905, Dr. Charles A. Bundsen founded the Swedish Consumptive Sanitorium (now Swedish Hospital) in Englewood. At first a collection of one-room cottages, the sanitorium built a sixteen-room pavilion with open sleeping porches in 1920. The need was so great that a few years later about 3,000 patients applied for the thirty available beds.

About the time that Dr. Bundsen's sanitorium opened, another religious group of about a dozen families, the Dutch Reformed, also began arriving in Denver from the Netherlands or other Dutch settlements, called *kolonies,* in the United States. They, too, had at least one member of each family seriously ill with tuberculosis or asthma. A few settled in Berkeley in northwest Denver and began informal church services in the Dutch language at the home of Klaas van Wyk. Berkeley was advertised as a healthful suburb with clear air; the Dutch may have chosen this location for the tuberculosis tent colony at about Forty-fifth and Zenobia streets as well as its liquor restrictions. Later, other immigrants in South Denver and Englewood joined them in the basement of the English (formerly German) Reformed Church at Seventeen Avenue and Emerson Street for Christian Reformed worship services. In the summer of 1907 the little congregation received a welcome visit from a man who was to lead them for the next forty years, Reverend Idzerd Van Dellen, minister of the Christian Reformed Church. Van Dellen's wife, Margaret, suffered severely from tuberculosis in the Netherlands, and in 1893 she emigrated alone to the Territory of New Mexico on her physician's advice to live with a Dutch Reformed kolonie near Maxwell City. Idzerd stayed behind to finish his seminary training. They were married in Maxwell City, where he pastored a small congregation and built a small tuberculosis sanitorium. The community failed to develop, however, and the settlers moved away. The sanitorium closed as well.

During Van Dellen's visit he urged the Dutch settlers to live together in a *kolonie* of their own in an agreed-upon neighborhood and called for a vote among the ten men (patriarchal heads of families) who had voting privileges. At this historic meeting, five chose Berkeley and five chose South Denver. Van Dellen, in the gentle, persuasive manner he would use so convincingly again and again to build churches, schools, and another sanitorium, managed to sway a

St. Thomas Seminary. *Photo by Millie Van Wyke*

Berkeley vote to "perhaps the more desirable" South Denver, and the seeds of the present Dutch neighborhood in South Denver were planted. One Saturday afternoon whole families in their buggies followed a realtor to pick out a site suitable for a church and parsonage. At last they chose the corner of South Emerson Street and Colorado Avenue and built an inexpensive, almost temporary, Christian Reformed Church structure there in 1908. Most of the families kept their promise to relocate around their new church, and before long other Dutch Reformed families joined them, building their homes mostly along Clarkson, Emerson and Ogden streets, from about Louisiana to Evans avenues. Dutch merchants opened shops, grocery stores, and a bakery.

The Dutch Reformed church traditionally educated their children in their own schools, and Denver was no exception. As soon as Van Dellen had their first temporary church established in 1910, he organized twenty-two *begunstigers* (contributors) into the Denver Christian School Society. For six years they held summer schools in the Fleming's Grove School building until they could build a school of their own. In 1916 they erected the Denver Christian School on the corner of Florida Avenue and Clarkson Street. This structure housed all grades until the Denver Christian High School was built at Pearl Street and Evans Avenue in 1949, and later the Van Dellen Elementary School at Warren Avenue and Ash Street. The original building at 735 East Florida Avenue was sold to the Waldorf Schools.

By 1916 enough Dutch Reformed families had joined the Denver kolonie from other parts of the country, severely overcrowding their temporary church

First Christian Reformed Church, 1910, with the Van Dellen home on the left. Photo courtesy of First Christian Reformed Church.

building. Because most of the members were poor and sick, the little congregation was unable to gather enough funds to erect a new one. Reverend Van Dellen assured them that a new church would be built somehow. He moved the congregation into Alkire's Hall on the corner of Pearl Street and Iowa Avenue while he went on the road to raise the money from Reformed congregations in the Midwest. Speaking tirelessly and eloquently for several months, Van Dellen came home with $12,000 for a new church. The congregation built a new Christian Reformed Church at 1814 South Emerson Street and dedicated it in 1917. The beautiful electric pipe organ was purchased from W. J. Lameris's nearby Holland Music and Radio Store at 1469 South Pearl Street, just down the block from the Hotel Lincoln established in 1912 at 1475 South Pearl. Lameris sold pianos, organs, stringed instruments, and sheet music in his store, and he was the authorized Crosley radio dealer. He had learned piano tuning as an apprentice in the Netherlands and engaged in piano tuning in South Denver for several years before opening his popular shop. The Holland Bakery in the same block provided the community with its wonderful Dutch almond-filled pastries and Dutch Rusk, a thick toasted round eaten with a generous slab of cheese.

As the Dutch kolonie grew, it attracted enough Hollanders to warrant the beginnings of the Mission of the Reformed Church (a sister congregation to the Christian Reformed Church). This little band met also at Seventeenth and Emerson in 1911 with Rev. H. Vander Ploeg their pastor, but the next year they established the mission in the Odd Fellows Hall on Colorado Avenue and South Broadway. Rev. D. H. Fouse also served as pastor. On October 31, 1921, the First Reformed Church was formally organized and its forty-six members held services in the Alkire Hall at South Pearl and Iowa Avenue. Rev. J. N. Trompen and Rev. J. J. Vander Schaaf were its first pastors. Two years later the congregation built a basement church of their own at 1600 South Clarkson Street and completed the structure in 1925. Several additions have been added since then. These congregations held services in both Dutch and English for a number of years.

With so much illness, the people clamored for a consumptive hospital of their own, but after the failure of the sanitorium in New Mexico, Van Dellen hesitated to recommend building a second time. Denver already had twenty-one sanitoriums by 1911, including Swedish close by. Nevertheless, the Christian Reformed denomination opened the Bethesda Tuberculosis Sanitorium at 4400 East Iliff Avenue in 1913, and Reverend Van Dellen and the minister of the First Reformed Church served as spiritual advisors for many years. Affectionately known as "The San," Bethesda provided not only medical care for tuberculosis patients but also jobs for the Dutch community. When new antibiotics eradicated the disease, Bethesda converted to a mental hospital in 1948 and today serves the Denver community as a psychiatric health center.

By 1936, the Christian Reformed Church on South Emerson Street could no longer contain its thriving congregation and needed a second structure. Somehow it heard that the Cameron Methodist congregation was about to default on its $15,000 debt, so the Dutchmen stood ready, money in hand, to take over the 1600 South Pearl Street property from the bank. This unsettled the Methodists and galvanized them to save their church. An energetic group of fund-raisers organized and began soliciting. In just five months the group was able to pay off the mortgage and save the building. The Dutch residents then built the Second Christian Reformed Church, at 1895 South Ogden, at the opposite end of the block from the First Christian Reformed Church.

By 1950, some 500 Dutch families lived roughly between Downing and South Broadway streets and Evans to Louisiana avenues. South Emerson Street, where three of their churches and two schools existed within a five-block radius, was nicknamed Dutch Boulevard. The neighborhood itself was known as "Little Holland."

One Dutch immigrant who was so ill that he was not expected to live past the age of forty played a vital part in the development of Denver's beautiful park system. Trained as an engineer in the Netherlands, Saco Rienk De Boer developed tuberculosis; he then turned instead to studying botany in Holland and horticulture in Germany and opened his own landscape architecture office. But his doctors and family thought he would die, so they sent him first to Maxwell City, New Mexico, and then to Denver. De Boer was horrified by America's ugliness and determined to beautify his little corner in some way "before he reached forty" and would die, as his physician predicted. De Boer secured a job with the Denver parks office and in 1910 he was chosen to replace Reinhardt Schuetz as parks planner for Mayor Robert W. Speer's administration. For the next several years Speer and De Boer worked to give Denver's parks and roadways a thorough face-lift. De Boer didn't like the way engineers had staked out a winding road at the north end of Washington Park, so one evening he and a helper stealthily pulled out the stakes and reset them into graceful, flowing lines. De Boer realized that automobiles and parks did not mix, so he surrounded the huge lawn with posts to keep motorists out.

De Boer happily laid out flower gardens and planted trees in Washington Park until 1912, when Mayor Speer was voted out of office and the new administration ordered all work in the park stopped. De Boer had already brought in trees for Evergreen Hill at the north end, so he disobeyed orders and planted them anyway.[37] When Speer was once again elected as mayor in 1916, De Boer was reinstated as landscape architect. In 1919, De Boer opened his own landscape office in the tramway building in partnership with Walter Pesman. Five years later they dissolved the partnership and De Boer set up his own business in the chicken house next to his red brick house at 515 East Iliff Avenue. He planted a small show garden in front of it, built a freestanding tower similar to the tower in his hometown in the Netherlands, and opened for business as S. R. De Boer & Company, City Planners and Landscape Architects.

In 1962, the city of Denver named a narrow park at Harvard Avenue and High Street De Boer Park in his honor. The city had purchased the land on February 14, 1957, for $1,000. De Boer remained active in his role of beautifying the city until his death in 1974 at the age of ninety-one.

Overland Park also flourished. Businessman Henry Wolcott laid out a nine-hole golf course around the racetrack in 1896, even though this was a time when golf was still new and ridiculed as a sissy game. The course, described as a "picturesque oasis in a sandy desert half an hour's journey from the center of the city," was popular with both men and women. Situated nicely between the Merchant Mill Ditch and the South Platte River, the course had plenty of water to keep its turf green. The clubhouse, shaded by tall cottonwood trees, was "the center of society life of Denver, the Mecca of temporary sojourners and of an extensive leisure class. To drive out in the afternoon, play a round or two, partake of supper on the spacious veranda, and enjoy the gentle snow-cooled breezes which float down from the peaks is sufficiently alluring to have brought up 300 members, with a discouragingly long waiting list."[38] The club also had two tennis courts, bowling alleys, and a small ballroom, making it a well-equipped country club.

But horse racing remained Overland's fundamental reason for its existence. "Railbirds" came to watch horses work out every morning, bettors won a little and lost a little, wealthy gentlemen raced each other down Broadway on the way home, and jockeys sometimes got into trouble. One June day a delighted audience watched as an angry jockey, ruled off the track for some irregularity, dashed up the stairs to the judges' stand and struck the starter with a vicious blow. In response, official judge Fred Mulholland's right foot "landed on the bosom of the obstreperous youth's pantaloons and his descent was meteorlike. The band then struck up 'A Hot Time,' and the people loudly cheered as the fresh strippling sneaked off."[39]

On racing days, South Broadway was crowded with "small traps weaving skillfully around the omnibuses and tallyhos. High-wheeled bicycles, later smaller wheeled, were sometimes barely visible through the dust."[40] Some of the more prosperous men who owned fast driving horses and vehicles with pneumatic tires even raced each other through the traffic. The *Denver Eye* remarked, "If these men were a lot of poor cusses they would be 'run in' forthwith for fast driving, but being of the soft-hand and kid-glove persuasion gives them license to set any kind of a pace without fear of being molested."[41] One of these gentlemen was undoubtedly millionaire judge Ernest A. Colburn of Colorado Springs. The discovery of gold in Cripple Creek was influential in the state's recovery from the 1893 depression and made fortunes for mining investors such as Colburn. With his Cripple Creek money, he moved his family to Denver and built a now-demolished house at 973 Logan as well as the Colburn Hotel in front of the house and the Cosmopolitan Hotel downtown. He also bought fifteen of the finest horses (the fastest was "Katie Medium") and beautiful vehicles and entered them in trotting races at Overland Park with himself in the driver's seat. Lacking stables for his horses, he decided to build barns and stalls near the track, at South Broadway and Florida Avenue. But attempts in 1899 and 1901 to erect a corrugated barn and twenty-five-stall training stables met with fierce opposition from Alderman Frank Bailey, the Southside Improvement Society, and property owners who feared stables would depreciate property values. But Colburn finally prevailed and built the two barns with haylofts, probably the next year. From here he trotted his thoroughbreds down South Broadway and Jewell Avenue into Overland Park for a few years, until racing was outlawed in 1908.

By this time Colburn had become interested in automobiles, had formed his own company, and with his sons Ernest, Jr., and H. C. Colburn, had produced the Colburn automobile between 1907 and 1911. The judge sold his South Broadway stables in 1926, and since then the barns have housed antique stores. When horse racing was legally restored in 1948, Colburn raced his trotters at City Park until he was ninety years old.

Overland Park went through many changes when automobiles and airplanes replaced golfing and horse racing in the early 1900s. A sturdy new grandstand with twenty private boxes replaced the old one in 1901, but a new betting shed erected at the same time was a bit more flimsily built. That summer a freak wind picked up the shed and dropped it down on the people

Saco R. De Boer. *Denver Public Library, Western History Department*

inside, breaking bones and bruising heads in the process. In 1902 Wolcott moved his golf club to First Avenue and University Boulevard, which became the Denver Country Club, and the once-elegant Overland clubhouse housed jockeys, later became a boardinghouse for cotton mill workers, and then burned down in January 1903. The stables were used until racing was outlawed and then were used again during World War I when the Colorado Cavalry tented there. They burned down in 1934.

The public turned from racing horses to racing anything mechanical that came to be invented. Although members wheeled out to the club on their bicycles over a pleasant path along Broadway, bicycle races were not held at Overland because of the sand. But motorcycles were. In 1913 a thousand members of the Federation of American Motorcyclists competed on Overland's one-mile dirt track for professional and amateur races, the first and only time the national motorcycle races were held in Denver.

As automobiles became popular, Denver men vied with each other on the track at speeds up to thirty-five miles an hour. Local mechanics built special engines and chassis for these early race cars, but other cars were little more than wagons equipped with two-cylinder engines. In 1904 "Dusty Daredevil" set a record by making his car go a mile a minute—on an unbanked track. Auto races were held at Overland for several years, the last big one in 1925, when a one-hundred-mile race lured eight of the greatest auto racers of the time, who vied for the $10,000 cash prize money.

Once machines appeared at Overland, it was only a matter of time until someone took a machine into the air, making Overland Park the scene of the very first airplane flight in Denver. In 1909 a fair and exposition at Overland Park featuring Derby Day for horse lovers, auto races, mineral exhibits, and prizes for best jellies drew 110,000 paid admissions for the week. Many were drawn there by the promise that balloonist Ivy Baldwin would hang suspended from the gas bag of his balloon in a Stanley steamer auto going at full speed. But on the first day Baldwin's gas generator failed, and on the second day it filled the balloon until it burst.

Playing golf at Overland Park, about 1897. *Denver Public Library, Western History Department*

In February 1910 a French aviator named Louis Paulhan assembled his Farman flying machine at Overland Park while hundreds of people watched all day, shivering in the grandstand. At sundown, the plane started up, shot up a runway, and disappeared toward Ruby Hill—all in a matter of seconds. They had seen a historic flight, nevertheless. In November three American barnstormers flew their Wright biplanes in a three-day show that was far more satisfactory. Arch Hoxsey stayed in the air a full twenty minutes the first day. But the second day, November 18, 1910, Ralph Johnstone plummeted to his death when a wing collapsed as he made two spiral turns over the park and the plane crashed on Delaware Street.

In 1917 Colorado's National Guard trained intensively at Overland, and the park was renamed Camp Baldwin for the duration of World War I. Over 1,100 members of the First Colorado Cavalry Regiment trained there and housed their mounts in the old stables. After the war the City and County of Denver bought Rufus Clark's old homestead "for a great athletic field and park and for a great new bathing beach," according to an excited editor in the February 8, 1919, *South Denver Eye and Bulletin*. The city paid $40,000 in cash for the west fifty-five acres along the river with intentions to use the gravel from the riverbed to resurface streets. After excavating the gravel, the *Eye* reported, the city would fill the cavity with "the greatest outdoor swimming pool in the country and a bathing beach, the Platte river furnishing the water." The city had eighteen months to pay the balance of $45,500 for the remaining 105 acres of the 160-acre tract. For a few years the park was a popular motor camp for tourists, with vacationers often settling in for long stays. The tourist camp was free and included a three-story clubhouse, ballroom, restaurant, bathrooms, a barber shop, a grocery store, and laundry. The park's main entrance was on South Santa Fe Drive at Colorado

Louis Paulhan flew his yellow Farman biplane, the first airplane to fly in Colorado, at Overland Park in February 1910. *Littleton Historical Museum*

Motor-camp entrance to Overland Park in the 1920s. *Denver Public Library, Western History Department*

Vacationers from other states camped at Overland Park, where they enjoyed all the necessary amenities free of charge. *Denver*

Avenue. In the early 1930s the city closed the auto camp and plowed up the track for the turf of the nine-hole golf course, which opened to the public in 1932. The course was enlarged to eighteen holes in 1957.

Rufus Clark, farmer, landowner, town trustee, prohibitionist, community builder, and in his own way one of Denver's movers and shakers, died in 1910 at the age of eighty-seven. He had lived to see his potato field transformed into a park, his prairie land into a fine university campus, and the Town of South Denver into one of Denver's prime locations. He had witnessed the conversion of horsepower to machines and, had he lived a little longer, would have seen the rise of industry along South Broadway, just blocks from the little shack he had built on the bank of the South Platte River nearly fifty years before.

Rufus Clark left the bulk of his nearly $500,000 estate to the Rufus Clark and Wife Theological and Training School of Shenge, Sierra Leone, West Africa, that he and Ella had established in 1886. Clark also left a curious bequest of $3,500 to the federal government to settle a forty-seven-year-old account. He stated in his will that he "knew a man in 1863 to have then defrauded the U.S. government of [this amount]. The fact was never reported by me, which I now feel in honor bound to do." Even his executor, Frederick S. Sweet, claimed that he had not the slightest idea as to the nature of the swindle on the government, nor did anyone else step forward to reveal whether an unknown person or Rufus Clark himself—in his preconversion life—was responsible for the crime. "The secret . . . went to the grave with the late Rufus Clark," said the *Denver Post*.[42]

Two of Rufus Clark's wives, Lucinda and Ella, and his daughter Mary Clark Walker are buried in the family plot at Denver's Riverside Cemetery. An inscription carved into the red stone says simply, "They lived and gave of their substance for the redemption of Sierra Leone, West Africa."

South Denver Gets Down to Business

The arrival of "forty carloads of prosperity" in the form of Ford automobile parts signaled the beginning of South Broadway's transformation into a major industrial district. During the summer of 1913 the Ford Motor Company of Detroit, Michigan, built a $200,000, four-story regional assembly plant at 900 South Broadway and the Ford Motor Company name went up on the white trim of the red brick building in December. The company had decided it would be cheaper to ship parts from Detroit than entire automobiles, and the Denver plant was one of the first of several such regional plants to be finished. The first forty train cars filled with automobile parts came in, festooned with banners that "advertised to the rest of the continent the fact that it was destined for Denver," and the shipment was met with great excitement. Three shifts of men unloaded six carloads of machinery and equipment for the plant, nineteen carloads of motors, three of wheels, two of tires, two containing auto tops, and one car each of paint and curled hair for upholstery, windshields, frames, hoods, lamps, radiators, and gas tanks. En route were another 110 carloads containing front and rear axles, fenders, and car bodies. Altogether there were enough parts to assemble 2,100 automobiles, and the entire lot was valued at half a million dollars.

The 150–200 employees turned out their first Model "T" Ford on December 11, completely put together on an "endless belt apparatus" on the second floor. From here the cars were distributed throughout Colorado, Wyoming, Utah, and New Mexico as well as selected counties in South Dakota, Nebraska, Kansas, Arizona, Nevada, and Idaho. The initial payroll of $15,000 per month with promises of more employment when the plant would run to capacity gladdened many a South Denver home that Christmas. The plant opened an up-to-date $300,000 addition "with every convenience and the best light and ventilating features of the finest factory buildings now erected" in 1916, raising production to about fifty Model T cars a day. This handsome structure of 130 x 223 feet had 140 feet fronting on South Broadway.

By 1917, the factory needed every inch of space for assembly work so the managers moved the sales and service department and the distribution agencies to eight different locations around Denver. A year later the United States entered World War I. Because the Ford Motor Company held large army contracts, it closed twenty-three assembly plants around the country, including Denver's, and switched to manufacturing war materials in Detroit. The Denver plant closed August 1918, putting 300 men out of work; only the stockroom remained open so that car repairs could continue in Denver. Although the employees hoped that the factory could be converted into making war products, this never materialized and it remained closed for five years. In 1923 the Ford Motor Company hired an additional 100 men and

Looking north on South Broadway, with the Gates Rubber Company and Montgomery Ward store on the left and the Ford assembly plant on the right. *Denver Public Library, Western History Department*

reopened the plant, intending to produce 150 cars per day. Workers assembled trucks, runabouts, coupes, touring cars, and limousines on a newly installed assembly line that featured three starting stations. "Workmen along the moving belt fit the various pieces of the car together, each part following the other until a complete machine comes off the end of the belt. Rollers whirl beneath the back wheels at the starting station and crank the engine. The car then goes out under its own power." To handle this increased output, Ford built a new steel and glass railroad loading station 387 feet long at the south end of the plant, and cars were put aboard trains for shipment throughout the region.[1]

By 1927 the plant had slowed down, but the company reorganized and enlarged it, providing work for between 600 when work was slow and 1,100 persons when it operated at full capacity. But the Great Depression affected the company adversely, and Ford virtually shut it down in January 1933. The little factory maintained about 100 employees through World War II, but when car sales boomed at the end of the war, the plant was regarded as outdated and too small. The Ford Motor Company closed it in 1947 and sold it to the Gates Rubber Company, which housed its print shop and rubber-hose division there. The remodeled 1913 building is now the Gates Corporation headquarters.[2] Today motorists rounding the I-25 curve

over South Broadway can clearly see the Gates name on the white trim of the red brick building that once bore the Ford Motor Company name and churned out Model T automobiles for the entire West.

A year after the Ford Motor Company opened its assembly plant on South Broadway, Charles Gates moved his Colorado Tire and Leather Company into a new building just across the street. Charles Gates had purchased a little retread shop at 1025 Broadway in 1911 and he and his brother John manufactured a steel-studded band of leather they called Durable Tread, which fastened onto the flimsy tires of the day to extend their mileage. Although Durable Tread proved a solid product, Denver had only a little more than 5,000 cars in the whole city, so the brothers launched aggressive marketing promotions. In 1912 they persuaded Buffalo Bill Cody to try the horse halters the Gates brothers made from leather scrap. With Buffalo Bill's help, the company became the largest halter manufacturer in the West.

In 1914 they made the first of their famous retreads out of fabric and rubber and the tire shop became a major enterprise. Charles and John bought six lots superbly located between the streetcar line and the railroad tracks, at 999 South Broadway. They constructed a small two-story building there, believing that would be ample space for a long time to come, and manufactured halters as well as a new product, the

The Town of South Denver

Half-Sole, a kind of rubber retread that was cemented over worn tires. Because the Half-Sole helped conserve rubber, the U.S. government classified it as a priority product during World War I, and sales boomed.

In 1917, the year the United States entered the war, Charles Gates also invented the first rubber and fabric V-belt. By September 1917 the Colorado Tire and Leather Company employed 535 men and added a new unit containing 100,000 additional square feet, which would increase to more than 1,000. In 1919 the company came out with the balloon tire, and its tire sales increased 40 percent in the next two years. When the automobile generator was introduced, the Gates corporation developed twenty belt sizes to fit 95 percent of all cars, setting an industry standard and doubling V-belt sales. The company "completed the factory" in 1919 by adding two new buildings and increasing the work force to over 1,500. But it expanded even more during the 1920s and was able to keep its employees and maintain profitability even during the 1930s, emerging from the Great Depression virtually unscathed. By 1934 the company had annual sales of $13 million, employed 2,500 people, and manufactured 4,000 items.

During World War II the Gates Corporation made belts for invasion boats; tires for jeeps, trucks and planes; parts for bombers, fighters, tanks, and ships; rubber buckets to hold TNT; and hoses to load and unload ships. When rubber became scarce, the company produced the country's first totally synthetic rubber belt and also used synthetic rubber in tires and other products. Research and engineering, together with aggressive promotions, propelled the company along, so that by 1948 the Research & Engineering Building was erected at 1001 South Broadway, and sales skyrocketed. From 1946 to 1954 sales grew from $59 million to $82 million, and the company employed 5,500 people in more than thirty interconnected buildings on fifty-three acres. The company diversified in the 1960s, buying the Learjet Corporation in 1967 and building Learjets for many years.

In 1974 the company phased out the tire business and produced the first completely sealed lead-acid rechargeable battery as well as several other products. By the end of the next decade Gates was a truly international company, and by 1989 it employed 18,000 people in forty-seven factories all over the world,

making V-belts, hoses, hydraulic products, batteries, fiber products, and auto accessory drive systems. The Gates Corporation recently ceased all manufacturing of automotive V-belts in Denver and moved its production operations out of Colorado. A few workers are producing about 450 sealed-lead batteries for automobiles and trucks per day in an experimental pilot project with Energy Products Company at its Denver plant, but most of the Gates Corporation's 1,800 remaining Denver employees work in headquarters and administrative positions.[3]

A different kind of industry also moved into the area at the same time as the Ford assembly plant and Gates arrived. After Horace Tabor's smelter at Virginia and the Platte River burned down in 1901, the site was occupied by the Colorado Zinc Company and Sutton, Steele and Steele Mining, Milling Machinery Company, which manufactured ore concentrators. In 1905 the South Platte River was rechanneled to accommodate these industries, and Merchants Mill ditch was filled in.

In 1914 the National Radium Institute constructed the United States' first experimental plant for radium processing on the Bailey-Tabor smelter site. Colorado had produced its own radium-bearing ores from mines in western Colorado as early 1903, but the carnotite ore had to be exported abroad because there was no facility in the United States to produce radium. Enormous costs prohibited the medical profession from importing the finished product—radium—for use in medicine and scientific research. The U.S. Bureau of Mines and Dr. Howard Kelly, a Johns Hopkins University cancer specialist, incorporated the National Radium Institute as the vehicle for this endeavor, and the facility went into operation in August 1915. The bureau quickly developed the nitric acid leach process, recovering over 90 percent of the radium contained in the carnotite. The process was so successful that a second building was added, but the plant now produced concentrate instead of processed ore. A total of 8.5 grams of radium and 298 tons of concentrate were produced before the plant closed in 1917. Eight grams went to Dr. Kelly and Dr. James Douglas of New York's General Memorial Hospital, and 0.5 grams to the Bureau of Mines. In 1923, the Minerals Recovery Company, a company engaged in treating and sacking metallic ore insulation, bought the plant but went out of business two years later. Petroleum companies

National Radium Institute. *Colorado Historical Society*

occupied the site through the 1930s, and the Platte River was rechanneled again.[4]

In 1941 the present owners, Robinson Brick and Tile Company, opened a brickyard on the site. George Robinson had founded the company before 1880 on several locations. In 1898 the company purchased Alex Miller's South Denver Brick Manufacturing Company near Mexico Avenue and Vine Street and operated it until the Valley Highway (I-25) was constructed through the property.

In the 1950s Robinson demolished the old National Radium Institute and built a grinding plant. In 1979, widespread low-level radioactive contamination was discovered at forty-four different locations in the Denver area, and the source was found to be the waste from production of radium on the Robinson property. The Bailey-Tabor smelters and various other chemical plants perhaps contributed to what is now recognized as one of the most polluted spots in Denver. Robinson moved its main yard to Englewood, and cleanup of the site, where John Simpson Smith and his Spaniards searched for gold along the banks of the pristine South Platte River in 1858, is under way.

Next to the Gates Corporation stands the former E. Burkhardt & Sons Steel & Iron Works, which built its plant at 787–795 South Broadway in 1917. Ernest Burkhardt had learned the trade in 1889 as a fence maker, and in 1914 he became part owner of the Denver Wire and Iron Works at 1401 Market Street. The next year he bought out his partner and employed his sons Harry, Herman, Louis, and Otto as draughtsmen,

superintendent, and credit manager. He renamed the company E. Burkhardt & Sons Iron and Wire Works and later to E. Burkhardt & Sons Steel and Iron Works to reflect the addition of steel in its products. Two years later Ernest and his sons moved into their new fabrication plant on South Broadway.

Ernest Burkhardt ran the company for two decades, until his death in 1938. Two of his sons, Ernest, Jr., and Louis, had preceded their father in death, and Herman and Otto and Otto's two sons, Alfred and William, took over operations. During World War II they convinced the U.S. Navy to use the Burkhardt plant to make parts for destroyer escorts. From 1942 to 1944 it manufactured diesel engine bases, destroyer bulkheads, hawser reels, vertical ladders, landing barges, and equipment for the destroyer vessels at their "shipyard of the Rockies." The Burkhardt company's production of "one of the most difficult and complex parts for fabrication" was of such uniformly high order that it was honored with the Army-Navy "E" (for excellence) award in 1943.

The plant expanded across Ohio Avenue, but in 1948 Vierling Steel Works of Chicago bought a large share of its stock and gained control of the steel fabricating, warehouse, and ornamental iron shops. The plant ceased production shortly afterward, and the plant remained vacant until the Regional Transportation District (RTD) purchased the property in 1976 for use as a maintenance facility.

The Burkhardt company's structural steel and ornamental iron can be seen on the City and County Building, South High School, Montgomery Ward, the Auditorium Annex, the State Capitol Annex, the police building, the Paramount Theater, and the Colburn Hotel.

The Shwayder Trunk Manufacturing Company (Samsonite Corporation) joined the Ford Assembly Plant, Gates Rubber Company, and the Burkhardt plant on South Broadway in 1924. Jesse Shwayder had discovered the potentials of luggage manufacturing many years earlier when selling trunks for a used furniture store owned by his father, Isaac. Jesse found the trunks easy to sell and opened his own retail luggage outlet in downtown Denver in 1903 at the age of twenty-one with $153 in savings and the promise of a month's free rent. He was successful enough selling several lines of hand luggage and trunks, which he

The Shwayder Trunk Manufacturing Company in 1924, renamed the Samsonite Corporation in 1965. *Denver Public Library, Western History Department*

manufactured himself, to pay himself $10 a week, open two more stores, and hire his father and brother Mark to run them.

But Jesse grew restless and convinced the Seward Trunk and Bag Company of New York to let him sell their products in the West. His first trip to Colorado Springs, Texas, Los Angeles and the West Coast, east to Butte, and back to Denver earned him $1,400 in profits. His father and brother Mark joined him and before long the three of them were selling $100,000 worth of merchandise a year. The company offered Jesse a job as sales manager in New York, so Jesse married Nellie Weitz in 1907 and moved to New York. A year later he was back in Denver preparing to start his own luggage manufacturing business.

Jesse bought used building materials from the company that was tearing down old buildings on the Civic Center site, and he built a tiny plant at 1050 South Santa Fe Drive in 1910 for his Shwayder Trunk Manufacturing Company. Jesse hired his brothers: Mark worked on sales, Maurice and Ben concentrated on manufacturing, and Sol was the company attorney. Jesse and Isaac went on the road selling trunks and inexpensive hand luggage. Jesse lost $2,000 the first year, broke even the second year, and began to show a profit by the third. Within seven years the company needed a larger plant, so Jesse and Maurice redesigned the Zang building at Sixteenth and Platte as a factory. Here Jesse created a suitcase that was as strong as the biblical Samson, giving the company its trade name of Samsonite. But the case retailed at $4.95, nearly $2 above comparable cases, so Jesse came up with a novel advertising gimmick to convince people to buy.

He had the suitcase photographed with Jesse, his three brothers, and his father—totaling 995 pounds—standing on it. Luggage sales boomed and from then on almost every product showed one or more Shwayders standing on it to show its strength.

By 1923 Jesse purchased seven acres of land at 1050 South Broadway from Gates Rubber Company to build a new plant. The 80,000-square-foot, one-story building was completed and equipped in 1924. Two years later Jesse realized $1 million in sales, and by 1927 the plant had 200 employees and was already the fourth largest luggage factory in the world.

During the depression years, the brothers changed the company name to Shwayder Brothers, Inc., and made everything they could think of to keep going in tough economic times, including sandboxes and license plates. Then Maurice bought two carloads of card table frames from an Idaho lumber company for little more than the cost to freight them to Denver, and by 1932 they had assembled and sold $100,000 worth of fiberboard-top card tables.

During World War II, the brothers retooled and converted the facilities to precision manufacturing of war materials. This included footlockers and ammunition boxes and later incendiary bombs, hand grenades, and fire generator units for the Chemical Corps. The bombs and grenades were armed elsewhere. Through research, the company found ways to speed up production, improve quality, and save money to boot, and for these efforts Shwayder Brothers, Inc., received the coveted Army-Navy "E" award. From 1941 through 1945 the company manufactured war goods worth more than $5 million. A decade later they geared up once again for war, this time in Korea, and produced more incendiary bombs during this three-year conflict than it had during all of World War II. In addition, they once again manufactured thousands of footlockers for all branches of the service. Following this war, the Shwayder brothers developed rocket carriers and fiberglass launching tubes for the Chemical Corps.

Between 1910 and 1970, Samsonite made more than 115 million pieces of luggage, introducing its classic tapered case in 1939, its hallmark Silhouette line in 1958, and its classic attaché case in 1962, a year after Jesse's son King David Shwayder became president of the fifty-year-old company. In 1965 the company name changed to the Samsonite Corporation; the company now employed 3,500 people. Two years later the company had a sales volume of $100 million and turned out 17,500 pieces of luggage a day. The seven-acre factory on South Broadway was bursting at the seams. In 1971 the company that had provided southsiders with jobs for forty-six years moved its plant out of South Denver to Montbello and sold its South Broadway property back to the Gates Corporation.[5]

As these large factories established themselves, other businesses located up and down South Broadway as well. Automobile-related businesses sprouted around the Ford assembly plant and H. L. Davis opened the South Denver Chrysler Company at 351 South Broadway in 1918, the first automobile sales agency to exist south of Cherry Creek. Linde Air Products manufactured nitrogen-filled tanks used in welding and steel cutting at their $100,000 plant at Exposition and South Broadway, built in 1917. And the Tramway Company employed 125 men at its car barns and repair and paint shops.

But travelers south of Alameda still contended with dust and chuckholes on Thomas Skerritt's dirt and graveled—and crooked—Broadway. The Denver Tramway Company had straightened the road and installed curbing in 1900 in order to lay new streetcar rails, paying nearly $7,000 in damages to storefronts, to avoid what the *Denver Eye* said would otherwise look like a streak of lightning. Now, twenty years later, businesses and civic associations, determined "to have better streets or know the vulnerable spots in the anatomy of folks who oppose them," campaigned for a paved road all the way to Littleton so that motorists could stop along the way to make purchases in South Denver "with smiles instead of frowns, without riding on a road that can sink in or throw you." By August 1923 Broadway was paved to Yale Avenue, making the six-and-a-half-mile boulevard the longest stretch of paved road in the city.[6]

In 1920, Union Park at Broadway and Center Avenue, home of baseball and football games, bicycle races, field and track events, circuses, outdoor concerts, and shows for nineteen years, was closed, and its tents, dance pavilion, and grandstands were torn down. Clinton A. Bowman's Merchants Biscuit Company purchased the park site for a new "Supreme Bakers" plant. However, Bowman decided not to build there after all, and the grounds remained idle for two years.

In the spring of 1922, the Denver Baseball Company, which planned to revive the defunct Western League baseball team at the Broadway and Sixth Avenue athletic field, found itself scrambling for a new site when the baseball company could not resolve a contract dispute. The six-acre Union Park, roomy and strategically located, was chosen over a dozen other possible locations, and president Al Price, secretary Arthur Oberfelder, and three other men began negotiations with owner Clinton Bowman. Within the space of one month, the baseball company agreed to lease the grounds for five years, to solicit the $20,000 needed for construction, and to fork over a large advance rental. Price convinced the Optimist Club and Rotary Club to work with similar organizations to raise the funds, which in turn may have persuaded Bowman to make a substantial contribution in exchange for naming the park after his company.

Architect Charles Redding drew up plans for a new athletic field, to be called Merchants Park, and contractor Henry Samson removed the stones and gravel from the old Union Park ball diamond and replaced it with smooth loam. Samson was forced to complete the park and its 8,000-seat grandstands within twenty-seven days, under threat of forfeiture if the structure was not ready three days prior to the opening of the first Western League game scheduled for April 25. Perhaps it was this haste that resulted in what one sportswriter called an ill-conceived "makeshift affair built with 'short dough, . . .' a dog heaven of pillars and posts that hinder the view from every seat, a playing field little better than a chunk of concrete, a

Babe Ruth pleases Denverites in an exhibition at Merchants Park. *Denver Public Library, Western History Department*

nightmare to spectators and players, and the worst ball park in America."[7] Home plate was in the southeast corner and "perhaps because of the higher value of property fronting Broadway, the right-field foul line measured a mere 318 feet . . . the left field measured 390 feet at the foul pole and it took a prodigious clout of 457 feet to reach the fence in dead center field," and the batters faced into the late afternoon sun.[8] The grassed infield was rock hard, and the outfield had no grass at all, which helped earn Merchants Park the nickname of "the brickyard."

The paying public, however, flocked to Merchants Park that first year to watch the Denver Bears, even though the team finished the season with a 63-105 record. The consortium of Colorado businessmen who owned the Bears sold the team to Denver businessman Milton Anfenger after the first season. Milton ran the front office for the Bears while his brother Fred operated the concessions and kept the grandstands in repair. An average of 5,000 fans poured in to Merchants Park each time the Denver Bears played or to watch the Young America League and the Old Timers and Legion games. But attendance began to fall in the late 1920s; to revive it, Anfenger installed electric lights around the ballpark in 1930. The first night game drew 6,000 fans into Merchants Park, and the Bears averaged 4,000 fans per contest over the next fifteen home games, winning nine of the games. But the success was short-lived; by August 1931 the Western League was in a shambles. The Anfengers were crushed by lack of support, even though the Bears achieved a combined 83-64 record in 1932, and that year the team folded again. Anfenger's Bears "had provided thrills and memories, but neither pennants nor consistent profits" in Anfenger's decade of ownership.

When professional baseball left Denver in 1932, Anfenger converted Merchants Park into a motorcycle track and spectators flocked to the races in the same numbers they had for baseball. The cycles traveled around the track at fifty to sixty miles per hour, providing enough thrills and spills to keep the spectators coming. With a heavy mortgage and no regular tenants, the Anfengers opened the park up to virtually any promoter who could pay some kind of rent. A series of events took place at the ramshackle stadium in the 1930s that defy description. The ballpark where fans had witnessed league baseball now held

exhibitions of donkey baseball and even motorcycle baseball, where everyone but the catcher and pitcher had to be on motorcycles, including the "runner." Anfenger added thirty-lap midget auto races to the "brickyard," further packing the already hardened outfield surface into the consistency of a speedway.

In 1944 Merchants Park became the home of the local semipro Victory League, a wartime baseball league that provided some of the best baseball played in the nation during World War II. But in 1943 high winds had torn loose a large section of the grandstand roof and sailed it across South Broadway, showering the street with debris. The press box also crashed into the street during the storm. The structure deteriorated further over the next two years and in 1945 the city condemned Merchants Park and ordered it to be torn down, citing defective bracing, rotting columns, defective railing, and seats and flooring defects that were extensive enough to be dangerous to life and limb. However, Milton and Fred Anfenger repaired the structure to the extent that the city withdrew its condemnation order and the park opened as usual for Victory League baseball the following spring.

The next year the Anfengers sold Merchants Park to realtors Arthur T. Cowperthwaite and J. F. McNaul, Jr., and the new owners spent nearly $20,000 on a new all-sod ball diamond, spacious restrooms, a new press box, better lighting, and new grandstand boxes to bring the Bears back to Merchants Park.

The Western League Denver Bears did return in 1947, but by this time Denver citizens wanted a larger, more modern athletic park. The move to relocate the Bears to a new ballpark quickly became a political issue as the 1947 municipal elections approached. The irrepressible *Denver Post* sports columnist Jack Carberry warned his readers against believing the "hogwash" of politicians who promised Denver voters a new ballpark because, he scoffed, only one of the nine councilmen knew the difference between a caddy and a third baseman. Incumbent mayor Benjamin Stapleton showed his support for baseball by stepping up to the Merchants Park home plate just before the election to swing a bat at a pitch from a young California congressman by the name of Richard Milhous Nixon. The seventy-seven-year-old mayor swung, missed, and fell flat on his face. Camera shutters clicked and the photograph of Denver's mayor sprawled in the dust appeared in *Life* magazine with the caption, "Mayor Strikes Out."[9]

Once the choice was made to build a new stadium, various sections of town vied for its location. The South Denver Civic Association, founded in 1913 as a political group "to see that politicians . . . did not slip one over on the people when they are not looking,"[10] resolved to keep the ballpark in South Denver. The group campaigned hard to convince the city to build a stadium between South High School and the University of Denver, but the city chose a site west of downtown for Bears Stadium. All was not lost, however; the South Denver Civic Association did convince the Denver Public Schools officials to establish its athletic fields on the site.

At the time of the 1947 election, the city also considered replacing the city auditorium. The South Denver Civic Association proposed that a new $2 million City Auditorium be erected at Mexico Avenue and University Boulevard. But although they won the backing of the Denver Centennial Auditorium Committee, the new mayor, Quigg Newton, decided instead to repair the decrepit city auditorium downtown. The association's grand plan to establish both the city ballfield and an auditorium between Franklin Street and University Boulevard and Mexico Avenue and the highway failed. A police station, Veterans' Park, and the Denver Public School athletic fields occupy the area today.

The Bears played at Merchants Park until the new Bears Stadium (Mile Hi) was finished in 1949. McNaul and Cowperthwaite sold Merchants Park to Richard L. Mark, who buried the historic ballpark under Denver's first suburban shopping center in the early 1950s. The single-story, L-shaped Merchants Park Shopping Center included Miller's Supermarket, Walgreen, Woolworth, and Joslin's stores. Together with the giant Montgomery Ward store next door, the sixteen stores served South Denver shoppers well for more than thirty years. Arthur Cowperthwaite later became chairman of the Colorado National Bank at Mississippi Avenue and South Broadway, which opened at that location in 1964, and retired in 1985 at the age of eighty.

While most companies built conventional manufacturing plants, stores, or baseball parks along South Broadway, Richard Pinkett spiced up the neighborhood by building a Normandy castle with steep roofs and two towers—what architect John Ohnimus thought a creamery should look like—at 1125 South Broadway in 1924. Pinkett called it the Bredan (bread 'n' butter) Creamery and sold dairy products from this unique structure for more than half a century. For a time he manufactured ice cream and also provided a drive-up window in its North Tower. Although these two innovations did not last long, the staple cottage cheese, buttermilk, and butter were delivered in brown and yellow dairy trucks as far as Greeley by 1940. During World War II, more than half of Bredan's butter production went to the government. In its last years as a creamery, Bredan was still turning out as much as ten tons of butter every week before being purchased by Beatrice Foods and closing in 1976. Attempts by civic groups to save the castle failed, and it was later demolished.

The phenomenal development of South Broadway as an industrial center convinced the Chicago-based Montgomery Ward company to build its eighth combination catalog and retail store at 555 South Broadway in February 1929. Fifty thousand people were on hand for the grand opening, an "epochal event amid blare of band and gasps of wonderment." Employees guided visitors on tours of the $2 million, eight-story, Spanish-style structure with its sixteen acres of floor space. The retail department on the first two floors handled department store merchandise in addition to auto supplies, tires, hardware, furniture, and drugs. The catalog department took up the next five floors, and the executive offices and employee cafeteria occupied the eighth floor. By 1937 the store employed over 1,500 people and had an annual payroll in excess of $600,000. Customers could order from the catalog over 190,000 items ranging from clothing and furniture to tombstones. Orders were shipped from the Denver store to sixty-five small towns in Colorado, Wyoming, Utah, and portions of nine other area states.

Montgomery Ward, a nonproducing business, did not have to convert to war measures during World War II, as did their steel, rubber, and footlocker manufacturing neighbors down the street. Instead, the Denver store became a victim of a long and nasty dispute between its Chicago headquarters and the president of the United States that resulted in a temporary takeover of the store by the U.S. Army. At issue was a December 1942 War Labor Board directive

The Montgomery Ward store on opening day. *Denver Public Library, Western History Department*

that ruled that all employee wages must be increased and that the union must be maintained in connection with war production. Sewell Avery, chairman of the Chicago board, protested that the government had no authority over a nonwar business such as Montgomery Ward and refused to comply. Because of Avery's refusal to hike wages, union members struck at stores in other cities but did not strike at the Denver store. After two years of fruitless negotiations and fearing that the strikes threatened the war effort, an exasperated President Franklin D. Roosevelt declared Avery guilty of "consistent and willful defiance" and of threatening the War Labor Board's "structure for impartial adjudication of disputes." The president then issued an executive order to the War Department to seize Montgomery Ward stores in seven cities, including Denver.

At 9:00 A.M. on December 28, 1944, six U.S. Army officers and a corporal, led by deputy war department representative Captain Harry W. Helioff from the prisoner of war camp in Greeley, marched into Montgomery Ward's South Broadway store and seized the retail department. (The catalog section was not affected.) When store manager T. O. Haugen arrived fifteen minutes later and found his office occupied by an army captain, he was urged to remain on the job and assist the army in running the store. The bewildered manager, caught in a fight he had nothing to do with and really didn't understand, put up a feeble protest at the injustice of it all. "I don't really know a great deal about the dispute which led up to this," he said. "The trouble apparently started in Chicago and will have to be settled there."[11] Nevertheless, he promised to cooperate, perhaps believing the occupation would be short-lived.

While Captain Helioff met with Haugen and union officials, soldiers posted notices of the government seizure throughout the store:

By direction of the President, the War Department has taken possession of this and certain other Montgomery Ward establishments in various parts of the country. I have been given the responsibility of operating these

The Town of South Denver

establishments and I expect the co-operation of every one of you.

You are to keep on performing your normal duties. . . . It is the duty of every Montgomery Ward employee and supervisor, as patriotic Americans, to assist the Army in carrying out this mission. We have a job to do and we are going to do it. Any person who interferes with our operation is subject to severe penalties under the law. I hope we will not have to invoke these penalties against anyone. I am counting on your help.

The directive was signed by Joseph W. Byron, Major General, USA, War Department Representative. The 350 employees went about their business as usual, and a clerk at the record counter even added a comic note by playing "The Army Made a Man Out of Me" repeatedly until her superiors ordered her to stop.

The next day Captain Helioff posed for photographs seated at Haugen's desk and a few days later, on January 3, 1945, the army announced that the government had assumed full control of the store. Haugen, who had remained as manager, soon found the situation impossible and refused to remain if the war department took over active operations. That same afternoon Haugen was "handed a notice which stated his services were no longer required and a few minutes later he voluntarily left the store."[12] Major Charles A. Ryan, executive officer of the special service branch of the U.S. Army's Seventh service command based in Omaha, replaced Haugen as store manager. In civilian life Ryan was assistant vice-president of the Kroger Grocery & Baking company, and prior to that a merchandise manager of a Brooklyn department store. Captain Helioff and five other army officers assisted Ryan, and most of the top Montgomery Ward officials also agreed to stay.

Major Ryan increased employees' wages according to the president's directive and tried to make enough profit to pay two years' worth of retroactive wages. In April 1945, Major Ryan's staff was replaced by Major L. M. Hinshaw, one other officer, and two civilians, and six months later Chairman Avery and the War Department settled out of court. On October 18, 1945, Major Hinshaw handed control of the store back to operations manager D. A. Hawkins, and the U.S. Army soldiers left for good. The War Department had only one regret about the whole business: they failed to make a profit in any of the stores they had seized.

Back in civilian hands, the South Broadway store

Army Occupation of the Denver retail store of Montgomery Ward & Co. was accomplished quietly at 9 a. m. Thursday as seven officers and one corporal "took over" on orders of the president. Capt. Edward E. Floyd, assigned as administrative officer of the store, is shown posting the first notice announcing the government seizure. This was the army's first official act. Corp. Jack Clem is standing by with other signs to be posted thruout the store. Both are stationed at Camp Carson.

MILITARY TAKES OVER CONTROL OF DENVER WARD RETAIL STORE

prospered for nearly forty more years. It expanded and remodeled in 1969 and served as a drawing card to South Broadway's "miracle mile" of shopping for Denver's middle class. Ward's was the place to shop: its congenial restaurant was also a meeting place for shoppers and neighborhood merchants alike. But in the early 1980s Montgomery Ward's sales began to drop drastically and the catalog center closed in July 1983, leaving only the two retail floors still operating. In the spring of 1984 Montgomery Ward sold the building, the nearby warehouse, and twenty-six acres of land to Realities, Inc., for well over $10 million. The plan was to convert the first two floors of the sprawling white Spanish-style building into luxury retail stores and the top six into offices. Realities also bought the adjacent Merchants Park Shopping Center, and the company planned to turn it into a "design-oriented" retail complex for shops selling posters, antiques, and jewelry. Although a few new shops were built and occupied for a short time, the properties went into receivership in 1990. The landmark Montgomery Ward building will be demolished.

While Henry Ford, Charles Gates, Jesse Shwayder, Ernest Burkhardt, the Montgomery Ward company, and other healthy businesses provided South Denver with its earliest economic base, other Denver leaders were caring for its social needs.

The concern of Elizabeth Byers for homeless boys was paralleled by the Sisters of the Good Shepherd for girls. In the early 1880s girls as young as ten were being exploited by pimps, so the Sisters offered refuge to "penitents, magdalens, and preservates" in two frame houses on Galapago Street in 1883, moving to a larger home between Cedar and Byers avenues at South Cherokee Street in 1885. By 1900, 300 girls lived at this House of the Good Shepherd, only blocks from the E. M. Byers Home for Boys on Alameda Avenue.[13]

In 1911, a new home was built on twenty acres of land at East Louisiana Avenue and South Colorado Boulevard that sheltered 650 girls. Four hundred Knights of Columbus sponsored the laying of the cornerstone on a cold, rainy March 13, and Bishop N. C. Mats, Governor Shafroth, Senator McCue, and other dignitaries spoke to 2,000 spectators. The three-story home was built for $200,000; some of the funds were contributed by sisters who had fasted in order to make donations to better "train the motherhood of a nation." The main structure was divided into two parts, one for orphaned or dependent children below the age of twelve years, and the other for "wayward girls sent there for reform purposes." The latter were instructed "both in books and in manual training" and required to share in the laundry work, cooking, and dining room duties, as well as learn sewing, music, and stenographic skills. Their playground was enclosed by a high cement wall at the rear of the building.

The House of the Good Shepherd was a small municipality in itself, with its own water system, lighting plant, heating system, and hospital. An industrial building housed the laundry, power plant, and other mechanical departments. With the help of $60,000 donated by Mrs. J. A. Osner, the building was remodeled and a new chapel and Magdalen Home were erected.

A fire in 1931 made considerable headway in the home before being discovered by one of the girls, but it was quickly extinguished by the girls under direction of Sister Mary of the Visitation. When firemen arrived, the entire roster of the home was giving thanks in prayer in the chapel. The Sisters of the Good Shepherd sold the home to a construction company in 1968 and relocated the home to East Quincy Avenue. Suspected arsonists started a spectacular three-alarm fire in the vacant building in January 1969 that completely destroyed what had been home to perhaps thousands of girls for fifty-seven years.

House of the Good Shepherd. *Photo courtesy Archdiocese of Denver Archives*

Entrepreneur, merchant, investor, and philanthropist Henry M. Porter gave the thriving town its second hospital. (Dr. Pool's short-lived Broadway Park Sanitarium was the first.) Porter fell ill while in San Diego on vacation in 1928 and was cared for at a Seventh-Day Adventist sanitarium. Impressed with the quality and integrity of care, he recalled an incident twenty-five years earlier at a similar sanitarium operated by the same church, and he decided that Denver needed one too. Already ninety years old, Denver's Grand Old Man threw himself into this new venture with his customary vigor. Porter had strung telegraph wires with his brother John when Colorado was still Kansas Territory, shipped groceries and mining tools over hundreds of miles with Charles Stebbins, helped start the Boettcher Company investment company with Charles Boettcher, and founded the Denver National Bank (United Banks of Colorado) and the Denver Museum of Natural History. On October 16, he and his daughter Dora Porter Mason gave forty acres of land that they had purchased from Henry's brother John L. Porter's estate to the regional Central Union Conference of the Seventh-Day Adventist Church. The two added $315,000 in cash to build a 100-bed sanitarium on it and later another $50,000 for nurses' quarters, the Dora Porter Mason Hall, west of the hospital. Henry Porter himself drew the plans for the brick, 142-room Porter Sanitarium and Hospital on plain brown paper, and contractor M. E. Carlson began its construction. Mayor Benjamin F. Stapleton broke ground in February 1929, fourteen weeks before the stock market crash that set off the Great Depression. The hospital was dedicated February 16, 1930, on grounds beautifully designed by landscape architect Saco R. De Boer and his associate Andrew Larson.

Rolland J. Brines, M.D., was the first medical director, and Otis A. Hudson its first business manager. The hospital struggled through the Depression, when few patients could pay the $7–$10 for a private room with bath, $5–$7.50 for a room without a bath, or $4 for a bed in a four-bed ward. Porter had stipulated that the Seventh-Day Adventist Church operate the hospital for fifteen years and so long as it could be done profitably, and the brethren assured him they would run it free of indebtedness. But the hospital survived and added a south wing in 1950 and a west addition in 1960. When Henry's son William E. Porter died in 1959, he bequeathed approximately $1 million to the institution. Augmented by additional donations and other funds, the institution built the east wing in 1964. The north wing was added in 1976, and remodeling continued until the original structure had been absorbed into the newer additions.

From its beginnings Porter's institution followed the sanitarium philosophy of similar Seventh-Day Adventist sanitariums, providing vigorous physical therapy,

Porter Sanitarium and Hospital. *Denver Public Library, Western History Department*

personal counseling, and a vegetarian diet in restful surroundings. Patients frequently stayed several weeks, taking advantage of its heliotherapy and hydrotherapy treatments. As economic and social conditions changed, Porter shifted the sanitarium's emphasis to acute hospital care and changed its name to Porter Memorial Hospital in 1969.[14]

South Denver never really conquered the saloon, even during the Town of South Denver's existence in 1886 when prohibition laws governed it. After annexation in 1894, Shattuck's fears that saloons would be licensed openly proved correct and they flourished once more. But the hardcore prohibitionists never gave up hope, and they campaigned for a national prohibition law.

Colorado went dry on New Year's Day of 1916, but that didn't stop the revelers. The *South Denver Eye and Bulletin* reported gleefully on a raid at "Dip" Evans' roadhouse at Mississippi and South Santa Fe in February 1919, where "society women, shop girls, business and professional men were caught with scarlet women and other denizens of the underworld, when the night's revelry was in full swing, with 'booze' flowing freely and men and women of all stations of life joining in a drunken revel." The next day, the paper reported, "there were rumors that the divorce courts would shortly be invaded by angry wives of sorrowful businessmen and the wrathful husbands of repentant wives" and that "projected marriages of certain society girls may be indefinitely postponed while they were shipped off to some school for girls in the East, there to repent and try to forget."[15] To this day, when a rumor that a neighborhood restaurant has applied for a liquor license circulates, southsiders are spurred to action.

The last corner of the former Town of South Denver developed during the 1920s. George W. Olinger began purchasing property between Mississippi and Exposition avenues and Steele Street and University Boulevard in 1923, erected stone pillars at the west street entrances, and named it Bonnie Brae (Scottish for Pleasant Hill). His Associated Industries company designed a unique pattern that featured streets that curved for beauty's sake, focusing on the lovely Bonnie Brae Boulevard and an elliptical-shaped park at its center. He also set up building restrictions and put in curbs, gutters, sewers, and graveled streets.

Buyers were few at first, however, and George Olinger divested himself of Associated Industries in 1925 after platting all five of the parcels. Associated Industries tried to develop the new community, but the company went bankrupt in 1928 and most of Bonnie Brae fell into the city's hands for tax debts. The next year two of Associated Industries's officers were sentenced to prison terms for looting the company of at least $5 million.[16]

A few homes existed at the time the developers went broke, but the owners paid heavy taxes for the existing improvements. Electricity was brought from the House of the Good Shepherd but there was no natural gas service. Nevertheless, some businesses opened along University Boulevard, notably the Bonnie Brae Tavern, which Carl and Sue Dire opened in 1934 at the end of Prohibition while the town was still in the midst of the Great Depression. Landscape architect Saco De Boer designed Bonnie Brae Park in 1936, but few houses were built in the area during the Depression. By 1940, however, fine homes, many designed in the new International and Art Moderne styles, were erected, and building continued until the last of the sites was filled about 1956.

Those first Bonnie Brae home owners could amuse themselves by watching ponies and their riders practice for polo matches across Exposition Avenue. Denver's polo clubs organized in about 1897 and the "Freebooters" played matches at City Park as well as performing exhibitions during the Overland Park harness races. By 1907 the players had fields and horse stables at the new Denver Country Club, but ponies and golfers didn't mix well, so in 1923 Lafayette Hughes and Ira Humphreys helped buy land bordered by East Alameda and East Exposition avenues, South University Boulevard, and South Steele Street for a place of their own. Here Denver's first families built the Denver Polo Club, including an 11,000-square-foot stable for 125 horses and an elegant Spanish Colonial Revival clubhouse. The Denver Polo Club also boasted tennis courts, a swimming pool, and lovely gardens. Some members built homes on the grounds. Lafayette Hughes's home overlooked the polo grounds, and William Berger, son of banker William Lewis Bart Berger, who had bought the Polo Club site from the Kansas Pacific Railroad in 1874, also built there. Until 1941, the club played U.S. Army teams, the Colorado

Springs Polo Club, and other touring players, but the Denver Polo Club closed and residences graced the grounds where ponies had galloped hard for eighteen years. In 1946 the residents incorporated a home owners association and declared the entire acreage private land. The clubhouse was converted to private use after World War II but was destroyed in 1978. Today, high stone walls, iron gates, and signs warning intruders to halt protect the Denver Polo Club residential area.[17]

Lawrence Cowle Phipps established the third neighborhood, Belcaro (Italian for "beautiful dear one"), in 1931, after completing twelve years in the U.S. Senate. Phipps moved from Pittsburgh to Denver after retiring as vice-president and treasurer of Carnegie Steel when it merged in 1901 with U.S. Steel, and he was a millionaire many times over. His Belcaro Realty and Investment Company added to the original plat in 1948 and 1950, the total subdivision bordered by Exposition and Tennessee avenues and South Steele and South Harrison streets. The Belcaro Shopping Center occupies the strip along South Colorado Boulevard.

Phipps hired Fisher and Fisher architects and consultant Charles Adams Platt of New York to design a fifty-four-room Georgian mansion on his six-acre estate at 3400 Belcaro Drive. The Phipps mansion of red brick with Indiana limestone trim was completed in 1933 and features a marble central hall, wood-paneled

Lawrence C. Phipps house, now the Lawrence C. Phipps Memorial Conference Center, University of Denver. *Denver Public Library, Western History Department*

rooms, Flemish tapestries, and a giant console organ. When Senator Lawrence Phipps died in 1958, his third wife, Margaret Rogers Phipps, bequeathed the estate to the University of Denver as the Lawrence C. Phipps Memorial Conference Center.[18] The mansion was placed on the National Register of Historic Places in 1975 and designated a Denver Landmark in 1977.

This last area to be developed settled rapidly and soon found itself badly in need of schools. Residents from Belcaro and Bonnie Brae neighborhoods helped plan the contemporary Stephen Knight Elementary School at 3245 East Exposition, erected in 1951. The school was named in honor of Stephen Knight and his son Stephen J. Knight, both of whom were presidents of the board of education. In 1983 the Denver Public School system converted Stephen Knight Elementary School into its first, and only, fundamental school. It was renamed the Knight Fundamental Academy to reflect its new emphasis on basic skills in reading, arithmetic, and writing for kindergarten through sixth grade students who function best in a traditional, structured environment. The school stresses patriotism, good citizenship, the work ethic, honesty, pride, courtesy, and respect for self, others, and authority; these values are reinforced by specific conduct and dress codes. The school has an enrollment of nearly 500 in grades one through five, having dropped kindergarten and sent its sixth grade pupils to middle schools.

Cory Elementary was built in 1952 at 1550 South Steele Street, just five blocks west of the area's very first school, the one-room Coronado School built sixty-six years earlier, in 1886. Designed by architect Victor Hornbein, Cory School is named for John J. Cory, a graduate of the Colorado School of Mines who was principal of South High School for twenty years until he was promoted to assistant superintendent in charge of secondary schools as well as the Emily Griffith Opportunity School in 1939. John Cory died in 1945 after serving thirty-four years in the Denver Public School system.

About 800 area junior high school students who had been crammed into Byers Junior High got a school of their own in 1953, when Merrill Junior High School opened at 1151 South Monroe Street, just east of Cory. Students from Grant Junior High School, also overcrowded, made up the rest of the student body.

Temple H. Buell designed this building and A. A. and E. B. Jones constructed it for $1,355,545. An addition was built the next year.

The school was named for a pioneer in the field of junior high education, Louise A. Merrill, who began her teaching career at Franklin School in 1897. For ten years Merrill was also with the Colorado State Home's Dora Reynolds School as teacher and then principal. She became principal of Byers when it opened in 1921 and retained the post until her death in 1940.

The development of the northeast corner of James Fleming's Town of South Denver represents the final chapter in the settling of the old town. Today, South Denver, as defined by its incorporated boundaries—the South Platte River on the west, Colorado Boulevard on the east, Alameda Avenue on the north, and Yale Avenue on the south—is a collection of neighborhoods. From 1858 Montana City's log cabins to the 1940s Polo Grounds estates, each community reflects its historical era, the architectural trends of the day, and the people who settled it.

The walled mansions and lovely grounds of the former polo fields reflect the elegance of the days when Denver's business leaders enjoyed spirited games and relaxed in a luxurious clubhouse. Bonnie Brae's Art Moderne residences, curved streets, and quiet loveliness preserve its 1920–1930s flavor, as does adjacent Belcaro, with the Phipps mansion as its focal point.

To the south, St. Thomas Seminary reminds us that institutions of learning have always been important; the neighborhood designation, Cory-Merrill, reflects the honor given to two of Denver's most dedicated public school educators.

University Park's beginnings as an academic center of higher education is symbolized in Bishop Warren's Fitzroy Place, the epitome of what the University Park Colonization Society had in mind for their university town. Several fine residences, the observatories, and the university campus itself have left a cultural heritage that sets University Park apart. Evanston, on the west side of the university, never got off the ground as an elite adjunct to University Park, but it did provide affordable housing for moderate-income families much later.

Washington Park's turn-of-the-century bungalows give this neighborhood its pleasant, unpretentious character. Home owners cherish the existence of South Denver's fabulous turn-of-the-century park and its long history as a center of the neighborhood. Washington Park includes Carrie Bailey's 1887 Myrtle Hill and its renovated Old South Gaylord Street.

The Platt Park (Fleming's Grove) community lies in the heart of the old Town of South Denver, symbolized by the historic Fleming mansion, which was occupied by four mayors. It is not difficult to imagine the Denver Circle trains stopping at Fleming's Grove train depot or to visualize horse-drawn firewagons charging out of the little hose house. "Little Holland" no longer dominates this neighborhood, but many former Dutch shops have been revitalized as Old South Pearl Street.

The early 1880s subdivisions on both sides of South Broadway—a portion of Baker; the Lincoln and Sherman subdivisions that William Loveland, Theodore Henry, Horace Tabor, and Rufus Clark fought over so bitterly; Rosedale; and Overland—have endured through economic booms and busts, social upheavals, and the ever-present saloons for more than a century.

Industrial Overland, dominated by the golf course of that name, claims the very first planned neighborhood in all of South Denver: Montana City, at Evans Avenue and the South Platte River. Three separate attempts to resurrect the memory of Montana City have been made since the Lawrence party settled this first Anglo town along the Front Range in 1858. The Sons of the American Revolution erected the first monument on the site on October 30, 1924, "to perpetuate the memory of the founding of Montana City, September, 1858, the first organized town in this region and the beginning of Denver." These words were etched on a bronze plaque attached to a five-foot granite boulder. The monument was set on a six-foot square concrete base "so that it will stand for centuries as a monument to the vanished Montana City founded sixty-six years ago this fall."

The hope of a lasting memorial was dashed less than twenty years later when someone removed the bronze plaque from the Montana City monument in 1943 during the World War II metal shortage. The granite boulder remained faceless for a decade until the Colorado Historical Society hauled it to Overland Park about 1949 and gave it a new tablet that commemorates not only Overland Park (the most historical of Denver's municipal parks) but also

Jacob Reithman, a Montana City resident in 1858, at ceremonies commemorating the site in 1924.

Montana City, Rufus "Potato" Clark, (who homesteaded the Overland Park site), and the Spanish (Mexican) Diggings at Virginia Avenue and the South Platte River.

Meanwhile, in 1939 John and Sara Robbins bought part of the old Montana City site and discovered a dilapidated log cabin on the premises—the last remaining 1858 home. The Robbinses tore down the cabin but stored the logs in a warehouse while Sara searched unsuccessfully for funds to restore it to its historical spot. The fifty logs remained in storage until 1959, when physician and historian Dr. Nolan Mumey convinced the city to create Pioneer Park on the Montana City site during Denver's centennial celebration. Mumey rebuilt the log cabin on its exact spot, at the north end of the park, and added a mining

display. Mumey had grand plans to build a heritage center in Pioneer Park and envisioned a gold mine with a tunnel and tipple, an early water wheel and mill, a fur-trading post and fort, an early Denver hotel, a narrow gauge train and early railroad station, and other vestiges of the 1859 days, when the land was still Kansas Territory. Funds for the project could not be raised, however, and a 1960 bond issue to raise funds for trails, tennis courts, and a sprinkler system was also defeated; the fenced park fell into disrepair for another decade.

The 1970s ecology movement was indirectly responsible for the park's restoration. Alan Wuth and Carl Crookham (Grant Junior High School science teachers), Geoffrey Muntz, and a small ecological club renamed the park "Frontier Park" and began cleaning, repairing, and landscaping it on Earth Day 1970. They adopted the park as one of their permanent projects. As the 1976 Colorado centennial approached, the teachers secured funds to beautify the park and institute an outdoor educational center for schoolchildren on the site. The first student groups to visit the park in early November 1975 were instructed in history, water chemistry, gold panning, plant collecting and conservation, and rock and mineral collections. Grant students from all departments helped with cleanup and repaired the fence and gate. Art students sketched, and English students wrote histories. Dr. Mumey contributed a stone-grinding wheel and a bank donated fifty trees.

On November 21, Grant students acted as hosts and guides at the ground-breaking ceremonies and participated in gold panning and water tests in eight-degree temperatures. By 1976 the students had daubed the cracks on the outside of the log cabin and chinked the logs inside.

In appreciation of the hard work and dedication of the students and teachers, the park was renamed again, to Grant-Frontier Park. For several years Grant teachers and students conducted outdoor education classes for Denver Public Schools children as part of the public school curriculum, but this program has since been discontinued.

The following tribute to the Montana City and other 1858 pioneers was printed in the *Denver Republican* on January 26, 1881, and reminds us of their accomplishments:

> The Roman Caesar conquered Britain, but you, gentlemen, the advance guard of the great Western pioneer column, you, the uncrowned Napoleon of the West, have conquered by your indomitable perseverance and energy, an empire greater than that of the imperial Caesar. You have wiped out from the map of the American continent the Great American desert. Out of that desert you have made a flower garden. . . . From the wild solitudes of this terra incognita you have produced the richest golden empire of the world. You have produced a . . . civilization which is alike gratifying to you individually, a proud record of our glorious common country, another star on the bright azure field of your country's flag, a wonder to the advanced civilization of European countries, and when, at the last hour, you have laid your head on the last pillow which the soft hand of love, friendship and affection may have smoothed for you, you can proudly remember that your epitaph will be written and your name blazoned high in the pantheon of history—a proud heritage to your children and your children's children.

Notes

CHAPTER 1

1. *Appleton's Journal* 15 (January–June 1876), p. 564–565 (Fort Garland papers), Colorado Historical Society Archives.

2. Jerome C. Smiley, *History of Denver* (Denver: Times-Sun Publishing, 1901), p. 191.

3. William B. Parsons, "Pike's Peak Fourteen Years Ago," *Kansas Magazine,* January–June 1872, p. 558.

4. Letter by William B. Parsons to *Lawrence Republican,* October 1, 1884, in *Kansas Historical Collection Transactions* 7, 1901–1902, p. 451.

5. *Rocky Mountain News,* January 18, 1860.

6. Carl Crookham, Geoffrey Muntz, and Alan Wuth, *Teacher's Guide to Grant-Frontier Park,* 1976. See also Geoffrey L. Muntz and Alan S. Wuth, *The Path of Time: A Guide to the Platte River Greenway* (Frederick, CO: Jende-Hagan Bookcorp, 1983).

7. *Rocky Mountain News,* January 18, 1860.

8. *Rocky Mountain Herald,* November 30, 1872.

9. William B. Parsons, "Pike's Peak," p. 552.

10. Eugene Parsons, "John Easter and the Lawrence Party," *The Trail* , no. 7 (December 1914), p. 6.

11. *Denver Republican,* January 26, 1881.

12. William B. Parsons, "Pike's Peak," p. 533.

13. Members of the Lawrence party were: First wagon: John H. Tierney (captain of the wagon train); William Prentiss, Peter Halsey, William McAlister. Second wagon: George W. Smith, William Parsons, Frank Bowen, Robert Peebles. Third wagon: John Easter, Roswell Hutchins, William Miles. Fourth wagon: Jack Turner, Pap Maywood.

Fifth wagon: George Peck, John D. Miller, Augustus Voorhees, William Copley. Sixth wagon: Charles Nichols, Adnah French, John A. Churchill, Charles Runyon, W. T. Cross. Seventh wagon: Josiah Hinman, Jason T. Younker, Howard Hunt, William Boyer. Eighth wagon: A. F. Bercaw, Andrew C. Wright, Frank M. Cobb, William "Nick" Smith. Ninth wagon: Robert Middleton, wife and child, Cassidy, George Howard. Tenth wagon: James Holmes, Mrs. Julia Archibald Holmes, Albert Archibald. Eleventh wagon: William Regan, Joseph Brown, William Hartley, James White, Giles Blood, William McKay. (Compiled from Voorhees/J. D. Miller lists.)

14. William B. Parsons, "Pike's Peak," p. 552.

15. Ibid., p. 553.

16. Ibid, pp. 553–61.

17. Ibid., p. 557.

18. Frank Cobb, "The Lawrence Party of Pike's Peakers (1858) and the Founding of St. Charles (Predecessor of Denver)," *Colorado Magazine* 10, no. 5 (September 1933), p. 194. Cobb, Miller, and Voorhees had been preceded in their ascent of the peak by Dr. James and companions of the Major Long expedition of 1820 (p. 195, n. 1).

19. *Lawrence Republican,* October 7, 1858. See also Julia Archibald Holmes, *A Bloomer Girl on Pike's Peak, 1858,* ed. Agnes Wright Spring (Denver: Denver Public Library, Western History Dept., c. 1949).

20. William B. Parsons, "Pike's Peak," p. 558.

21. *Kansas City Journal of Commerce,* December 14, 1858. For Katrina Murat story, see "Katrina Wolf Murat, the Pioneer," *Colorado Magazine* 16, no. 5 (September 1939).

22. Eudochia Bell Smith, "Women," in *Colorado and Its People*, ed. LeRoy R. Hafen (New York: Lewis Historical Publishers, 1948), p. 557.

23. William B. Parsons, *The Gold Mines of Western Kansas, Being a Complete Description of the Newly Discovered Gold Mines, Different Routes, Camping Places, Tools and Outfit and Containing Everything Important for the Immigrant and Miner to Know.* Lawrence, Kansas Territory: *Lawrence Republican* Book and Job Printing Office, 1858.

24. William B. Parsons, "Pike's Peak," p. 560.

25. William McGaa, "Statement on St. Charles and Denver Town Companies," *Colorado Magazine* 22, no. 3 (May 1945), p. 127.

26. *Private Laws of the Territory of Kansas*, Fifth Session of the Legislative Assembly, begun at the City of Lecompton, on the lst Monday of Jan'y, 1859, and held and concluded at the City of Lawrence (Lawrence, K.T: Herald of Freedom Steam Press, 1859), pp. 219–20.

The O'Donnell party, traveling just behind the Lawrence party, laid out a town on part of what is now Colorado Springs, called El Paso. But "it never developed anything more than one poor log cabin and a few tents and did not disturb Montana's title to having been the first real town in the region" (Smiley, *History of Denver*, p. 191).

The Auraria Town Company, which adopted a constitution on October 31, 1859, was never incorporated. Denver City Town Company also failed to get a charter and was never incorporated; it took over St. Charles instead.

27. *Denver Republican*, July 14, 1883.

28. *Denver Republican*, January 26, 1881.

29. O. J. Goldrick, "Historical Sketch of Denver, Colorado," a speech given July 4, 1876. Colorado Historical Society.

30. Eugene Parsons, "John Easter and the Lawrence Party," pp. 5–10.

31. *Denver Republican*, July 14, 1883.

CHAPTER 2

1. Allen D. Breck, *From the Rockies to the World* (Denver: University of Denver, 1989), p. 66.

2. *Denver Post*, December 31, 1935.

3. Louisa Ward Arps, *Denver in Slices* (Athens, OH: Swallow Press, 1959), p. 173.

4. James R. Harvey, "Cebert Alexander Trease, Engineer," *Colorado Magazine* 16, no. 6 (November 1939), p. 223.

5. Letter from William N. Byers to parents dated January 3, 1861. Western History Library.

6. Mrs. William N. Byers, "The Experiences of One Pioneer Woman," n.d. Western History Library.

7. Ibid.

8. Lyle W. Dorsett, *The Queen City: A History of Denver* (Boulder, CO: Pruett, 1977).

9. Byers, *The Experiences*.

10. Typewritten report by Julia Hudson, secretary, E. M. Byers Home for Boys. No date, but presented between January 1917 and January 1920. Edwin O. Martin was superintendent at this time. Western History Library.

11. Earl L. Mosley, "History of the Denver Water System to 1919." Compiled by Louisa Ward Arps, December 1969.

12. E. W. Robinson, typewritten manuscript of conversation with Rufus Clark, July 11, 1906. Colorado Historical Society.

13. *Rocky Mountain News*, October 23, 1874.

14. Arps, *Denver in Slices*, p. 72.

15. Petition of Thomas Skerritt et al. for road in Town[ships] 4 and 5, Range 68, filed April 25, 1871 with the Arapahoe County Board of Commissioners.

The petitioners were Thomas Skerritt, Robert Beeson, Maria L. Bryant, George Bryan, Thomas Lockard, R. H. Ostrander, Patrick Riley, Thomas Miller, Philip Riley, Gus Christmann, Hugh Smith, James D. Terry, Andrew A. Nichols, Henry Thompson, John Bell, Cassidy, William Maudlin, Nelson Phillips, H. H. Bryan, Jr., Rufus Clark, A. C. Upcint, and Peter Magnes. Colorado State Archives.

16. Report of Road Viewers on Petition of T. Skerritt et al. and Petition of R. Beeson et al., filed May 3, 1871 and adopted June 5, 1871. Colorado State Archives.

17. James O. Patterson, "History of South Denver," *South Denver Eye*, c. 1900. See also Alice Polk Hill, *Colorado Pioneers in Picture and Story* (Denver: Brock-Haffner Press, 1915), p. 218–219.

18. Patterson, "History of South Denver."

19. Ibid.

20. County Superintendent Frank Church Report excerpt, December 20, 1873, p. 17. Colorado State Archives.

District 7 school board officers were, 1874–1875: Elisha Bennet, president; Emmet Nuckols, treasurer (replaced by M. B. Corbin in 1875–1876). 1876–1877: John E. Hall, president; Frederick W. Johns, secretary, M. B. Corbin, treasurer. In November, Johns moved out of the district, and Rev. Levi Debusk was appointed to fill his term. 1877–1878: George H. Bryant, president; Amos A. Shell, secretary; M. B. Corbin, treasurer. 1878–1879: J. C. Jones, president; T. E. Stowe, secretary; M. B. Corbin, treasurer. Shell also served as secretary from February to May 1879. 1879–1880: J. C. Jones, president (to 1882); Amos Shell, secretary; Rufus Clark, treasurer (to 1883). 1880–1882: J. F. Weedman, secretary; R. H. Nelson then served the post until 1885. James A. Fleming was president 1883–1884, and J. A. Alkins for the 1884–1885 term, with Frederick W. Johns returning as secretary.

21. Arapahoe County School records, Colorado State Archives.

22. Fred J. Stanton was secretary of the district at first, and Levi Booth for several years afterward.

23. Gertrude Brown Working, *Levi Booth of Four Mile House* (Denver: 1986), p. 35.

24. Kenton Forrest, Gene McKeever, and Raymond McAllister, *History of the Public Schools of Denver* (Denver: Tramway Press, 1989), p. 44.

25. See Thomas J. Noel, *The City and the Saloon: Denver, 1858–1916* (Lincoln, NE: University of Nebraska Press, 1982).

26. Patterson, "History of South Denver."

27. *Rocky Mountain News*, April 23, 1880.

28. Patterson, "History of South Denver."

29. *Rocky Mountain News*, November 17, 1880.

30. *Daily News*, May 15, 1881.

31. Also James Duff, J. T. Cornforth, George Tritch, Richard Sopris, Colonel L. H. Eicholtz, A. J. Williams, William D. Todd, Henry R. Wolcott, A. H. Estes, J. Jay Joslin, George Clark, John Arkins, Dr. Moore, J. J. Riethman, W. Hall, Edward Eddy, Charles F. Hendrie, A.P.W. Skinner, Colonel D. C. Dodge, John L. Dailey, S. H. Elbert, J. W. Nesmith, S. F. Edmunds, W. H. Bush, Charles H. Smith, William Fisher, R. W. Woodbury, O. H. Rothaker, W. Q. Rice, J. Alden Smith, General H. B. Bearce, and Edward B. Light. Also, serving on the Resolutions Committee were John Arkins, S. F. Emmons, and A. C. Fisk.

32. *Daily News*, May 15, 1881, p.4.

33. Duane A. Smith, *Horace Tabor, His Life and the Legend* (Boulder: Colorado Associated University Press, 1973), p. 244.

34. Patterson, "History of South Denver."

35. Mark S. Foster, *The Denver Bears: From Sandlots to Sellouts* (Boulder, CO: Pruett, 1983), p. 7.

36. Property owners, sensing rising land values, platted one subdivision after another around the Exposition Hall in 1881. Lucy Pomeroy platted Pomeroy's Broadway subdivision (Broadway to Logan Street, Dakota Avenue to Virginia Avenue), George W. Currier and John Knox the Knox and Currier Subdivision (Virginia to Exposition and Logan to Clarkson Street) and John L. Dailey and Arthur Pierce "and other capitalists" Broadway Heights (Alameda to Exposition avenues and Franklin to University streets). Charles Bohm platted Bohm's Addition (Exposition to Kentucky and Franklin to University) on February 6; Elizabeth Smith platted Lake View (Alameda to Virginia and Clarkson to Franklin) on February 28; George W. and William M. Clayton Bryn Mawr (Exposition to Kentucky avenues and Clarkson to Franklin streets) May 5; and Edward A. Reser laid out Reser's Subdivision (Franklin to University Boulevard and Mexico to Jewell, plus Race Street to University Boulevard and Florida to Mexico) on October 7. Francis G. King platted Maplewood (Mexico to Jewell Avenue and Colorado Boulevard to Steele Street) January 25, 1883.

37. *Daily News*, June 30, 1882.

38. *Daily News*, February 13, 1899.

39. Joseph G. Rosa, and Waldo E. Koop, *Rowdy Joe Lowe, Gambler with a Gun* (Norman: University of Oklahoma Press, 1989).

40. *Daily News*, February 13, 1899.

41. *Rocky Mountain News*, May 25, 1883.

42. Noel, *The City and the Saloon*, pp. 37–39.

CHAPTER 3

1. James Alexander Fleming came from an old Pennsylvania family. His great-grandfather, James Fleming, had settled in Pennsylvania in 1771; his grandfather Thomas and his father, William P., who married Susanna Hill, had lived in Indiana County, Pennsylvania, since 1819.

2. *Denver Eye*, January 1, 1890, p. 8.

3. W. Weston, *Descriptive Pamphlet of Some of the Principal Mines and Prospects of Ouray County, Colorado*, August 10, 1881, pp. 24, 36. See also Robert A. Corregan and David F. Lingane, *Colorado Mining Directory* (Denver: Colorado Mining Directory Co., 1883), pp. 477–478.

4. *Daily News*, May 12, 1882, p. 3, col. 3.

5. Thomas J. Noel and Barbara S. Norgren, *Denver, the City Beautiful and Its Architects, 1893–1941* (Denver: Historic Denver, 1987).

6. J. O. Patterson, "History of South Denver," *South Denver Eye*, c. 1900.

7. Letter from Nellie J. Paddock to James A. Fleming dated October 22, 1884. Exhibit 4, Divorce Case No. 8455, Arapahoe County Court. Colorado State Archives, Denver.

8. Louisa Ward Arps, *Denver in Slices* (Athens, OH: Swallow Press, 1959).

9. *Rocky Mountain News*, June 25, 1883.

10. William M. Dailey was elected president; A. P. Taylor, vice-president; Brinton Gregory, secretary; and Arthur E. Pierce, treasurer. Trustees were John L. Dailey, George W. Allen, and George E. Kettle. Serving on various committees also were D. C. Wyatt (fire); G. S. Boughton, Daniel Polk, J. W. Bilbie (water); I. L. Killie, Avery Gallup, A. Scudemore (light); C. M. Butters, John L. Russell (streets); C. Von Trotha, J. W. Roberts, R. H. Nelson (mail); James O. Patterson, E. P. Varian, J. T. Harlow (numbering); W. D. Woodman (by-laws); A. M. Hunter, and A. E. Riddle (hall).

11. Alice Polk Hill, *Tales of the Colorado Pioneers* (Denver: Pierson and Gardner, 1884), pp. 158–159.

12. Jerome C. Smiley, *History of Denver* (Denver: Times-Sun Publishing, 1901), p. 477.

13. *Denver Republican*, April 23, 1887.

14. *Denver Republican*, April 9, 1888.

15. *Colorado Live Stock Record*, April 25, 1884.

16. Arps, *Denver in Slices*, pp. 174–175.

17. Robert L. Perkin, *The First Hundred Years: An Informal History of Denver and the Rocky Mountain News* (Garden City, NY: Doubleday, 1959), p. 256.

18. See Jim Norland, *The Summit of a Century: A Pictorial History of the University of Denver, 1864–1964* (Denver: University of Denver, 1963) and its companion, Allen D. Breck, *From the Rockies to the World* (Denver: University of Denver, 1989).

19. Contract between Colorado Seminary and Rufus Clark, February 2, 1886. Colorado Historical Society.

20. David Boyd, *Greeley and the Union Colony* (Greeley, CO: Greeley Tribune Press, 1890), p. 14.

21. Charles M. Deardorff, "History of University Park." Handwritten manuscript, University of Denver archives.

22. Denver Circle Railroad Company Resolution dated March 3, 1886. Colorado State Archives.

23. James Edward Le Rossignol, "History of Higher Education in Colorado." *U.S. Bureau of Education Circular of Information No. 1* (Washington, D.C.: Government Printing Office, 1903), p. 36.

24. Testimony of F. C. Millington, Arapahoe County District Court case No. 8506, Frank W. Loveland et al. vs. Rufus Clark et al., filed May 12, 1887, pp. 179–181.

25. Smiley, *History of Denver*, pp. 188–189.

26. *Rocky Mountain News*, September 6, 1879, p. 2, col. 1.

27. *History of Denver Public Schools*, Denver Public Library, 1957.

28. G. B. Coulter served as president of District 7 (1888–1891), Amos Shell (1888–1889) and Alex Miller (1890–1892) treasurers; and Samuel H. Seccombe, secretary (1888–1890). By 1888, District 7 had sixty-five children between the ages of five and twenty-one eligible as students.

29. Arps, *Denver in Slices*, pp. 68–69.

30. Saco R. De Boer, *University Park Report*. Prepared for the University Park Community Association, 1923.

31. The petition was signed by Ed Hammlyn, William Franklin, William Brian, Thomas Wyette, R. B. Mulford, William Bolles, Theodore Petzoldt, W. B. Simms, and William E. Thompson.

32. *Denver Eye*, January 1, 1890.

33. *Denver Eye*, January 1, 1890.

CHAPTER 4

1. *Denver Eye*, January 1, 1890.

2. *Denver Eye*, January 1, 1890.

3. The forty petitioners for incorporation of the Town of South Denver were James A. Fleming, Henry F. Jolly, F. S. W. Gleason, Samuel H. Seccombe, J. D. Munn, Joseph R. Atkins, G. Hallatt, Elias H. Broadwell, Jesse E. Fleming, Adam Kohankie, John Hamlet, William Bradley, Mark W. Moe, George E. Dunlap, Max Werner, John W. Gerrito, John Berry, Charles Newlander, James F. Foster, S. E. Thompson, G. B. Coulter, C. G. Jolly, George Scholls, E. H. Provost, Charles W. Stokes, August H. Gamage, C. Sherwood, Avery Gallup, Alex Miller, John L. Russell, Joe Purcell, F. A. Moe, Erick Englund, Gus Rollins, Frederick W. Johns, F. M. B. Norman, Robert H. Nelson, Amos A. Shell, E. A. Cuem, and Rufus Clark.

4. The 104 voters in order of balloting were George E. Taylor, Alexander H. Frye, Amos A. Shell, Edward Gary, James A. Fleming, H. W. Wyman, R. McNeal, N. S. Dow, James Foster, A. C. Kinyon, Alex Miller, William E. Thompson, James Rose, Louis York, Charles Stokes, John L. Russell, Rufus Clark, John S. Babcock, Frederick W. Johns, Samuel H. Seccombe, Bartley Green, Griff Jones, Irvin Waite, Charles E. "Pap" Wyman, Avery Gallup, F. F. Lucas, J. Berngan, Val Clorley, George Smith, Miller Thorpe, F. S. W. Gleason, J. Kuhn, J. S. Lucas, J. Stevens, Joe Lowe, Erick Englund, T. M. F. Bush, Elias H. Broadwell, E. A. Cotis, Bernard Hovey, George H. Krome, E. H. Madison, Frank S. Stoddard, D. Evans, Max Werner, S. J. Kid, Joseph R. Atkins, Markle Moe, F. A. Moe, J. Dewey, Charles Johnson, George

Dunlap, C. H. Caswell, Thomas McManee, W. C. Duncan, Calvin Fleming, William Davidson, Frank McKinny, David Lauster, William Bradley, J. E. Arnold, Jesse E. Fleming, George Osten, J. D. Mun, John Berry, J. F. Vandougen, J. Groves, Gus Rollins, F. B. Otis, J. W. McCausland, Henry D. Meier, Joseph Kerstem, George E. Pierce, C. G. Jolly, Fred Norman, B. A. Noble, E. H. Provost, Henry F. Jolly, James Jongatt, J. Alderfer, Emil Austin, Joe Purcell, August H. Gamage, Charles Newlander, C. Sherwood, George Shaw, Adam Kohankie, J. Hamlet, M. Melvin, Thomas Wood, L. A. Dow, Harry Scranton, D. F. Spaulding, M. Lewis, H. E. Johnson, J. P. Bachelor, Gus Johnson, George Noble, E. A. Coon, James Shanon, Helmam Huston, S. Lewis, and John Makin.

5. *South Denver Journal (Proceedings of the Board of Trustees, South Denver, Colorado),* October 12, 1886. Colorado State Archives.

6. Arapahoe County District Court Case No. 8206, filed November 27, 1886. Colorado State Archives.

7. *Denver Tribune-Republican,* November 28, 1886.

8. Arapahoe County Criminal Court, People vs. Alexander Miller, Case No. 3669. Colorado State Archives.

9. *Denver Republican,* November 25, 1890.

10. Colorado Supreme Court Case No. 2042, filed April 5, 1887. Colorado State Archives.

11. "History of the University of Denver," *Kynewisbok* (Denver: University of Denver, 1912).

12. *Denver Times,* August 1, 1887.

13. Colorado Supreme Court Case No. 2042.

14. *Denver Eye,* January 1, 1890.

15. University Park Colony Brochure, Dove-Pabor Printing Co., n.d. University of Denver archives.

16. *Denver Republican,* April 18, 1888.

17. *Denver Tribune-Republican,* November 12, 1885.

18. *Denver Republican,* May 28, 1887.

19. *Denver Republican,* June 26, 1891.

20. Horace A. W. Tabor vs. Rufus Clark, John R. Hanna, Charles B. Kountze, the Denver Circle Real Estate Company, T. C. Henry, and W. A. H. Loveland. Arapahoe County District Court Case No. 7864, filed June 29, 1886. Colorado State Archives.

21. Arapahoe District Court Case No. 8506, filed May 12, 1887. Colorado State Archives.

22. Arapahoe County Court Case No. 8506, p. 132–33.

23. Colorado Supreme Court Case No. 2153, filed December 7, 1887.

24. *Overland Park Club Handbook, 1898,* quoted in Louisa Ward Arps, *Denver in Slices* (Athens, OH: Swallow Press, 1959), p. 175.

25. *Denver Eye,* January 1, 1890.

26. *Denver Times,* August 16, 1895.

27. Robert L. Perkin, *The First Hundred Years: An Informal History of Denver and the Rocky Mountain News* (Garden City, NY: Doubleday, 1959).

28. *Denver Times,* August 16, 1895.

29. *Denver Eye,* January 1, 1890.

30. James O. Patterson, "History of South Denver," *South Denver Eye and Bulletin,* c. 1900.

31. *Denver Eye,* January 1, 1890.

32. Rocky Mountain Railroad Club, *Steam Tramways of Denver* 3 (June 1950).

33. Stephen J. Leonard and Thomas J. Noel, *Denver: Mining Camp to Metropolis* (Niwot: University Press of Colorado, 1990), map on p. 63.

34. *Denver Times,* August 16, 1895.

35. Minutes of the Forty-first Session of the Colorado Annual Conference of the Methodist Episcopal Church, August 26–31, 1903.

36. Advertisement, c. 1888–1889, source unknown. Western History Library.

CHAPTER 5

1. *Denver Eye,* January 1, 1890.

2. *Denver Republican,* March 30, 1890.

3. *Denver Republican,* April 2, 1890, p. 2.

4. Trustees were John S. Babcock, August H. Gamage, Avery Gallup, Benjamin F. Niesz, John L. Russell, and Samuel H. Seccombe. Also Charles H. Peters, clerk and recorder; Henry Abel, Jr., treasurer; De Witt C. Webber, attorney; H. W. Spangler, police magistrate; Thomas D. Robinson, town engineer; Temple D. Kuykendall, street commissioner; Thomas H. Fleming, water commissioner; and W. P. Thompson, marshal.

The treasurer, clerk and recorder, attorney, marshal, and police magistrate were bonded to ensure that they "will at the end of their one-year term pay over all moneys and deliver up all property in their custody belonging to said town." The treasurer's annual salary was $300; the marshal, magistrate, clerk, and attorney each drew $500; and the clerk and recorder earned $600.

5. Jerome C. Smiley, *History of Denver* (Denver: Times-Sun Publishing, 1901), p. 757.

6. P. R. Otis installed T. J. Weekes, George Corkett, C.

H. Miller, E. F. Titcomb, William Lawson, W. P. Thompson, E. R. Pierson, and T. H. Cleveland as I.O.O.F. officers.

7. *Denver Republican*, August 3, 1890.

8. *Denver Republican*, August 2, 1890.

9. *Denver Republican*, July 21, 1891.

10. *Phoenix Herald*, April 14, 1893, p. 1.

11. The trustees for 1891–1892 remained as they were for 1890–1891: John S. Babcock, August Gamage, John L. Russell, Avery Gallup, Benjamin F. Niesz, and Samuel H. Seccombe. Charles H. Peters was clerk and recorder; Henry Abel, street commissioner; Temple D. Kuykendall, water commissioner; De Witt C. Webber, attorney; W. P. Thompson, marshal; W. D. Robinson, engineer, and W. G. Smith, fire chief.

12. *Denver Times*, May 7, 1891.

13. Fleming's son, Charles, went on to California, where he married and had a son. Fleming's third son, William Porter, stayed in Denver with his grandmother Susanna Fleming.

14. *Arizona Republican*, April 14, 1893, p. 5.

15. James H. McClintock, *Arizona, the Nation's Youngest Commonwealth Within a Land of Ancient Culture* (Chicago: S. J. Clarke, 1916), p. 342.

16. Arizona State Board of Health Death Certificate No. 290, filed February 29, 1917. In Globe, James Fleming worked as a mine superintendent. His sons Richard and Charles, Charles's wife, Blanche, and their child, Porter, lived there with them, also working in the copper mines. Fleming's brother, George, had also moved from Denver to Globe and worked the copper mines.

17. *Denver Times*, April 2, 1891.

18. Petition to the "Honorable Mayor and Board of Trustees of the City of South Denver, in Common Council Assembled," handwritten and undated. Colorado State Archives.

19. *Denver Republican*, June 25 and 26, 1891.

20. *Rocky Mountain News*, August 16, 1891, p. 6.

21. The six trustees were John L. Russell, August Gamage, John S. Babcock, Frank Bailey, William Lawson, and Benjamin Niesz. George H. Crosby was clerk and recorder; Henry Abel, Jr., treasurer; E. J. Short, attorney; J. E. Harper, police magistrate; George W. Reed, marshal, and T. C. Robinson, engineer. Commissioners were George R. Parker, streets; Temple D. Kuykendall, parks; and George E. Dunlap, water.

22. *Daily News*, December 7, 1892, p. 2, col. 6.

23. *Denver Republican*, December 4, 1892, p. 6, col. 1.

24. *Daily News*, December 6, p. 3, col. 2, and December 7, 1892, p. 2, col. 6.

25. *Denver Republican*, February 19, 1893.

26. *South Denver Eye*, November 17, 1900.

27. Articles of Incorporation, The Broadway Park Sanitarium Company, August 23, 1892, and Certification of Amount of Capital Stock, November 30, 1892. Directors were Dr. R. N. Pool, Carleton Ellis, Charles E. Skiles, R. H. Scribuen, C. A. Whitescarver, E. R. Morris, and T. G. Horne.

28. *Denver Republican*, December 15, 1892.

29. "History of Rosedale," Milton-Rosedale PTA paper, author unknown, c. 1935.

30. *The Coloradan*, December 15, 1892, p. 26.

31. Haines, Dorothy, "May Centennial Celebration." Typewritten manuscript, University Park School files, Denver, n.d.

32. *Denver Republican*, April 5, 1890.

33. Jim Norland, *The Summit of a Century: A Pictorial History of the University of Denver, 1864–1964* (Denver: University of Denver, 1963).

34. *Rocky Mountain News*, February 23, 1892.

35. *The Hesperus*, March 1, 1892.

36. *Denver Times*, January 18, 1902.

37. Robert C. Shattuck, *University Park, Octogenarian Memories* (Denver: University Park Methodist Church, January 1, 1986).

38. Francine Haber, Kenneth R. Fuller, and David N. Wetzel, *Robert S. Roeschlaub, Architect of the Emerging West 1843–1923*, Colorado Historical Society, 1988.

39. Alberta Iliff Shattuck, "Singer Comes to Colorado," February 17, 1976, p. 19.

40. Shattuck, *University Park, Octogenarian Memories.*

41. Ibid.

42. *Minutes of the Forty-first Session of the Colorado Annual Conference of the Methodist Episcopal Church*, August 26–31, 1903, p. 233.

43. Lydia Terrell Lort, *A Church Bell Rings in Denver* (Denver: Otto J. Stockmar, 1951), p. 20.

44. *Minutes of the Forty-first Session*, p. 374.

45. John Alton Templin, "A History of Methodism in Denver 1876–1912," Ph.D. dissertation, Iliff School of Theology, 1956, p. 626.

CHAPTER 6

1. *Daily News*, December 6, 1892, p. 3, col. 2.

2. *Denver Republican*, February 19, 1893.

3. *Denver Republican*, February 17, 1893, p. 2.

4. *Denver Republican*, February 17, 1893, p. 1.

5. *South Denver Journal*, March 4, 1893.

6. *Denver Republican*, March 14, 1893.

7. *Denver Republican*, March 25, 1893.

8. In the end the 1893 council consisted of Solomon Barcus, mayor, and trustees Frank A. Bailey, Benjamin F. Niesz, Albert E. Riddle, William Lawson, Walter P. Miller, and Daniel H. Pike. George H. Crosby was clerk and recorder; Charles H. Peters, treasurer; De Witt C. Webber, attorney; F. A. Woodson, police magistrate; Henry W. Scott, marshal; Thomas D. Robinson, engineer; and George E. Dunlap, water commissioner.

9. McCarthy, Joan, "There Was More Than Golf at Overland Park," *Washington Park Profile*, October 1983.

10. *Denver Republican*, June 18, 1893.

11. Mayor and Trustees of the Town of Valverde vs. Shattuck et al., Colorado Supreme Court Case No. 3293, September 1893 term. Colorado State Archives.

12. Court Order No. 21027, in the matter of the annexation of the Town of South Denver to the City of Denver, December 5, 1893. Colorado State Archives.

13. Report to the Honorable Mayor, City of Denver, Colo., by William H. Young, dated April 18, 1894. Colorado State Archives.

14. Second Annual Report, Gold and Silver Extraction Mining and Milling Company, April 30, 1892. Colorado Historical Society Archives.

15. Duane A. Smith, *Horace Tabor: His Life and the Legend* (Boulder: Colorado Associated University Press, 1973), p. 276.

16. *Denver Times*, January 7, 1901, p. 3, col. 6.

17. James Edward Le Rossignol, "History of Higher Education in Colorado." *U.S. Bureau of Education Circular of Information No. 1.* (Washington, DC: Government Printing Office, 1903).

18. *Denver Times*, February 21, 1899.

19. Personal letter of A. H. Briggs, dated April 20, 1900. Warren papers, Iliff School of Theology Archives.

20. Thomas Russell Garth, *The Life of Henry Augustus Buchtel* (Denver, Peerless Printing, 1937), p. 197.

21. *Denver Times*, March 26, 1902, p. 3, col. 5.

22. Thomas J. Noel, and Barbara S. Norgren, *Denver, the City Beautiful and Its Architects, 1893–1941* (Denver, Historic Denver, 1987).

23. Ibid.

24. "Platt Park Recreation Center Building," a typewritten paper, Decker Branch Library archives.

25. *Denver Republican*, August 16, 1890.

26. *Daily News*, October 24, 1897, p. 4, col. 1.

27. *South Denver Eye*, June 17, 1899.

28. *South Denver Eye*, July 15, 1899.

29. Joan McCarthy, "Growing Up in Washington Park," *Washington Park Profile*, February 1981.

30. *Denver Times*, March 26, 1902, p. 2, col. 5.

31. Denver Landmark Preservation Commission files, Denver Planning Office.

32. Louisa Ward Arps, *Denver in Slices* (Athens, OH: Swallow Press, 1959), pp. 228–229.

33. Frances Melrose, "The Ol' Ball Game Has Long Been Part of Denver Lifestyle," *Rocky Mountain News*, December 7, 1986, p. 44.

34. *Denver Times*, March 28, 1903.

35. Denver Public School Interdepartmental Communication, March 8, 1948.

36. Thomas J. Noel, *Colorado Catholicism and the Archdiocese of Denver 1857–1989* (Niwot: University Press of Colorado, 1989), pp. 59, 60, 123, 125, 154–155.

37. Joyce Summers, "One Man's Vision," *Colorado Heritage,* Colorado Historical Society, no. 2, May 1988.

38. S. H. Thompson, Jr., "Golf in Colorado, 1901," in Mel Shapiro, Warren Dohn, and Leonard Berger, eds., *Golf, a Turn of the Century Treasury* (Secaucus, NJ: Book Sales, 1986).

39. *South Denver Eye*, June 17, 1899.

40. Arps, *Denver in Slices*, p. 182.

41. *South Denver Eye*, June 17, 1899.

42. *Denver Post*, November 2, 1911.

CHAPTER 7

1. *South Denver Eye and Bulletin*, September 27, October 11, and December 6, 1913; August 26, 1917. *Denver Post*, July 16, 1916. *Rocky Mountain News*, August 23, 1918. *Denver Times*, January 26, 1923.

2. Frances Melrose, "Denver's Ford Plant," *Rocky Mountain News* Sunday Magazine, November 20, 1988, p. 14; "Many Autos Cranked Out in and near Denver from 1904–1917," *Rocky Mountain News Sunday Magazine*, June 10, 1990, pp. 12–13.

3. *Gates Corporation, The Gates Story, 1800–1986* (Denver: Gates Corporation, n.d.); *Denver Post,* May 27, 1991, p. 1C.

4. William N. Fitch and Frederick K. Allgaier, "Robinson

Brick Company/Denver Radium Site," Workshop on the Management of Radioactively Contaminated Sites, U.S. Environmental Protection Agency, Albuquerque, New Mexico, May 3, 1989. Thanks also to Enid T. Thompson, researcher.

5. Walter B. Lovelace and Walter S. Lovelace. *Jesse Shwayder and the Golden Rule, First Fifty Years of Shwayder Bros., Inc., 1910–1960* (Denver: Lakeside Press, 1960); Olga Curtis, "Jesse Shwayder, Ageless Samson," *Denver Post Empire Magazine*, February 12, 1967, pp. 18–21; Samsonite Corporation, *The Samsonite Story*, n.d.; "Saga of Shwayder Family Opens with Child's Trunk," *Denver Monitor*, November 17, 1954.

6. *Denver Times*, September 28, 1917, p. 2.

7. Jack Carberry, "The Second Guess," *Denver Post*, April 17, 1945, p. 15; and June 25, 1947.

8. Mark S. Foster, *The Denver Bears: From Sandlots to Sellouts* (Boulder, CO: Pruett, 1983), p. 34.

9. Thomas J. Noel, ed., *Rocky Mountain Gold: Pictorial and Entertaining Commentary on the Growth and Development of Denver, Colorado* (Tulsa, OK: Continental Heritage Press, 1980).

10. *South Denver Eye and Bulletin*, August 30, 1913.

11. *Denver Post*, December 28, 1944, p. 5.

12. *Denver Post*, January 3, 1945, p. 1.

13. Thomas J. Noel, *Colorado Catholicism and the Archdiocese of Denver 1857–1989* (Niwot: University Press of Colorado, 1989), p. 32.

14. Marion R. Rymer, *Porter Memorial Hospital, Its Birth and Life* (Denver: Porter Memorial Hospital, 1978). Also, *Denver Times*, November 3, 1901, p. 5.

15. *South Denver Eye and Bulletin*, February 22, 1919.

16. *Washington Park Profile*, March 1986, p. 3.

17. Robert Johnson, "City Sports Mark O'Polo," *Denver Magazine*, September 1986, pp. 55–56. Also Thomas J. Noel and Barbara S. Norgren, *Denver, the City Beautiful and Its Architects, 1893–1941* (Denver: Historic Denver, Inc., 1987).

18. Noel and Norgren, *Denver, the City Beautiful.*

References

BOOKS

Arps, Louisa Ward. *Denver in Slices*. Athens, OH: Swallow Press, 1959.

Beardsley, Isaac Haight. *Echoes from Peak and Plain; or Tales of Life, War, Travel, and Colorado Methodism*. Cincinnati: Curts & Jennings, 1898.

Boyd, David. *Greeley and the Union Colony*. Greeley, CO: Greeley Tribune Press, 1890.

Breck, Allen D. *From the Rockies to the World*. Denver: University of Denver, 1989.

Brettell, Richard R. *Historic Denver: The Architects and the Architecture, 1858–1893*. Denver: Historic Denver, 1979.

Chamberlin, Thomas S., ed. *The Historical Encyclopedia of Colorado*. Denver: Colorado Historical Association, c. 1953.

Corregan, Robert A., and David F. Lingane, eds. *Colorado Mining Directory*. Denver: Colorado Mining Directory Co., 1883.

Denver City Directories, various publishers, 1873–present.

Denver Inventory, a Plan for Historic Preservation in Denver. Denver: Denver Planning Office, Historic Denver, Junior League of Denver, rev. 1977.

Dorsett, Lyle W. *The Queen City: A History of Denver*. Boulder, CO: Pruett, 1977.

Dyer, John Lewis. *The Snowshoe Itinerant: Autobiography of the Reverend John L. Dyer*. Breckenridge, CO: Father Dyer United Methodist Church, 1975. Reprint of 1890 edition published by Cranston and Stowe, Cincinnati, 1890.

Etter, Don D. *Denver, University Park 1886–1910: Four Walking Tours*. Denver: Graphic Impressions, 1974.

_____. *Denver Going Modern: A Photographic Essay on the Imprint of the International Style on Denver Residential Architecture*. Denver: Graphic Impressions, 1977.

Forrest, Kenton, Gene McKeever, and Raymond McAllister. *History of the Public Schools of Denver*. Denver: Tramway Press, 1989.

Foster, Mark S. *The Denver Bears: From Sandlots to Sellouts*. Boulder, CO: Pruett, 1983.

Garth, Thomas Russell. *The Life of Henry Augustus Buchtel*. Denver: Peerless Printing, 1937.

Goode, William H. *Outposts of Zion, with Limnings of Mission Life*. Cincinnati: Poe and Hitchcock, 1863.

Haber, Francine, Kenneth R. Fuller, and David N. Wetzel. *Robert S. Roeschlaub: Architect of the Emerging West 1843–1923*. Denver: Colorado Historical Society, 1988.

Hafen, LeRoy R., ed. *Colorado and Its People*. New York: Lewis Historical Publishers, 1948.

Hall, Frank. *History of the State of Colorado*. Chicago: Blakely Printing Company, 1889.

Hicks, Dave. *Englewood from the Beginning*. Denver: A-T-P Publishing, 1971.

Hill, Alice Polk. *Tales of the Colorado Pioneers*. Denver: Pierson and Gardner, 1884.

_____. *Colorado Pioneers in Picture and Story*. Denver: Brock-Haffner Press, 1915.

Holmes, Julia Archibald. *Bloomer Girl on Pike's Peak, 1858*. Agnes Wright Spring, ed. Denver: Western History

Library, c. 1949.

Jones, William C., and Kenton Forrest. *Denver: A Pictorial History from Frontier Camp to Queen City of the Plains.* Boulder, CO: Pruett, 1973.

Kelsey, Harry E., Jr. *Frontier Capitalist: The Life of John Evans.* Boulder, CO: State Historical Society of Colorado and Pruett, 1969.

King, Clyde Lyndon. *The History of the Government of Denver with Special Reference to Its Relations with Public Service Corporations.* Denver: Fisher Book Company, 1911.

Kynewisbok. University of Denver Yearbook. Denver: University of Denver, 1912.

Leonard, Stephen J., and Thomas J. Noel. *Denver: Mining Camp to Metropolis.* Niwot, CO: University Press of Colorado, 1990.

Lort, Lydia Terrell. *A Church Bell Rings in Denver.* Denver: Otto J. Stockmar, 1951.

Lovelace, Walter B., and Walter S. Lovelace. *Jesse Shwayder and the Golden Rule, First Fifty Years of Shwayder Bros., Inc., 1910–1960.* Denver: Lakeside Press, 1960.

McClintock, James H. *Arizona, the Nation's Youngest Commonwealth Within a Land of Ancient Culture.* Chicago: S. J. Clarke, 1916.

Mumey, Nolie. *History of the Early Settlements of Denver (1599–1860).* Glendale, CA: Arthur H. Clark, 1942.

Muntz, Geoffrey L., and Alan S. Wuth. *The Path of Time: A Guide to the Platte River Greenway.* Frederick, CO: Jende-Hagan Bookcorp, 1983.

Noel, Thomas J. *The City and the Saloon: Denver, 1858–1916.* Lincoln: University of Nebraska Press, 1982.

————. *Colorado Catholicism and the Archdiocese of Denver 1857–1989.* Niwot: University Press of Colorado, 1989.

————, ed. *Rocky Mountain Gold: Pictorial and Entertaining Commentary on the Growth and Development of Denver, Colorado.* Tulsa, OK: Continental Heritage Press, 1980.

Noel, Thomas J., and Barbara S. Norgren. *Denver, the City Beautiful and Its Architects, 1893–1941.* Denver: Historic Denver, 1987.

Norland, Jim. *The Summit of a Century: A Pictorial History of the University of Denver, 1864–1964.* Denver: University of Denver, 1963.

Parsons, William B. *The Gold Mines of Western Kansas, Being a Complete Description of the Newly Discovered Gold Mines, Different Routes, Camping Places, Tools and Outfit and Containing Everything Important for the Immigrant and Miner to Know.* Lawrence, Kansas Territory: *Lawrence Republican* Book and Job Printing Office, 1858.

Perkin, Robert L. *The First Hundred Years: An Informal History of Denver and the Rocky Mountain News.* Garden City, NY: Doubleday, 1959.

Portrait and Biographical Record of Denver and Vicinity, Colorado. Chicago: Chapman Publishing Company, 1898.

Private Laws of the Territory of Kansas. Lawrence, KS: Herald of Freedom Steam Press, 1959.

Rosa, Joseph G., and Waldo E. Koop. *Rowdy Joe Lowe, Gambler with a Gun.* Norman: University of Oklahoma Press, 1989.

Rymer, Marion R. *Porter Memorial Hospital, Its Birth and Life.* Denver: Porter Memorial Hospital, 1978.

Shapiro, Mel, Warren Dohn, and Leonard Berger, eds. *Golf, a Turn of the Century Treasury.* Secaucus, NJ: Book Sales, 1986.

Smiley, Jerome C. *History of Denver.* Denver: Times-Sun Publishing, 1901.

Smith, Duane A. *Horace Tabor: His Life and the Legend.* Boulder: Colorado Associated University Press, 1973.

Sprague, Marshall. *Colorado: A Bicentennial History.* New York: W. W. Norton, 1976.

Steam Tramways of Denver. Denver: Rocky Mountain Railroad Club, 1950.

Stewart, J. T. *Indiana County, Pennsylvania: Her People, Past and Present.* Chicago: J. H. Beers, 1913.

Stone, Wilbur Fisk, ed. *History of Colorado.* Chicago: S. J. Clarke Publishing, 1918.

Swords, C. L., and W. C. Edwards, eds. *Sketches and Portraitures of the State Officers and Members of the Ninth General Assembly of Colorado.* Denver: Carson, Hurst & Harper, 1893.

Ubbelohde, Carl, Maxine Benson, and Duane A. Smith, eds. *A Colorado History.* Boulder, CO: Pruett, 1988.

Van Dellen, Idzerd. *In God's Crucible.* Grand Rapids, MI: Baker Book House, 1950.

Vickers, W. B. *History of the City of Denver.* Chicago: O. L. Baskin and Company, 1880.

Wiley, Samuel T. *Biographical and Historical Cyclopedia of Indiana and Armstrong Counties, Pennsylvania.* Philadelphia: John M. Gresham, 1891.

Working, Gertrude Brown. *Levi Booth of Four Mile House.* Denver: 1986.

Zamonski, Stanley W., and Teddy Keller. *The '59ers: Roaring Denver in the Gold Rush Days.* Denver: Westerner, 1957.

JOURNALS AND PERIODICALS

Appleton's Journal, 1876.
The Coloradan, 1892.
Colorado Heritage, 1988.
Colorado Live Stock Record, 1884.
Colorado Magazine, 1933, 1939, 1945.
*Colorado Reports: Cases Adjudged in the Supreme Court of
    Colorado,* 1889, 1891, 1893.
Denver Magazine, 1986.
Denver Monitor, 1954.
Denver Westerners Roundup, 1967.
Kansas City Journal of Commerce, 1858.
Kansas Historical Collection Transactions, 1901–1902.
The Kansas Magazine, 1872.
*Minutes of the Forty-first [and Forty-second] Session of the
    Colorado Annual Conference of the Methodist Episcopal
    Church,* 1903, 1904.
Sons of Colorado Bulletin, 1929.
The Trail, 1914.

NEWSPAPERS

Arizona Republican. Phoenix, Arizona, 1893.
Colorado History News. Denver, Colorado, 1988.
Colorado Prospector. Denver, Colorado, 1989.
Daily News. Denver, Colorado, 1881, 1882, 1892, 1897, 1899.
Denver Eye. Denver, Colorado, 1887–1890.
Denver Post. Denver, Colorado, 1911, 1916, 1935, 1944, 1945,
    1947.
Denver Post Empire Magazine. Denver, Colorado, 1967.
Denver Republican. Denver, Colorado, 1881–1893.
Denver Times. Denver, Colorado, 1887–1923.
Denver Tribune-Republican, Denver, Colorado, 1885, 1886.
Freedom's Champion. Atchison City, Kansas, 1858.
The Hesperus. Denver, Colorado, 1892.
Indiana Times. Indiana, Pennsylvania, 1880.
Lawrence Republican. Lawrence, Kansas, 1858.
Phoenix Herald. Phoenix, Arizona, 1893.
Rocky Mountain Herald. Denver, Colorado, 1872.
Rocky Mountain News. Denver, Colorado, 1860–present.
South Denver Eye. Denver, Colorado, 1890–1901.
South Denver Eye and Bulletin. Denver, Colorado, 1910–1921.
Steam Tramways of Denver, Denver, Colorado, 1950.
Today. Denver, Colorado: University of Denver, 1989.
Tombstone Daily Prospector. Tombstone, Arizona, 1917.
University of Denver Clarion. Denver, Colorado, 1900.

Washington Park Profile. Denver, Colorado, 1981, 1983, 1986.
Yuma Sentinel. Yuma, Arizona, 1896.

REPORTS AND PAMPHLETS

De Boer, Saco R. *University Park Report,* 1923.
Gates Corporation. *The Gates Story, 1800–1986,* n.d.
Le Rossignol, James Edward. "History of Higher Education in
    Colorado." *U.S. Bureau of Education Circular of
    Information No. 1.,* Washington, D.C.: Government
    Printing Office, 1903.
Samsonite Corporation. *The Samsonite Story,* n.d.
Shattuck, Robert C. *University Park, Octogenarian Memories,*
    1986.
University Park Colony Brochure. Denver: Dove-Pabor
    Printing Company, c. 1886.
Weston, W. *Descriptive Pamphlet of Some of the Principal
    Mines and Prospects of Ouray County, Colorado,* 1881.

UNPUBLISHED MANUSCRIPTS AND MATERIALS

Arapahoe County Commissioners Road Reports, 1871.
    Colorado State Archives.
Arapahoe County Commissioners School Superintendent
    Reports, 1871, 1873. Colorado State Archives.
Byers, Mrs. William N. "The Experiences of One Pioneer
    Woman," n.d. Byers collection, Western History Library.
"Centennial Celebration 1861–1961: Grand Lodge A.F.& A.M.
    of Colorado," 1961.
Crookham, Carl, Geoffrey L. Muntz, and Alan S. Wuth.
    "Teacher's Guide to Grant-Frontier Park," 1976.
Deardorff, Charles M. "History of University Park," c. 1899.
    University of Denver Archives.
Denver Circle Railroad Company Resolution, 1886. Colorado
    State Archives.
Etter, Don D. "The Denver Park and Parkway System," 1986.
    Colorado Historical Society.
Fitch, William N., and Frederick K. Allgaier. "Robinson Brick
    Company/Denver Radium Site," 1989. U.S.
    Environmental Protection Agency, Albuquerque, NM.
Goldrick, Owen J. "Historical Sketch of Denver, Colorado."
    Speech given July 4, 1876. Colorado Historical Society.
Haines, Dorothy. "May Centennial Celebration," n.d.
    Typewritten manuscript, University Park School files,
    Denver.
"History of Denver Public Schools," 1957. Denver Public
    Library, Western History Department.

"History of Rosedale," c. 1935. Milton-Rosedale PTA paper, author unknown.

Hudson, Julia. Typewritten report by secretary of E. M. Byers Home for Boys, n.d. Denver Public Library, Western History Department.

Mosley, Earl L. "History of the Denver Water System to 1919." Compiled by Louisa Ward Arps, 1969. Denver Public Library, Western History Department.

"Ninth Annual Report of the Denver Chamber of Commerce and Board of Trade, Denver, Colorado, for the Year Ending December 31st, 1891." Denver Public Library, Western History Department.

"Platt Park Recreation Center Building," a typewritten paper, Decker Branch Library archives.

Robinson, E. W. Typewritten manuscript, 1906. Colorado Historical Society.

"Second Annual Report, Gold and Silver Extraction Mining and Milling Company." 1892. Colorado Historical Society.

Shattuck, Alberta Iliff. "Singer Comes to Colorado." 1976. University Park School files, Denver.

"South Denver Journal," 1886–1894. Board of Trustees, Town of South Denver. Minutes of meetings. Colorado State Archives.

Templin, John Alton. "A History of Methodism in Denver 1876–1912." Ph.D. dissertation. Iliff School of Theology, Denver, 1956.

Trimble, Anna G., ed. "Origin of Denver Streets," 1932. Denver Public Library, Western History Department.

Young, William. "Report to the Honorable Mayor, City of Denver, Colorado," 1894. Colorado State Archives.

MAPS

Bennett & Abbott Map of Denver, 1888.

Clason Map of Denver, Colorado, c. 1922.

Denver Land and Improvement Company's Map of the City of Denver, 1882.

Denver World's Map of Denver, April 1888.

H. L. Thayer's City of Denver Map, 1883.

Rollandet's Guide Map and Street Index to Denver, 1892.

Rollandet's Map, City of Denver, 1889.

Thomas Skerritt Map, Petition for Proposed Road, 1871.

Town of South Denver Incorporation Map, 1886.

Willits Farm Map, February 1899.

Index

Fleming, Nettie, 29, 47
Fleming, Richard, 29, 46, 68, 136n16
Fleming, Sadie, 29, 47
Fleming, Susanna Hill, 29, 46-47, 133n1, 136n13
Fleming, Thomas Calvin, 29
Fleming, Thomas H., 27, 29, 47, 61, 135n4
Fleming, William Porter, 29, 133n1, 136n13
Fleming Ammons, Elizabeth (Lizzie), 29, 46-47
Fleming Block, 29
Fleming Brothers Bank, 29
Fleming Building, 69
Fleming Duffies, Martha (Mattie), 29, 46
Fleming mansion, 46, 71, 89, 97; photo of, 28, 68
Fleming's Broadway Addition, 46
Fleming's Grove Methodist Episcopal Church, 55; photo of, 57
Fleming's Grove School, 36, 55, 60-63, 74, 85, 105
Fleming's Grove Subdivision, 22, 28, 29, 36, 46, 55, 68, 95
Fleming's Grove Union Sunday School, 55
Ford, Henry, 124
Ford Motor Company Assembly Plant, 113-14, 116
Fort Garland, 1, 2, 7
Fort Worth and Denver Railroad, 36
Foster, James F., 134n3, 134n4
Four-Mile House, 18
Fourier, François Marie Charles, 33
Fouse, D. H., 106
Franklin School, 128
French, Adnah, 8, 9, 131n13
Frizzele, J. Wellington, 82
Frontier Park, 10, 130; photo of, 4
Fuller and Wheeler, architects, 79, 80

Gaff, Mary, 11
Gallup, Avery, 39, 40, 42-44, 56, 58, 61, 78, 134n3, 134n4, 134n10, 135n4, 136n11; photo of, 19
Gallup, Charlotte, 20, 57, 97
Gallup, Perry, 97
Gallup country estate, photo of, 18
Gallup Nursery, 80
Gallup-Stanbury building, 20
Gamage, August H., 40-42, 67, 134n3, 135n4, 136n11, 136n21
Gambling, 43, 69
Gang Ticket, 60, 67
Garrison, J. G., 74
Gates, Charles, 114-15, 124
Gates, John, 114

Gates Corporation, 114-16, 118
Gates Rubber Company, 114, 116, 117; photo of, 114
Gentlemen's Club, 72, 73
German National Bank, 36, 92-93
Gibbons, James J., 69
Gibbs, Ada B., 75
Gilpin, William, 22, 24
Gleason, F. S. W., 134n3, 134n4
Gold and Silver Extraction Mining and Milling Company, 92, 93
Gold Mines of Western Kansas . . . , The (Parsons), 7
Goldrick, Owen, 9
Golfing, 107-9, 112; photo of, 109
Gonner, John and Amalie, 43
Gonner, John, 84
Goodfellow, Bertha M., 85
Gow, Leonard, 92
Grace, J. M., 73
Graham, H. J., 9
Grant-Frontier Park, 130
Grant Junior High School, 61, 127, 129-30
Grant School, 61-63, 74, 98; photo of, 63
Grant Subdivision, 58, 63
Grasmere Lake, 98, 100
Gray, William E., 46
Gray Real Estate and Mines, 46
Great Depression, 114, 115, 125, 126
Greeley, Horace, 34
Gregory, Paul, 88
Grey Gables, 35, 55, 76, 77

Haish, Jacob, 79
Haish Manual Training School, 79
Hallack, E. F., 31
Hallett, Moses, 22, 50, 51
Halsey, Peter, 8, 131n13
Hamlet, John, 134n3, 135n4
Hammond, E. P., 12
Hanna, John R., 50, 51
Harper, J. E., 67, 73, 136n21
Harris, Kate D., 36
Hartley, William, 1, 8, 131n13
Hartley, William, Jr., 8
Harvard Gulch, 37-38
Harvard Park and Golf Course, 66
Haugen, T. O., 122-23
Hawkins, D. A., 123
Hegner, Casper F., 76
Heinrich, Julius, 29-30
Helihoff, Harry W., 122-23
Henry, Stuart, 51
Henry, Theodore C., 23, 25, 36, 40, 50, 51, 92, 128
Hicks, J. R., 63
Highlands, 87

High Line Canal, 37
Hill, Alice Polk, 16, 31
Hill, Henry, 21
Hilltop Stadium, 82
Hinman, Josiah, 1-3, 8-10, 131n13
Hinshaw, L. M., 123
Hipp, John, 38, 40, 42, 44, 45, 57, 61
Holland Bakery, 106
Holland Music and Radio Store, 106
Holmes, James, 6, 7, 131n13
Holmes, Julia, 6-7
Hopkins, D. M., 73
Hornbein, Victor, 127
Horse racing, 49, 108, 109, 126
Hose House No. 1, 90
Hospitals, 74, 104-7, 125-26
Hotel Lincoln, 106
House of the Good Shepherd, 124, 126; photo of, 124
Howe, Herbert A., 55, 78, 94
Hoxsey, Arch, 110
Huddart, John J., 101
Hudson, Otis, A., 125
Hughes, Lafayette, 126
Hughes, Louis C., 69
Humphreys, Ira, 126
Hunt, Howard, 8, 10, 131n13
Hutchins, Roswell, 4, 5, 8, 9, 131n13
Hyde, Ammi B., 83

Iliff, Alberta, 83
Iliff, John Wesley, 33, 35, 79
Iliff, John Wesley, Jr., 33
Iliff, Louise, 33
Iliff, William Seward, 33, 79, 80, 82, 83
Iliff Hall, 79
Iliff School of Theology, 79, 83, 86, 94; sketch of, 79
Incorporation, 40, 42-46
Independent Order of Odd Fellows (I.O.O.F.) Silver State Lodge #97. See Odd Fellows Hall
Indignation meetings, 73, 87
Industrial district, 22, 87, 113-18

Jack, J. H., 63, 65
James Fleming's Town, 128
James Sudler and Associates, 101
Jefferson, May L., 74
Jefferson Block, 74
Jefferson Building, 74
Jewell, Charles A., 23, 25, 40
Jewell Park, 25, 32, 49, 95; photo of, 39
John Collins Methodist Episcopal Church, 85-86; photo of, 86
John Collins United Methodist, Home of the Olde Methodist Church, 85
Johns, Frederick W., 40, 42, 43, 132n20,